New 7th Edition

NEW JERSEY DAY TRIPS

A GUIDE TO OUTINGS IN NEW JERSEY, NEW YORK, PENNSYLVANIA & DELAWARE

Revised and Updated

BARBARA HUDGINS

The Woodmont Press
P.O. Box 108
Green Village, N.J. 07935

If a copy of this book is not available at your local bookstore, you may order one by sending $12.95 plus $2.00 shipping to:

The Woodmont Press
P.O. Box 108
Green Village, N.J. 07935

ISBN 0-9607762-6-5
Printed in the United States of America

DEDICATION

To all the friends and family who trudged through countless amusement parks and reconstructed villages to help me with my book.

ACKNOWLEDGEMENTS

Much gratitude and thanks to:

All the driving companions who searched out New Jersey's nooks and crannies with me. In particular: Gail Davies, Sheila Di Marsico, Alexandra Knox, Nancy Boucher, Doug and Ralph Milnes, Pam Morse, Betty Murphy, Carol Potter, Kathy Slack, Laslo Vasko, and the Wemple family.

Those who helped with the book production beyond the call of duty, particularly: Pam Morse for copyreading, Jack Krug and Irene Rich for editorial help and Linda Kimler for pictures and general support.

And to Lani and Robert for their help and comments.

FOREWORD

There are several ways to put together a guidebook. One can do it regionally (e.g., all attractions in Sussex County are listed together), chronologically (everything open in winter is listed in one section) or by subject (all zoos are listed together, and all museums are listed together). There is no perfect way.

My book is set up primarily by subject. However, there are chapters that differ from this approach. The first chapter, "Unique Towns, Places to Browse" covers such towns as Atlantic City, New Hope, Princeton and various walking tours. Here I write about the town as a whole and include all the sites available. In the chapter "Museums of All Kinds," the listings proved to be so huge that I subdivided the sections geographically (N.Y., N.J. and PA.) and then subdivided New Jersey museums.

You will find some of my listings to be purely arbitrary. When a particular place could belong to more than one category, I simply chose the one I felt it fit in best. Pennsbury Manor, for instance, the reconstructed estate of William Penn, could fit in either the chapter titled "Homes of the Rich and Famous" or the one on restored villages.

The advantage of listing attractions by subject is that someone interested in a particular sport or hobby can easily find what is available at a glance. A newcomer wants to know what ski areas are near — a garden club president wants to know where to take her group on a trip — a parent asks a history teacher what Revolutionary War sites are around — and so forth. However, because many people want to know what is available in their immediate geographical area, I have included a regional index in the back of the book. Here the listings for New Jersey are under each county, and those for out-of-state are under a specific area (such as the Poconos, the Hudson Valley or New York City). One caution however — always check the main listings before you set out. There are many attractions that are open on a limited basis. For example, a well-done Colonial restoration — the Miller-Cory house — is open only on Sundays during the school year. Other places change guise with the season. Just as a weasel becomes an ermine in winter, summer action parks become winter ski areas, and August fairgrounds become September flea markets.

I wish you many hours of pleasurable day-tripping in and around New Jersey.

A WORD ABOUT PRICES

Prices are accurate for the year of publication of this guidebook. Since we do a new edition every two years, there will of course be increases during this time period.

Although prices have zoomed for amusement parks, entertainments, and even local museums and zoos, there are a few ways you can save money.

1. Use coupons and "two-fers". Most amusement parks have marketing arrangements with certain companies — Coke, Pepsi, Roy Rogers, Burger King, etc. where you get a two-for-one admissions with the requisite can or coupon. (Coupons for weekends are usually not as good as for weekdays.) Also check for coupons in brochures.

2. Go on free days. New Jersey State Parks are free on Tuesday and off-season. The Philadelphia Museum is free Sunday mornings. Certain other museums have free or reduced price hours.

3. Buy season tickets. This only makes sense if you live within close range and are available weekdays, but it certainly explains why certain water parks and amusement centers are filled on weekdays.

4. Use your corporate or organizational clout. Most corporations give money to local museums, zoos, etc. Their employees get a free "corporate" day — or a standard discount. Members of AAA and AARP usually get some discount.

5. Check with your town's Recreation Department. They often have discount tickets for any number of events.

6. Become a member of a local museum, garden, zoo. Especially with families it works out price-wise — and you often get discounts for the gift shop and trips.

7. "Suggested donation" means just that. If you are visiting for a short period of time or have a large family with you, you do not have to pay the full "suggested donation", although you must pay something.

8. Watch out for "extras", like parking fees and sales tax. Always take along more money than you think you will need.

CONTENTS

UNIQUE TOWNS,
PLACES TO BROWSE,
GUIDED WALKING TOURS

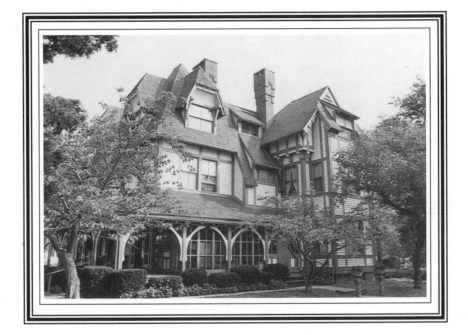

Photo: Cape May County Division of Tourism

1

In This Chapter You Will Find:

Atlantic City, N.J.
Princeton, N.J.
New Hope, PA
Lahaska, PA
Cape May, N.J.
Chinatown, N.Y.
Other N.Y. Tours

Guided Walking Tours for:
  Paterson, N.J.
  Bordentown, N.J.
  Burlington, N.J.
  Mount Holly, N.J.
  Other N.J. Tours
  Philadelphia, PA

ATLANTIC CITY

Atlantic City is revving itself up as a convention center again, with less emphasis on gambling alone. A new Convention Hall is slated to open early in 1997. Even now there is more variety in the offerings, more hotels opening without casinos and even the return of amusements to the Steel Pier. In the casinos, you can now find Keno, horse-racing simulcasting, and an amazing variety of slot machines. Best of all, you can find chairs in front of the slots, so you can at least be comfortable while you are losing your money.

There are now twelve casino-hotels in Atlantic City and they have changed their names more often than Hollywood stars change husbands. Changed their decor also. The famed boardwalk is still a pastiche of monolithic hotels, huge parking lots, hole-in-the-wall arcades, concession stands and ordinary stores. In warm weather there are crowds of people, lots of rolling chairs, even boardwalk concerts. The beach is bumpy with sand dunes.

Here's a short run-down on what you will find:

Parking: Valet parking is available at the hotels if you are staying over or using the casino. Most offer free parking for a 3 or 6 hour stay. However, getting into town on a busy summer weekend can be full of traffic delays.

Transportation: Once you have parked your car, the best way to get around town is to take the small jitneys that operate along Pacific Avenue. They come frequently and cost $1.25. On the boardwalk you can walk on a nice day or take the push-along rolling chairs that cost about $5 for every six blocks. Cabs are plentiful if you want to get away from the boardwalk area. And NJ Transit buses serve the length of the island 24 hours a day. They run along Atlantic Ave.

Bus Tours: Still the favorite way for most people to make a one day visit — fares vary from point of embarkation. It costs around $19 from north Jersey but the casinos give you quarters and other freebies when you arrive. You must stay 6 hours if you take a bus tour. These casino-subsidized buses travel to Atlantic City every day of the year. Groups can charter their own buses. Regular NJ Transit buses and trains also service the town.

The Hotels: Prices are high in the sparkling casino hotels. On the boardwalk they stretch from Bally's Grand on the south (formerly the Golden Nugget) to the Showboat on the north at Delaware Ave. Over at the marina (a few miles away) Harrah's and the Trump Castle overlook a flotilla of docked boats. However, if you don't mind visiting A.C. off-season, there are some very reasonable weekday packages available. Once the summer season hits, though, be prepared to pay. Of course if you are a casino regular, you can use your card "comps" for free rooms and food. Actually, almost every shore resort in Jersey has a bus tour to A.C. nightly, several nights a week, so it is not necessary to stay in town in order to play in town. There are many older motels along Pacific and Atlantic Avenues which have been refurbished. For a package listing hotels, restaurants and information call 1-800-262-7395.

The Casinos: If your idea of a casino is garnered from the movies and you expect evening dresses and tuxedos, leisurely gaming tables and James Bond types floating around, forget it. This is supermarket gambling, where little old ladies with shopping bags hover over the slot machines, longshoremen and bewildered bus groups from Delaware wander around and the hotel employees all seem to have taken a vow of silence. Roulette and blackjack and craps tables are placed side by side, and rows of slots glisten in the artificial light. It's all very confusing. However, minimum bets are posted at each table, and gaming guides are sometimes available at the hotel desks.

As for slot machines — you change your paper money into coins at the elevated change booths in the slot area. But to transform a bucketful of coins into dollars, you must hike over to the Coin Banks, usually located way across the room. The slots come in all varieties: from nickel and dime (not too many of these) to the one, five and ten dollar, poker and progressive.

The casinos try mightily to keep their customers loyal. The gimmick of choice right now is a card (something like a credit card) which you get by joining a particular casino's "club". This card gives you back points every time you use the slot machines or tables, so that eventually, if you spend enough money, you get enough "comps" to eat in the fancy restaurants, buy in the gift shops or sleep in the hotel rooms. This allows the middle class to enjoy some of the privileges once reserved for the high rollers. It also keeps people pushing quarters into machines.

Food: There are many excellent restaurants in Atlantic City. From the old *Knife and Fork Inn* to the French, English and Japanese eating rooms in the large hotels. The better restaurants absolutely require reservations. However, the daytripper will more likely end up at the buffets at almost any hotel. They're not as elegant as they were ten years ago, but they're cheaper. But, oh,

4

the lines! Reserve your time as soon as you land. And now there's **Planet Hollywood** at Caesars which should start a whole new trend. There are also 24-hour coffee shops that are mediocre and a few New York style delis that are good. And fast food courts are available everywhere.

Entertainment: First class shows, chorus girls and big name stars appear at the hotels, and this, above all, has brought a certain zing to the resort. Shortened versions of Broadway shows have become a favorite form of entertainment. Besides the big shows, there are lounges with brassy singers, lounges with tinkling pianos, big boxing matches and all sorts of tournaments. As for teenagers, they will find video game rooms in the hotels and some on the Boardwalk also. Families can enjoy the **Tivoli Pier** in the TropWorld Hotel which offers a miniature version of boardwalk amusements (including a ferris wheel) and the supersized bowling alley over at the Showboat hotel.

Across the boardwalk from the Taj Mahal, the newly re-opened **Steel Pier** offers a collection of amusement rides plus some of the daredevil stunts that once made it famous. No diving horses, but they have had high wire stunt walkers. Further down the boardwalk you can often find entertainment at the amphitheater at Indiana Avenue. At **Ocean One Mall** (it looks like a cruise ship berthed across the boards from Caesars) there are three floors of middle-class stores and a profusion of restaurants and fast food joints. The first floor of this mall also has a back section devoted to arcade games, virtual reality basketball, air hockey and other teenage diversions.

For nostalgia buffs, there's a museum devoted to Atlantic City history, plus an art museum at **The Garden Pier**, which is on the boardwalk north of the Showboat hotel.

For those who want to venture beyond the Boardwalk, there are a few summertime attractions. One is **Lucy, the Margate Elephant**, an architectural oddity that is six stories high — complete with howdah. You can walk through Lucy (which is tin-plated outside and wood inside) with a guided tour during the summer — for a fee. You can even step outside on top and get a view. It is located at 9200 Atlantic Avenue in Margate — two towns down from Atlantic City. The wooden elephant is open weekends May and September and daily from late June to Labor Day.

On the inlet side, Atlantic City offers **Historic Gardener's Basin** which began life as a miniature fishing village in the manner of Mystic, Connecticut. But the square riggers and boutiques have disappeared. What is available now is a number of special events such as concerts and clambakes. Also, a speedboat ride.

Other standard sidetrips from Atlantic City are the winery tours at Renault and Gross's Highland Winery, the Historic Towne of Smithville and Wheaton Village, all of which are mentioned elsewhere in this book. And of course, in the summertime, there is always the Atlantic City beach, which is free.

DIRECTIONS: Garden State Parkway to Exit 40 and 38S, or NJ Tpke. to Atlantic City Expressway.

PRINCETON

Shades of F. Scott Fitzgerald! Golden lads and lasses walk the well-clipped paths between venerable University halls while russet leaves flutter overhead from rows of sturdy trees. Time, scholarships, and the inclusion of girls have changed the atmosphere at this Ivy League bastion somewhat. But still, for a trip to a true University town that combines history, culture and typical collegiate Gothic architecture, nothing beats a visit to Princeton.

The best way to see the campus sights is to take the free tours offered by the *Orange Key Guide Service.* Just go to MacLean House on campus in time for the tours which leave at 10 AM, 11 AM, 1:30 PM, and 3:30 PM weekdays and Saturdays. Sunday tours are 1:30 and 3:30 P.M. The telephone number is 609-258-3603 but it is not necessary for individuals to reserve in advance. Here are some campus sights included in the tour:

1. **Nassau Hall:** Built in 1756, this Georgian stone structure has survived pillage and fire (by the British, not the students) over the years. It served as a barracks and hospital for troops of both sides during the Revolutionary War. In 1783 Congress met here and drafted the Constitution while Princeton was still the capital. It now serves as an administrative office for the University. A painting by Charles Willson Peale of Washington at the Battle of Trenton is to be found here.

2. **Firestone Library:** A beautiful two-million volume library built in 1948, it is the embodiment of the Collegiate Gothic style. Major collections include the papers of F. Scott Fitzgerald, Adlai E. Stevenson, John Foster Dulles, Woodrow Wilson and other famous graduates. A changing exhibit of rare books is also on display.

3. **Woodrow Wilson School of Public and International Affairs:** Guides will show you the outside of this striking building, one of the few modern structures on campus. Designed by Minoru Yamasaki, it includes a reflecting pool and the Fountain of Freedom by James Fitzgerald.

4. **The University Chapel:** Built in a Gothic design by Ralph Adams Cram in 1928, it is the third largest university chapel in the country, seating 1800. A 16th Century carved oak pulpit and some of the finest stained glass to be seen this side of the Atlantic Ocean make the Chapel an outstanding part of the Princeton trip.

5. **The Putnam Sculptures:** These are a series of massive metal and stone sculptures scattered around the campus as if a giant had decided to distribute his toys among the college buildings. Almost all are abstract in design and they stick out like sore thumbs among the ivy-walled buildings. You can't miss them, so you might as well examine them. Sir Henry Moore, Jacques Lipchitz, Louise Nevelson and Pablo Picasso are among the biggies represented there.

6. **The Prospect:** A Tuscan villa built in 1949, it is now used as a Faculty Club and not open to the public. However, the formally designed garden to the rear is open for browsing and is very pleasant.

Not included in the tour, but an important stop, is the **Princeton Art Museum**. This is a first rate museum and a wonder of wonders — it's free! Paintings include a generous sampling of Americana, Italian Renaissance and French Baroque. You'll find a good collection of Chinese bronzes as well as artifacts from Central and South America. A top collection of prints and a separate medieval room that includes part of the stained-glass window from the Cathedral at Chartes are also "must sees." Special changing exhibits are of a high order. Call 609-258-3788 for more information. And don't forget Guyot Hall with its Museum of Natural History and dinosaur bones. Call 609-258-5807 for hours.

Besides the university, Princeton has pleasant shopping along Nassau Street and many good restaurants (among them *"Lahiere's," "The Nassau Inn"* and the *"Alchemist and Barrister"*). You might also want to look at the Princeton Cemetery at Wiggins and Witherspoon, which holds the remains of Aaron Burr and Grover Cleveland among its many notables. The Princeton Battle Monument, a fifty-foot structure, stands imposingly at Nassau and Mercer Streets, while a walking tour of the area will take you past many lovely old houses. Albert Einstein's former home, at

112 Mercer St., is not open to the public. However, many people take a photograph of it as they pass by. A short drive away is Princeton Battlefield Park.

Morven, at 55 Stockton Street is open to public tours on Wednesdays from 11-3. This lovely Georgian mansion has lost most of the beautiful furnishings it had as a governor's mansion. Drumthwacket, the present governor's residence, and the Bainbridge House have separate listing in this book. Self-guided tour maps can be picked up at the Bainbridge House (158 Nassau St.). And anyone can join their walking tours on Sundays at 2 PM.

The **McCarter Theater** runs a full program of professional plays, movies, ballet and concerts from September to June. There are also a good number of fairs and community doings going on.

DIRECTIONS: Route 206 or 27 to Princeton. The University is on Nassau Street.

NEW HOPE, PENNSYLVANIA

There are a number of small towns in the United States that seem to survive simply by being picturesque. A combination of natural beauty, historical significance and the establishment of an art colony (followed inevitably by a writer's colony and a rustic theater) creates that certain atmosphere that brings the tourists out in droves. Whether the original tourist impetus was the antiques in the historical part of town or the artworks in the art colony, the more people arrive, the more craftshops, antique stores, boites, boutiques and charm-laden restaurants open.

New Hope, Pennsylvania has long been the cultural and picturesque capital of Bucks County. On any fall weekend the narrow sidewalks of this sophisticated oasis set in Pennsylvania farm country are simply jammed. People come to browse or just wallow in the atmosphere.

In the 1920's landscape painters settled here, bringing with them the excitement of the creative world. By the Thirties, Bucks County had become well known as a quiet weekend haven for novelists, poets and playwrights. And in 1939 a grist mill in the center of town was transformed into the **Bucks County Playhouse**. The opening program was "Springtime for Henry" with Edward Everett Horton, and the playhouse has remained a stalwart of the "Straw Hat Circuit" ever since. The season now begins in the late spring and extends well into the fall. Since the theater offers family musicals and matinee performances it is one of New Hope's biggest draws. (Telephone: 215-862-2041)

Another warm weather attraction is the **New Hope Mule Drawn Barge Ride** which offers a one-hour ride down the old canal works. It is a slow and easy way to see the town. It departs from the barge landing at New Street, and usually several rides are offered during the afternoon. Call 215-862-2842 for details.

A popular pontoon ride is **Coryell's Ferry** which offers scenic rides on the Delaware. It loads behind Gerenser's Exotic Ice Cream Store, 22 S. Main St. And railroad enthusiasts will enjoy the **New Hope 1890 Steam Railway** which operates between May and October. It leaves from West Bridge and Stockton Streets. The schedule varies so call 215-862-2332 beforehand.

Historic house lovers will enjoy the **Parry Mansion** at South Main and Parry Streets. Guided tours of ten rooms that run the gamut from Colonial to early 20th century are available. The rooms were furnished by a professional interior decorator and each reflects a period—Federal, Victorian, etc.— in the history of the house. It's quite well done. The house is open from May to October on Friday through Sunday from 1-5 PM. Tours cost a small fee. Call 215-862-5652 for additional information.

But even without these extras there is plenty to see in New Hope. Stroll along the leaf-strewn streets and visit the shops if you are interested in antiques. There are plenty of shops featuring memorabilia in town, and if you collect old sheet music, military hats or miniature dolls, you'll find much to pick from. If you're tired there are horse-drawn carriage rides which leave from The Logan Inn.

Art galleries can be found on Main Street, Mechanic Street and Route 202. Phillips Mill, just two miles outside New Hope, hosts an art festival and has galleries too. Besides the standard landscape of Pennsylvania red barn country you can find modernistic sculpture and paintings also. The kids will be more interested in the toy shops, the knickknack and the candy shops.

One of the charms of visiting a quaint, riverside town is eating in a quaint, interesting restaurant, and there are plenty of them in New Hope, most along the main drag. Whether you opt for the casual *Mother's*, the glossy *Hacienda*, or the cutesy *Picnic Basket*, you will be satisfied. The better places fill up on weekends, though, so you'd better make reservations as soon as you hit town. There's

9

a variety of night spots that gives the place a jazzier tone after 7 PM. Check the Information Center at 1 W. Mechanic Street, or call 215-862-5880.

Lambertville, on the Jersey side of the river, now rivals New Hope in restaurants and antique shops. Read more about Lambertville in the chapter on Flea Markets.

DIRECTIONS: Route 202 across Delaware River, Then 32S; or 179 to 29 to Lambertville and cross bridge.

LAHASKA, PENNSYLVANIA

Having gone as far as New Hope, you might as well go the extra four miles on Route 202 to Lahaska and the Peddler's Village area. The road is dotted with antique shops which is what brought this area to prominence in the first place. **Peddler's Village** is one of those reconstructed outdoor shopping malls that combine the brick walls and lamps of the 18th Century plus very pretty landscaping with astute 20th Century commercialism. In fact, it is very similar to a number of other Colonial style malls. This one has a great big waterwheel and lovely floral beds to give it the proper atmosphere. It even has its own Bed and Breakfast inn, one of the many in Bucks County.

Many people who visit New Hope like to go on to Lahaska to eat since Peddler's Village features free parking and several different eating and drinking areas. The Village also includes many shops which sell china, leather, children's clothes, handcrafts and so on, together with enough cheese, nut and candy shops to insure that you don't leave the grounds without buying something. There are special events here on special weekends — everything from a Strawberry Festival to a Teddy Bear Picnic.

A number of shopping areas have sprung up next to Peddler's Village. Across the street, a new outlet mall called Penn's Purchase has just opened.

LOCATION: Routes 202 & 263, Lahaska, PA.
HOURS: 10-5:30 daily for shops. Fridays until 9. Sun.: 1-5:30. Restaurants are open later.
TELEPHONE: 215-794-4000

CAPE MAY

When the Bed and Breakfast boom started in the 1970s, New Jersey was hardly mentioned in all those B&B books. But now, architectural buffs have discovered the Victorian summer homes of Cape May and have converted them into the latest thing in inns. Gone are the dull, old-fashioned guest houses whose porches always seemed to show peeling white paint. In their stead there is a whole array of Victorian homes, sporting the sprightly colors of pink, blue and maroon. Gothic cottages, Italian villas, Mansard and Stick style buildings have metamorphized into charming, whimsical Bed and Breakfast homes, restaurants, antique stores and art galleries. And the interest in this Victorian revitalization has led the town of Cape May to extend its season beyond the ten weeks of summer.

You can now take walking tours, house tours, trolley tours, and tulip tours on weekends from May through October. And a special Victorian Week, held in October, features ten days of antiques, crafts, fashion shows and tours. Another special is the Christmas candlelight tours. The group that runs many of these festivities is the *Mid-Atlantic Center for the Arts*, which operates out of the **Emlen Physick Estate**. The Physick house itself is the scene of a popular tour. This sprawling 1881 Stick Style home is typical of the late Victorian era both in its exterior and its somewhat fussy furnishings. A trolley car tour that leaves from the estate travels to the more colorful beachfront area, where houses trimmed in carpenter's lace and fancy restaurants await the visitor.

Cape May has long been a part of the summer scene (see the chapter on the Jersey Shore). And the beachfront still has a few modern motels and video game arcades among the older hostelries. But the major ambience of the town is the restoration of its Victorian past. The Washington Street Mall is a focal point for shoppers and you can find any number of boutiques and outdoor cafes in this pleasant outdoor mall. You can also catch both trolley and horse-drawn carriage rides at the mall entrance. For more information on the various tours and inns, contact: The Mid-Atlantic Center for the Arts, P.O. Box 340, Cape May, N.J. 08204, or telephone 609-884- 5404. For other information call the Chamber of Commerce at 609-884-5508.

DIRECTIONS: Garden State Parkway to Exit 0. Follow signs to historic area.

CHINATOWN, NEW YORK

There are many unique neighborhoods in nearby New York, but the one that stands out as the last of the true ethnic neighborhoods is Chinatown. Although there are some modern towers rising up in the area, most of Chinatown is still packed with six-story tenements that nestle within them a huge variety of shops and restaurants. Pagoda-shaped telephone booths, a Chinese movie, and Buddhist temples add touches of the Orient. But it is the smell of spices in the streets, the gnarled looking vegetables in the grocery shops and the tinkling brass bells in the curio shops that gives Chinatown its special flavor.

Most of all it is the restaurants that pull the crowds to Chinatown. You can find hot and spicy Northern cooking, the traditional (to New Yorkers) Cantonese cuisine, and the small tea shops that serve dim sum lunches. Sunday is the big day for tourists, so it gets awfully crowded, but weekdays it's just blah. Try Saturday, or get there early on Sunday if you want to find a parking space. This is the closest you'll get to a foreign country without leaving the United States.

DIRECTIONS: Use Holland Tunnel. Keep straight on Canal Street to Pell St. Chinatown lies in the general area between Pell & Mott streets in lower Manhattan.

NEW YORK TOURS

Since New York is a center for art and theater and New Yorkers are traditionally preoccupied with being "In", it is only natural that some of the most popular tours here are of the behind-the-scenes variety.

Lincoln Center, for instance, runs escorted tours through the whole complex. That means you get a peek at the Vivian Beaumont Theater, the opera and the State Theater all on the one ticket. You may buy tickets at the Tour Desk in the downstairs concourse. Call 212-875-5351 for information and reservations. For the one and one-half hour backstage tour of the **Metropolitan Opera** (which runs at 3:45 PM on weekdays and 10 AM on Saturday) you don't have to be a phantom but you do have to make reservations. Call 212-769-7020.

NBC Television Tours: these are extremely popular although very few programs still originate from this building. Anyway there is a lot of history and inside information on the way TV really works. The tours run every fifteen minutes from 9:30 to 4:30 and leave from the main floor of 30 Rockefeller Plaza. Tickets cost $8.25 per person and children under 6 are not permitted. It is best to get your tickets as early as possible, since the tours do fill up. Tickets go on sale at 9 A.M. For information on group tours call 212-664-4000.

For those interested in the backstage machinations of the Capitalist world, the **New York Stock Exchange**, 20 Broad St., in the Wall Street area, has been allowing visitors for years. You get a glimpse of the Exchange floor from a high window. Otherwise, there's plenty of information and hands on computer stuff to play with. It's free, but access is limited. Call 212-656-5167 for further information.

There are a number of private walking tour groups operating in the New York area, but they change name and number so frequently I hesitate to mention them. However, one tour guide who is extremely popular in my area is Lou Singer of **Singer Tours**, 130 St. Edward St., Brooklyn, NY 11201. Mr. Singer's "noshing" tours (where you stop and sample knishes, canneloni, Chinese dumplings and such fare during walks through the lower or upper East Side) and his architectural tours of Brooklyn are justly famous. Singer works primarily with groups. Telephone: 718-875-9084 between 7 and 11 P.M. Howard Goldberg's **Adventures on A Shoestring** walking tours are also very popular. Telephone: 212-265-2663 for this one. As for other groups, it's best to check in the most recent copy of the Manhattan Yellow Pages, to find groups that are operating at the moment.

NJ GUIDED TOURS

There are two kinds of walking tours. One is the self-guided type where you begin with a map and a brochure (usually provided by the local historical society) and hoof it yourself. The other is the pre-arranged group tour wherein you reach your destination by bus or car and then proceed *en masse* down the street, following a highly knowledgeable leader who tells you what you are seeing. Group tours often include one or two private houses where you enter by special permission.

Here is a sampling of some of the many guided and self-guided tours available.

PATERSON TOURS

Do-it-yourself tours, guided group tours, visits to the variegated ethnic churches or simply a walking tour of the public statues of Gaetano Federici—these are some of the many tour possibilities you find in the city of Paterson. This industrial city is proud of its history as one of the earliest manufacturing sites in the United States. Its tours emphasize the historic district of *The Society for Useful Manufactures*, a section of the city that was planned for commerce by Alexander Hamilton back in 1791.

The Great Falls of Paterson, a spectacular waterfall completely surrounded by concrete and urban landscape, is the focal point of the S.U.M. Tours. The Society for Useful Manufacture's Historic District covers the area of mills and plants that were once the heart and breath of the city. Paterson's Golden Age began early in the 19th Century when power from the falls created an industrial bonanza. **The Colt Mill** with its cotton duck sails for the Navy, the **Rogers Locomotive Works** building (which now contains the Paterson Museum and a host of interesting exhibits), and the silk mills that made Paterson the center of that industry are included in the tour. Many of these brick and stone edifices are in various states of rehabilitation.

The **Great Falls Development Corporation** runs tours that take you to the scenes of Paterson's industrial past, but they also will custom-tailor tours to the interests of the group. Popular stops on all the tours is the Farmer's Market which offers vegetables, cheeses and other fresh items; or the great stone churches with their stained glass windows.

CONTACT: Great Falls Visitor Center, 65 McBride Ave., Paterson, N.J. 07501. Telephone: 201-279-9587

BORDENTOWN TOUR

One of the most historical towns in New Jersey, Bordentown is no longer the Quaker enclave it once was. Nor is it the large metropolis (the major boat and coach stop on the route to Philadelphia) of yore. Several famous citizens once made their abodes here — among them Clara Barton, Thomas Paine, Francis Hopkinson (another Revolutionary notable) and Joseph Bonaparte, brother of Napoleon. There are many Quaker buildings still standing and the homes of the famous are here but are private for the most part. And even though the town - which depends heavily on the Ocean Spray cannery for income - is primarily working class, there is still an aura of quaintness and history here.

Self-guided walking tours begin with a brochure from the Historical Society which is located in the **Old City Hall**. The hall itself has many interesting rooms - among them a one-room courthouse upstairs and a four-cell jail downstairs. The jail demonstrates how economically space was used in the old days — a criminal was sentenced upstairs and jailed within the same building, right away. The City Hall is open to the public Tues.- Thurs., 9:30-11 & 12:30-3; Fri.: 9:30-11; Sat.: 10-3. For those individuals who take the brochure and proceed from City Hall it is mostly a matter of looking at the outside of the historic buildings. However, if you book a group tour (ten or more) you may get a peek inside.

The group tour I took had as our first stop the **Gilder House**. As we entered the front hall, we noticed an elaborate rendition of a family tree that traced the line from Samuel Bunting to the Reverend Gilder for whom the house is named. But it is the furniture from Joseph Bonaparte's estate that creates the most interest here. An elaborate buffet, a blue couch with eagles and a gold-trimmed tea set in the Empire style are some of the remnants the rich and proud French family left in this small New Jersey town. The guide also pointed out a painting of sheep by artist Susan Waters. She is another Bordentown native whose fame is growing with the stronger appreciation of American itinerant painters.

From the Gilder House we proceeded to the **Clara Barton Schoolhouse**, a prime historical site in the town. Actually Miss Barton taught here for a very short time but she made quite an impact on the town. Up until that time, middle class children went to private school while public schools were considered to be for paupers. Miss Barton had to persuade the local school-children to attend. There was no fee, but each child was required to bring a stick of wood to keep the woodstove going. The small red brick building has benches and a raised platform where the teacher sat (in the back of the room, not the front).

Other houses included on the self-guided tour are: The Friends Meeting House, Shippen House, Francis Hopkinson House, Thomas Paine House and the Joseph Borden House. While most of these are private they are often opened up for Bordentown's *"Open House Tour"* which takes place in mid-October. The Gilder House is open some Saturdays in summer.

15

CONTACT: Bordentown Historical Society, P.O. Box 182, 302 Farnsworth Ave., Bordentown, N.J. 08505. Telephone: 609-298-1740 (12-3 PM except Mondays).

BURLINGTON

Another town that saw its heyday years ago at a time when it was the capital of West Jersey and a stronghold of Quakerism is Burlington. Among the many buildings that still stand are the **Friends Meeting House**, the **Revell House**, and the **Ulysses S. Grant House**, plus several prominent churches.

A very active Historical Society operates a museum here comprised of five houses. One is the house once rented by the family of America's first novelist and is named, appropriately, the **James Fenimore Cooper House**, although the writer only spent the first thirteen months of his life here. The **Captain James Lawrence House** is right next door and is dedicated to pictures and memorabilia of the War of 1812 hero who is best known for his words, "Don't Give Up The Ship!" (You find out, during the tour here, that they did give up the ship, and the British won the battle, but what the heck, a good phrase is hard to find.) Although small, this is a well furnished and very interesting place.

These side-by-side houses are located at 457 and 459 High Street. **The Pearson How House** (453 High St.) the **Alice Wolcott Museum** and the **Delia Pugh Library** make up the rest of the museum complex. For hours of visitation or special arrangements call 609-386-4773. Usually, they are Mon. - Thurs., 1-4; Sun., 2-4.

Aside from its historical district, Burlington also offers the *Burlington Coat Factory* on Route 130, which is home base for a well-known outlet chain. There is also a small mall of outlet shops called The Burlington Mart. And down by the riverfront you can find an old-fashioned walk with a nice view.

A brochure for a self-guided walking tour of the historical district is available from City Hall. You can also make arrangements for guided group tours from there.

CONTACT: Dr. Nicholas Kamaras, City Hall, Burlington, N.J. 08016. Telephone: 609-386-3993.

MOUNT HOLLY

The county seat of Burlington was a center of Quakerism in New Jersey. This quiet little town has several buildings of note on its walking tour. You may obtain a pamphlet for the self-guided tour from: Township Hall, 23 Washington St., Mt. Holly, N.J. 08060. Telephone: 609-261-0170.

Among the noteworthy buildings are: The **Burlington County Prison-Museum**, designed by Robert Mills, architect of the Washington Monument, the **Mill Street Hotel**, the **John Woolman Memorial** and a restored 1759 schoolhouse where Woolman, the famous Quaker abolitionist, once taught. Most of these are heavy old stone buildings that really set you back in time.

A few miles outside of Mt. Holly there stands the historic mansion of **Smithville** (not to be confused with the historic town of Smithville in Atlantic County). This large columned house includes a museum of bicycles and is open for tours Wed.-Sun. from April through November. Telephone 609-261-5068 for further information.

OTHER NEW JERSEY TOURS

SALEM TOUR: Salem was an early Quaker settlement in West Jersey in the county of the same name. The town boasts a large number of authentic 18th Century houses. The headquarters of the Historical Society is the **Alexander Grant** House at 79-83 Market Street. It is maintained as a museum and offers nineteen rooms of early American furniture and decorative arts. Living rooms, bedrooms, featherbeds, rooms full of dolls and much more are on view here Tues.-Fri. from 12-4 plus the 2nd Sat. of the month. There is a nominal fee for the museum. This is where you pick up the map for a walking tour of the local historic area. Among the important sights are the Old Court House and the ancient Salem Oak. And once every two years, Salem hosts an open house of its historic buildings. *Telephone:* 609-935-5004.

GLOUCESTER COUNTY: For those who wish to see the many historical buildings in the small towns that dot the county of Gloucester, the County Historical Society has prepared a map which lists forty-eight of them and gives a short history of each.

Many are privately owned, but the **Hunter-Lawrence House**, 58 North Broad St., Woodbury, is now a museum and open to the public Wed. & Fri., 1-4. The library at 17 Hunter St. is the headquarters of the Historical Society and you may stop there for the map before you set out. *Telephone:* 609-845-4771.

BRIDGETON: Yet another southwestern Jersey town trying for a Renaissance of its heyday. The town includes New Jersey's largest historic district with over 2000 homes and buildings from the Colonial, Federal and Victorian eras all in various stages of repair. The strongest ambience here is Victorian with many large homes on hand. The Cohansey River runs through town and a new riverfront plaza has been built to host concerts, fairs and walking tours. A large park, which includes the Nail Museum and a good-size zoo is on the other side of the river. A few boutique shops have opened in the riverfront area, but the town has a long way to go to rival Cape May in interest. Maps, a slide film and arrangements for guided bus and walking tours are available at the Bridgeton-Cumberland Tourist Association at Routes 49 & 77, Bridgeton. *Telephone:* 609-451-4802.

CRANBURY: A charming little town below New Brunswick, that has at various times been called Cranberry and Cranberrytown. Many of the houses standing on the tree-lined streets were built between 1820 and 1880. Washington dined here during the battle of Monmouth (although not at the Cranbury Inn which has a Dickensian ambience). The Historical Society runs a museum at 4 Park Place (open Sat.-Sun.: 1-4) with early Victorian furnishings. They also supply a walking map of the sites in the historic district. Write Cranbury Historical Society, 4 Park Place, Cranbury, 08512.

NEWARK: You can reserve walking tours through the Ironbound and visit the shops in this heavily Portugese and Spanish district. And for bus groups, a very knowledgeable guide will board the bus and give a tour of Newark that includes downtown, the Newark "subway", the parks, the slums, the grand old houses and the magnificent **Sacred Heart Cathedral** which you may enter. This huge Gothic cathedral rivals its European counterparts in beauty, if not in age. For the tours: Telephone: 201-621-8900, ask for Liz Del Tufo.

SEASONAL TOURS: Many towns (including a few that used to run regular tours) now concentrate their efforts on a once a year "Open House" type of thing. Among these are **Plainfield**, which boasts many beautifully restored Victorian homes. Its hospital tour, usually in May, includes some old-style wrap-around porch houses that makes this town so distinctive. **Hoboken** celebrates its railroad station in October with festivities, tours of the Byzantine station and walks through some of the newly renovated brownstones. November is the season for **Sergeantsville's** "Thanksgiving In The Country" tour wherein the whole town makes soup for the church luncheon and runs buses back and forth to the various open houses.

PHILADELPHIA TOURS

Probably the best known self-guided tour is that of Independence National Historical Park (Independence Mall) which is treated in the chapter entitled "Classics". Other popular tours in Philadelphia are:

UNITED STATES MINT: Within the downtown historic area (it's located at Arch & 5th Sts.) is the building where the coins we use are produced. No, they don't give free samples, but you can buy special sets and commemorative coins from the sales counter in the lobby. Self-guided tours are continous and last about 45 minutes. No cameras or videos allowed. Free. *Hours:* 9-4:30, Mon.-Sat. *Telephone:* 215-597-7350.

FAIRMOUNT PARK HISTORIC HOUSE TOURS: Fairmount Park cuts a wide swath through Philadelphia on both sides of the Schuylkill. It includes within its many acres, not only the usual playgrounds, pools and tennis courts, but such major attractions as the Philadelphia Zoo and the Philadelphia Museum of Art.

In the 18th Century, the park was a center for country homes of the gentry who wanted to escape the epidemics of the crowded city. Eight of these homes have been restored and are now open to the public. They include John Penn's Solitude, Robert Morris' Lemon Hill, and such Georgian classics as Woodford and Mount Pleasant. The houses, which are scattered about the park, are furnished with authentic antiques and hark back to the time when Philadelpha was the most important Colonial town in the world.

Guided tours for groups can be arranged beforehand to emphasize history, decorative arts or gardens. In early December, a special Christmas tour features the houses decorated in the manner of the 18th and early 19th centuries. Individuals may also visit the homes although they will not get a guided tour. Public hours and fees vary. There is also a special trolley which stops at several places in Fairmount Park, including the historic houses. The trolley can be boarded at the Visitor's Center at 16th and JFKennedy Boulevard. It costs $15.00 but it covers most tourist spots and you can get on and off at will.

For general information on Philadelphia write: Philadelphia Convention and Visitors Bureau, 1515 Market St., Suite 2020, Philadelphia, PA 19102 or call 215-636-1666.

See Also: *Lambertville* and *Chester* in the chapter on "Flea Markets and Outlets".

WHERE WASHINGTON SLEPT, ATE AND FOUGHT

Photo: Courtesy N.J. Travel & Tourism

In This Chapter You Will Find:

Jockey Hollow, N.J.
Washington's Headquarters (Ford Mansion, Revolutionary War Museum), N.J.
Dey Mansion, N.J.
Wallace House, N.J.
Old Dutch Parsonage, N.J.
Rockingham, N.J.
The Old Barracks, N.J.
Washington Crossing State Park, N.J.
Washington Crossing Historic Park, PA
Fort Lee Historic Park
Valley Forge, PA
Monmouth Battlefield State Park, N.J.
Covenhoven House, N.J.
Red Bank Battlefield, N.J.
Indian King Tavern, N.J.
Boxwood Hall, N.J.
Buccleuch Mansion, N.J.
Von Steuben House, N.J.
Other Revolutionary War Sites, N.J.

JOCKEY HOLLOW

The winter of 1779-1780 was the coldest in a century. On December 1, 1779, General George Washington entered Morristown and took up residence at the home of Mrs. Jacob Ford, Jr.

Meanwhile, four miles away at Jockey Hollow, 10,000 men chopped down six hundred acres of oak, walnut and chestnut trees to build hundreds of huts along the slopes of the "hollow". Severe snowstorms hindered their work and delayed the supply of meat and bread they needed to survive. Starvation confronted the army, which also suffered from inadequate clothing, disease and low morale. So terrible was the winter of the Morristown encampment that many troops finally mutinied.

But the history books only tell you about Valley Forge. Why? Because New Jersey has simply never had a very good public relations man. Not until recently, anyway.

Today there are a few reconstructed huts on the site which is administered by the National Park Service. However, the Visitor's Center gives full information about the encampment. If you go beyond the main desk you find a mini-theater where an eleven-minute film begins at the touch of a button. The story of typical foot soldiers huddled in a simple hut waiting for the rations and money that took so long in coming is unfolded. After the film, you can move on to the mock-up of the soldiers hut and see the straw beds, muskets and clothing used at the time.

From the Information Center, proceed out the back door to the **Wick Farm** where a Park Service employee is in residence. The farmhouse was occupied by both the Wick family (owners of the farm that included Jockey Hollow) and General Arthur St. Clair and his aide. A vegetable and herb garden, a well and a horse barn surround the wooden cottage.

Inside the smoky cabin, a Ranger dressed in Colonial garb will be cooking, melting down candles or just answering questions. A tour through the house shows the little bedroom of Tempe Wick, the General's office and bedroom.

From the Wick house, proceed to the open slopes called the Pennsylvania Line. There the simple soldier's huts and some hiking trails await. Special weekends there are often encampments or other doings. Free.

HOURS: 9-5 Daily. May be closed Mon. & Tues. in winter. Closed major holidays.

WASHINGTON'S HEADQUARTERS, MORRISTOWN

For another look at the details of the Morristown encampment, go to the **Ford Mansion** and **Revolutionary War Museum** which is part of the overall National Historic Site called Washington's Headquarters. It's a short drive away. You must enter through the museum and there you will find all the military paraphernalia - surgeon's tools, mess kits, muskets and cleaning rods - that accompanied the troops. The display of 18th Century weaponry is considered one of the best in the country. A new exhibit emphasizes the role of the citizens of Morristown and how they reacted to the encampment. There are some interactive elements here so that viewers can become involved.

Don't miss the fifteen-minute movie shown periodically in the auditorium. A professional film which was shot on location both here and in Jockey Hollow, it contrasts the warmth and food available to officers at the mansion with the hungry, freezing men camped four miles away. A lively ball scene was filmed in the central hall of the Ford Mansion which is right next door to the museum.

The Mansion itself is a solid frame Colonial house - by no means a mansion in the modern sense. As you enter the long central hallway, you notice how well such halls were suited to the line dances such as the Virginia Reel. The Ford home was offered as headquarters to Washington by Mrs. Ford, a widow with four children. The Ford family lived in two rooms while the General and his staff occupied the rest of the house. The furnishings are authentic to the period and many are true Ford family pieces. Beds include the canopied master bed used by Washington. Highboys, chest-on-chests, wall maps and lots of straw mattresses are all to be noted. The mansion is shown by hourly tours. National Park Service people, usually in colonial dress, take you through.

Despite the rigors of the Morristown encampment, the Ford Mansion looks like a warm, yet comparatively elegant abode for the Chief of Staff. It was here, also, on May 10, 1780, that the

Marquis de Lafayette was welcomed. And Alexander Hamilton, at that time Washington's aide-de-camp, used his time in Morristown to court Betsy Schuyler who was staying at the nearby Schuyler-Hamilton house.

HOURS: 9-5 Daily. May be closed Mon. & Tues. in winter. Closed major holidays.
ADMISSION: Adults: $2.00. Under 17 free.
DIRECTIONS: Route 287 to Exit 36 or 36A to Morris Ave. East. Follow signs to Washington's Headquarters.
TELEPHONE: 201-539-2016

DEY MANSION

A solid Dutch farmhouse built in the early Georgian style, the Dey Mansion was Washington's headquarters for three months during the summer and fall of 1780. Furnishings reflect the status of the Dey family who were quite well to-do. An unusual feature of this northern house is the separate kitchen. (There is a breezeway between it and the main house for use during the colder months.) According to the guide, the separate kitchen was practical, for if the hearth caught on fire, it would not take the rest of the house with it!

After an inspection of the well-stocked kitchen, you may tour the house which has two floors of well-kept furnishings and many family portraits. The third floor attic is used partly as a museum with varying exhibits.

Outside there are a few picnic tables placed about. You are so close to the neighboring golf course (for this historic site is part of a county park) that you might get a golf ball in your iced tea. There are also several outbuildings in various states of repair, including a spring house and a forge.

HOURS: Wed. - Fri.: 1-4:00. Sat.: 10-12 & 1-4:00. Sun.: 10-12, 1-4:00
ADMISSION: Adults: $1.00. Under 10 free.
LOCATION: 199 Totowa Rd., Wayne, Passaic County, (in Preakness Valley Park).
TELEPHONE: 201-696-1776

WALLACE HOUSE

Washington's headquarters during the winter encampment at Middlebrook (1778-79) is a two-hundred year-old clapboard Colonial now hidden away on a back street in Somerville. Once you discover the back street, you will find that the guide who administers the Wallace House also takes care of the Old Dutch Parsonage across the street. So if you knock and nobody answers, wait a while — he might be at the other house. He will usually leave a sign advising you of the fact. On busy days, there are usually volunteers who help out.

The headquarters itself is a nine room, solidly built wood structure with wide plank floors that creak curiously under modern weight. Although the furnishings are not those actually used by Washington and his staff, they are all of the period. A four-poster bed stands in the room where Washington probably slept. There are also typical toiletry articles there. The house is slowly being refurbished to reflect its state when the Wallaces lived there, after the war.

The formal parlor does not look large, but it is said up to thirty people ate there when General and Mrs. Washington entertained. It must have been awfully crowded. The Wallace House may have been the best home in the area, but the rooms are small and cramped compared to the high, airy drawing rooms at Mount Vernon. One can see why Washington was constantly pining for his old Virginia home. And although Martha spent part of the winter here she did manage to return to her Southern home once or twice. However, the house has an office, four bedrooms and two parlors, so there was ample room for entertaining.

The winter of 1778-79 was rather mild, much more pleasant than those at Valley Forge or Morristown, and the encampment at Middlebrook faced less disasters. Food, however, was never plentiful, so when the Washingtons entertained, they did so sparsely. Free. The house may be undergoing renovations.

HOURS: Wed.-Sat.: 10-12 & 1-4. Sunday: 1-4.
LOCATION: 38 Washington Place, Somerville, Somerset County.
TELEPHONE: 908-725-1015

THE OLD DUTCH PARSONAGE

This house was the home first of Pastor Frelinghuysen, minister of the Dutch Reformed Church. The bricks that built the house were brought over as ballast from Holland. Later it became the home of Rev. Jacob Hardenburgh who married Frelinghuysen's widow. Hardenburgh was one of the "Fighting Pastors" of the Revolutionary War who condemned the British from the pulpit. He founded Queens College which later became Rutgers University. He was a frequent host to General and Mrs. Washington when they lived close by during the Middlebrook Encampment. The house has since been moved so it is now across the street.

The displays at the parsonage reflect the life and times of this Dutch pastor. There are authentic relics, Colonial clothing to try on, exhibits on Dutch development, memoirs of the Frelinghuysen family and some handsome furniture.

HOURS, ETC., Check Wallace House entry.

ROCKINGHAM

A little beyond the quaint town of Rocky Hill, which in itself looks like it has slept since the Revolution, lies Rockingham. It was here that Washington stayed in 1783 while the Constitution was being hammered out at nearby Nassau Hall in Princeton. Actually, both George and Martha stayed here and entertained extensively. It is best known as the house where the "Farewell Address to the Armies" was composed.

A medium-sized Colonial with front porch, the house was once part of a fine estate of 360 acres with barns, stables, coachhouse and granary. It has since been removed from its original site (because of dynamiting in a nearby quarry) and is set a little ways off Route 518 in such a way that it takes a hardy traveller to find it. However, you will discover that the pillared porch of this Colonial is in the back, and that the vista from that side is quite pleasing. A nice kitchen garden, flowering trees and some outbuildings skirt the house.

Although there is a guide, you may roam through the house yourself. There are two stories of period rooms and some historical exhibits. Of course rooms were never huge in these New Jersey Colonials, but the ten rooms in Rockingham are good sized. The furniture is handsome. Period pieces include Chippendale sets, burnished bureaus, canopied beds and antique tea services. The Blue Room study where the Farewell Address was composed is left with the ink stand and green cloth still on the table.

There are often special exhibits, such as a display of handmade quilts, on view here. Free.

HOURS: Wed.-Sat.: 10-12 & 1-4; Sun.: 1-4.
LOCATION: Route 518 (Off 206) Rocky Hill, Somerset County
TELEPHONE: 609-921-8835

THE OLD BARRACKS

The Old Barracks has been undergoing yet another restoration in the last few years. This is the only standing barracks of the type used by the British to house foreign troops in colonial America. It is also the place where Washington and his troops surprised the Hessian soldiers after he crossed the Delaware.

The fieldstone building is U-shaped. When you enter there is a daily presentation and video. One of the restored rooms is the Squad Room with its bunk beds (where a live "soldier" may tell you what it's like to live and fight in those days). Another section is devoted to a restored officer's house, with its superior furnishings. One room is dedicated to Washington's triumphant return to Trenton as a hero.

The Barracks have quite a history. Just before the building was saved from demolition, the rooms were being used as a "Home for the Relief of Respectable, Aged and Indigent Widows and Single Women". Before that, the building had been chopped up into a series of private dwellings. Before that it was a hospital for wounded American soldiers in the Revolutionary War. And before that - well, the famous crossing of the Delaware on Christmas Day was for the express purpose of surprising the Hessian mercenaries who were sleeping off their Christmas cheer in this self-same barracks.

Originally, the Barracks were built in 1758 during the French and Indian War because American colonists objected to the billeting of British troops in private households. Later, in 1776, the British and Hessian mercenaries used it until the Americans gained control. The building went through a series of ups and downs until the Old Barracks Association saved it in 1899. Nowadays, interpretative history, with costumed guides in each room, is emphasized.

HOURS: Tues. - Sat.: 11-5; Sun.: 1-5. Closed major holidays.
ADMISSION: Adults: $2.00; Seniors: $1.00; Children: $.50
LOCATION: Barracks St. at West Front St., Trenton.
TELEPHONE: 609-396-1776

WASHINGTON CROSSING STATE PARK (N.J.)

This popular park, covering 807 acres that stretch from the banks of the Delaware in Titusville, commemorates the crossing that led to the most important victory of the war's early years. On Christmas night 1776, General Washington crossed the icy Delaware with 2,400 men, plus artillery and supplies. The crossing took nine hours and the men and officers converged on this spot on the Jersey side. The ensuing surprise attack gave a sweet taste of victory to the discouraged American troops.

Now at the park, you find a Visitor Center filled with information on the battle, the uniforms and muskets of the times. There are a variety of exhibits and some audio-visuals.

Outside there are open fields for frisbee throwing, a nature center (you must take a rocky road to get there), and an open air ampitheater for summer shows. There are many picturesque picnic groves here also. Near the Delaware River there is a monument marking the spot and two historic houses. One of these, the **Johnson Ferry House**, a refurbished building set up as an inn, offers guided tours at specific times. Nearby, the Nelson house, even closer to the river, is used as a gift shop for souveniers. Admission to the park, the center and the houses is free, but there is a parking fee on summer weekends ($3.00).

HOURS: Wed. - Sun.: 9-4:30. Shorter winter hours. Park open all the time.
LOCATION: Routes 29 & 546, Titusville, Mercer County.
TELEPHONE: 609-737-2515, 609-737-9304.

WASHINGTON CROSSING
HISTORIC PARK (PA)

Across the river the site of the embarkation is the focus for a large park that stretches up the Delaware River and includes several sections. In the first section, a modern Visitor's Center offers brochures, a theater for a film about the crossing and tickets for the historical buildings within the park. Some of these buildings are within easy walking distance. The first is the **McKonkey Ferry Inn** where Washington and his staff met and ate just before the crossing. It is fixed up as a travelers' inn with tables set with pewter and a bar and grill. In this section of the park there are two other historic houses plus replicas of the longboats that were used for the crossing.

Traveling north you come upon another section of the park which includes a wildflower preserve, the high observation tower on Bowman's Hill and the **Thompson-Neely House** (which is an original structure built of Delaware River ledgestone and looking as authentic as all get out). Tickets for all historic houses are reasonable and of course you get a guided tour through each.

Lots of picnic pavilions, walking paths and driving roads throughout the park. The Visitor Center and film are free.

HOURS: Tues.-Sat.: 9-5, Sun.: 12-5.
ADMISSION: Guided Tour: Adults: $4.00; Seniors $3.00; Children: $2.00; Under 6, free.
DIRECTIONS: Take bridge from Titusville, N.J., drive north on Pa. 32 for other sections of park.
TELEPHONE: 215-493-4076

FORT LEE HISTORIC PARK

Set in the scenic Palisades Interstate Park with a view of the Hudson, the George Washington Bridge and Manhattan, Fort Lee commemorates a defeat, not a victory. The park is only 33 acres but it contains a handsome, modern, Visitors Center, meandering roads, a picnic area, reconstructed gun batteries and an authentic 18th century soldier's hut. The park is actually a quarter mile east of the original Fort Lee (which was named after General Charles Lee who helped in the defense of New York City).

Washington planned Fort Lee as a defense against the British control of the Hudson River by its strong navy. With forts on either side of the river and sunken ships in the river channel, the British ships could be kept at bay. However, the British, under General Howe, forced the American Army out of Long Island and then New York City. In November, 1776, an orderly retreat from Fort Lee was planned. But before it could take place General Cornwallis struck first, ferrying over 6,000 men across the Hudson, north of the fort. Washington ordered an immediate retreat before his men could be cut off. Unfortunately, the cannon and other military supplies had to be left behind in this hasty retreat. This devastating blow ushered in the darkest days of the Revolution.

Nowadays you can see replicas of the abandoned cannon in the park, and view the story on plexiglas panels in the Visitors Center. A short film and displays of muskets are also on view. Down at the soldier's hut, costumed guides interpret colonial life on summer weekends and for school groups.

HOURS: Visitor Center: Wed. - Sun.: 10-5. Closed Jan., Feb.
ADMISSION: $3.00 parking fee.
DIRECTIONS: Hudson Terrace, Fort Lee. Take Palisades Int. Parkway to last exit before GW Bridge. Turn left on Hudson Terrace.
TELEPHONE: 201-461-1776

VALLEY FORGE

It is known as "The Crucible of Victory" because the 10,000 men who emerged from the harsh winter had coalesced into an efficient, well-trained fighting force. The encampment lasted from December 19,1777 to June 19, 1778. It is now commemorated at this huge park which is so vast you must start with a map or a bus tour.

The Visitor Center, where you can procure both, also offers a slide show and a small museum of Revolutionary swords and military equipment. It is here that you can board the buses which operate during the warm weather only. The bus tour, which stops at key sites, features a taped narration as you go along. Even better, you can rent or buy a tape for use as you drive along yourself. Among the important sites you will pass on the scenic drive are: the Memorial Arch, the earthen fortifications, statues of Anthony Wayne and Von Steuben, and of course, the soldiers' huts.

When staffing permits, (budget cuts have hit hard recently) costumed soldiers are at hand to welcome you at **Washington's Headquarters** and other historic houses. There is a small admission fee at these houses. There are often costumed personnel stationed at the soldier's huts also. They help to point out the hardships the soldiers endured. A friend's child was properly awed by the sacrifices of the Revolutionary soldiers when he saw one of the simple huts reconstructed here. "They didn't even have portable radios!" he told his mother.

For modern day visitors there are picnic grounds, bicycle trails, a snack bar and souvenir shop and lots of beautiful scenery. The park is free, but there is a fee for bus tours, tapes and historic houses.

> **HOURS:** Daily except Christmas 9-5. For buses: Memorial Day-Labor Day several times a day. April, May, Sept. Oct.: 3 times a day.
> **ADMISSION:** $5.50 per person.
> **LOCATION:** Visitor Center: Junction of PA 23 & 363, Valley Forge, PA.
> **TELEPHONE:** 610-783-1077

MONMOUTH BATTLEFIELD STATE PARK

Although it was not a complete victory, still the Battle of Monmouth proved that American troops, honed by the winter at Valley Forge, could hold their own against British soldiers. Today's park was the scene of a hot day's battle with a general who ordered a retreat (and was later reprimanded by Washington) and a lady named Molly "Pitcher", who became a heroine according to legend.

The fields of close-cropped rolling hills are empty at Monmouth Battlefield, but a large new Visitors Center gives you the necessary information. Three audio-visual screens offer the story of the battle from the night before to the day after. And a relief map, set with tiny lights, displays the position of the opposing forces.

Press a button and the lights move and "shoot" each other to the sound of rifle fire on the accompanying audio track. So much for the show.

Here at the center you can also pick up a map of the battlefield and other historic sites in the area. Also a refreshment counter and a picnic area are part of the building. If you drive around following the map you will find the **Craig House** (which may or may not be open, depending on staffing) where the wounded were cared for; **Tennant Church**, a good-looking, shake-sided Colonial edifice which was close to the battle; and **Molly Pitcher's Well**. Free. Once a year, in mid-June, a live re-enactment of the battle takes place.

> **HOURS:** Daily 8-4 Winter; 8-7 Summer (Park.)
> **LOCATION:** Route 9 to Route 33, just west of Freehold, Monmouth County.
> **TELEPHONE:** 908-462-9619

COVENHOVEN HOUSE

One of the four historic houses administered by the Monmouth County Historical Association, it is significant for its role in the Battle of Monmouth. Henry Clinton, commander of the British troops at the battle, stayed at the home from Friday, June 26 until Sunday, June 28, 1778. After the battle, he and his troops left Freehold and returned to New York.

The main section of the home is in Georgian style and is furnished according to a 1790 inventory of William A. Covenhoven, the well-to-do farmer who owned the property. A mural depicting a sea-battle and walls decorated in a blue-and-white Delft pattern were discovered in one bedroom during the restoration of the house. Extremely authentic and well-done — an interesting house to visit.

> **HOURS:** May-Oct.: Tues., Thurs., Sun.: 1-4; Sat.: 10-4.
> **ADMISSION:** Adults: $2.00: Seniors: $1.50; Children: $1.00; under 6 free.
> **LOCATION:** 150 West Main St., Freehold.
> **TELEPHONE:** 908-462-1466

RED BANK BATTLEFIELD

A small but decisive battle to defend Fort Mercer took place here on October 19, 1777. The Hessian army received many casualties at the hands of the American Army, which, up until this point had known mostly defeat. Since the Fort guarded the Delaware River and prevented British ships from entering occupied Philadelphia, the freedom of Fort Mercer was quite important. Although British ships eventually went through, the Red Bank victory helped France decide to join America in her fight against the British. The site is not to be confused with the town of Red Bank in Monmouth Country on the ocean side of New Jersey. The park contains old cannons and an historic house that is open for tours when guides are available (usually Memorial Day to Labor Day). Picnic areas. Free.

HOURS: Daily, 9-5.
LOCATION: 100 Hessian Ave., National Park, Gloucester County.
TELEPHONE: 609-853-5120

INDIAN KING TAVERN

Set in the little town of Haddonfield, which looks as if it stepped out of the past, this public house, or tavern, was the site of frequent meetings of the New Jersey State Legislature during the Revolutionary War. Among the rooms the guide shows off are the Colonial kitchen, the toy room, and the bedroom where Dolly Madison slept. (Her uncle was a one-time owner of the tavern). Groups by appointment only. Children under 12 must be accompanied by an adult. Guided tours for individuals are ongoing. You must wait at the door for the next tour if there is one in progress at the moment.

HOURS: Wed.-Sat.: 9-4; Sun.: 1-4.
ADMISSION: Donation ($1.00 suggested)
LOCATION: 233 Kings Highway, Haddonfield, Camden County.
TELEPHONE: 609-429-6792

BOXWOOD HALL

Also known as the Boudinot Mansion, this very nicely furnished Colonial house is not far from the main drag in Elizabeth. Built in 1750, it was the home, during the Revolution, of Elias Boudinot, president of the Continental Congress. George Washington had lunch here on the day he embarked for New York and his inauguration as President. House furnishings include both the Colonial and later Empire style. State Historic Site. Free.

HOURS: Call first.
LOCATION: 1073 East Jersey St., Elizabeth.
TELEPHONE: 201-648-4540

BUCCLEUCH MANSION

A handsome Georgian mansion which was recently refurbished (the surrounding gardens are very impressive). The house is set inside Buccleuch Park on a tree-lined street that is practically part of the Rutgers Campus in New Brunswick. Originally built in 1793, White House Farm, as it was then known, was sold to an English army officer in 1774.

The house was confiscated by the Americans in 1776, but by December the British troops re-occupied New Brunswick. The bannister still retains the marks of the soldiers' musket barrels from the time of this occupation, which lasted until 1777. After the war, Colonel Charles Stewart, Commissary General of the Revolutionary Army, became the owner. At this time, White House Farm was visited by Washington, Hancock and Alexander Hamilton, who all loved the setting.

Much of Buccleuch Mansion's furnishings today are of 19th Century origin. Of particular note is the striking wallpaper in the the downstairs and upstairs hallways. Rooms include a Victorian parlor and a drawing room with Queen Anne pieces. You can also inspect the bedrooms (including the one where Washington slept), a toy room, a craft room with spinning wheel, and an attic filled with assorted "significa", including side-saddles, hoops for hoopskirts and two centuries of whatnots. There are also changing exhibits in the house. Free (donations accepted). Group tours by appointment.

HOURS: Sun.: 2-4 June-Oct.

VON STEUBEN HOUSE

A Dutch Colonial home built in 1695 and further added to in 1752, this home is an example of early architecture in New Jersey. The house was confiscated by the Americans during the Revolutionary War because the owners (the Zabriskie family) were loyal to the British crown. Its position on the Hackensack River made it a strategic prize for both sides. (The house literally sits on the river's edge). It was later presented to Baron Von Steuben for his aid during the war.

One thing you notice in the furnishings here is the emphasis on local craftsmen, and on the Dutch influence in Bergen County. Some fine specimens of the local Colonial craft include a New Brunswick kas, a Hudson Valley kas, an old settle, etc. The house is maintained as a museum by the Bergen County Historical Society and includes Indian artifacts, dolls and toys. Next door there are two other historical buildings which are opened on weekends during warm weather. Free.

HOURS: Wed.-Sat.: 10-12 & 1-5; Sun.: 2-5
LOCATION: 1209 Main Street, River Edge, Bergen County (take River Edge exit from Route 4).
TELEPHONE: 201-487-1739

OTHER REVOLUTIONARY WAR SITES

Among the many other historic sites and buildings associated with the Revolutionary War are:

PRINCETON BATTLEFIELD STATE PARK: A short, decisive battle was fought here on January 3, 1777, just a week after the famous crossing of the Delaware. General Hugh Mercer was mortally wounded during this battle. Within the park, you can visit the Thomas Clarke House, used as a hospital following the battle. Open Wed. - Sat. 10-12, 1-4. Free. *Hours:* 9 AM to dusk. *Location:* 500 Mercer St., Princeton. *Telephone:* 609-921-0074.

BRANDYWINE BATTLEFIELD STATE PARK: This battle was a defeat for Washington's forces. It took place on September 11, 1777, and is commemorated by dioramas and audio-visuals at the Visitors Center. There are also two historic houses within the park. One was Washington's headquarters and the other was used by the Marquis de Lafayette. Free (fee for houses). *Hours:* Tues.-Sun.: 9-5, May 30-Labor Day. *Location:* Route 1, Chadds Ford, PA. *Telephone:* 610-459-3342.

DRAKE HOUSE: During the battle of the Watchung Mountains, Washington used this house as his command headquarters. Although there is a Colonial bedroom where he is supposed to have rested, the house was later remodeled. It now reflects the Empire and Victorian styles as well as the basic Colonial. *Hours:* Sun.:2-4. *Admission:* $1.00; *Location:* 602 West Front St., Plainfield, Union County. *Telephone:* 908-755-5831.

HANCOCK HOUSE: Scene of massacre of American troops by attacking British Rangers, this 1734 house has period furnishings. Free. *Location:* Route 49, 5 miles south of Salem, Salem County. *Telephone:* 609-935-4373.

SCHUYLER-HAMILTON HOUSE: Colonial home where Alexander Hamilton courted Betsey Schuyler. *Hours:* Tues. & Sun., 2-5. *Admission:* Adults: $1.50; Under 12 free. *Location:* 5 Olyphant Place, Morristown, Morris County. *Telephone:* 201-267-4039.

ALLEN HOUSE: Since this 1750 house was operated as the Blue Ball Tavern during the Revolutionary War, two major rooms here have been furnished in that manner. Tables are set with pewter, there is a bar and grill with whiskey jugs and so forth. Upstairs, changing exhibits *Hours:* April-Dec.: Tues., Thurs., Sun., 1-4; Sat. 10-4. *Admission:* Adults: $2.00; Children: $1.00; Seniors: $1.50. Under 6 free. *Location:* Route 35 & Sycamore Ave., Shrewsbury, Monmouth County. *Telephone:* 908-462-1466.

See Also: *Nassau Hall, Morven, Independence Hall* and several of the colonial homes mentioned in the chapter "Restored Villages and Homes".

HOMES OF THE RICH
AND FAMOUS

Photo: Courtesy Boscobel

In This Chapter You Will Find:

Nemours, DE
Kykuit, N.Y.
Hyde Park, N.Y.
The Vanderbilt Mansion, N.Y.
Edison Labs —Glenmont, N.J.
Historic Speedwell, N.J.
Grover Cleveland Birthplace, N.J.
Ballantine House, N.J.
Lambert Castle, N.J.
Ringwood Manor, N.J.
Lyndhurst, N.Y.
Sunnyside, N.Y.
Boscobel, N.Y.
Maccoulloch Hall, N.J.
Drumthwacket, N.J.
Bainbridge House, N.J.
William Trent House, N.J.
Kuser Farm Mansion, N.J.
Walt Whitman House, N.J.
Craftsman Farms, N.J.
Pennsbury Manor, PA
Andalusia, PA
Green Hills Farm, PA

NEMOURS

The fabulous homes of the super-rich are America's equivalent of the palaces and castles of Europe. And no home is more palatial than Nemours, the former residence of Alfred I. DuPont. Located outside Wilmington in the increasingly popular Brandywine Valley area, Nemours is the latest in a series of DuPont Estates now open to the public.

The mansion, built in 1909, is a modified Louis XVI French chateau. The landscaped gardens are in the French formal style and include marble statues, cascading fountains and a series of terraces and stairways to please the eye. In fact, the hand of Louis XVI seems to lie everywhere in Nemours — a tribute as much to the Gallic origins of the DuPonts as to the possibility that American millionaires in 1910 must have known the era of conspicuous consumption was about to end. A few years later the income tax and World War I helped destroy any notion of an American aristocracy. Like the French kings before them, the DuPonts may have realized this was the last chance to flaunt their riches.

Once you enter the chateau, you are led by a tour guide into a home of vast elegance. The gold and white dining room boasts ornate moldings on walls and ceilings, Rococco style paintings and a chandelier worthy of the Phantom of the Opera. The reception room, living room and other public rooms are equally fabulous with inlaid ceilings, marble tiled floors, rich oriental rugs and carved walls. Furniture includes both genuine antiques like George Washington's chair and fine copies of Louis XVI furnishings.

You rarely see the kitchens of "great homes," but at Nemours there's a downstairs tour of the restaurant-sized cooking area with its empty pantry and huge pots. A dumbwaiter is set up with a breakfast tray of Spode china as if ready to be sent up to the bedroom of Mrs. DuPont. Also, downstairs is the bowling alley (no, it's not automatic, they used real pin boys), the billiard room (with a table the size of a bowling alley) and the furnace room (ingeniously set up by Alfred himself, who was an engineer).

After the house tour you may either board a mini-bus for a tour of the gardens or walk around yourself. Fountains and pools, colonnades and balustrades, marble Cupids and Dianas, velvet lawns and clipped hedges create a mini-Versailles here.

Nemours doesn't exactly admit hordes of people. Numbers are limited and there are only four tours a day. Reservations are highly suggested. No children under 16. No picture-taking inside the mansion. And mind your manners — this here is DuPont territory!

HOURS: May-Nov.: Tues.-Sat.: tours at 9, 11, 1 & 3. Sunday tours: 11, 1 & 3.
ADMISSION: $8.00 ($10.00 - 1996)
LOCATION: Rockland Road (inside Alfred I. DuPont Institute) Wilmington, Delaware.
TELEPHONE: 302-651-6912 or write: Reservations Office, Nemours Foundation, P.O. Box 109, Wilmington, Delaware 19899

KYKUIT

You may never be as rich as Rockefeller, but at least now you can visit the family estate in Pocantico Hills, near Tarrytown, New York — if you can get a ticket. Since timed tours of this recently opened mansion are limited in number and are run only spring through fall, ticket demand has outnumbered supply. As time goes by, however, it should become easier to see this 87 acre enclave.

This was the country home of four generations of Rockefellers. John D., his son, John D. Jr., Nelson and Nelson's children. The furnishings inside and the magnificent terraced grounds show the influence of the first three generations. John D. Rockefeller, who started the fortune, did not believe in conspicuous consumption. The original stone house, called "Kykuit" which is Dutch for "lookout" was not particularly ornate. It was later remodeled in the Renaissance Revival style.

Inside the house you'll find rooms decorated in various ways - including a beautiful Adamesque side room. The most spectacular is the two-floor music room (it once housed an organ) which now has graceful balconies rimming the oculus - an oval ceiling opening. 18th and 19th century furniture along with Chinese vases from various dynasties are found in the first floor rooms.

What makes Kykuit unique is the incorporation of modern paintings and sculptures into classic and Victorian surroundings. Both Nelson Rockefeller and his mother, Abby Aldrich Rockefeller were strong collectors of modern art. So you will see a modern work or folk art mixed in with traditional furnishings. However, most of the modern paintings, rugs and lithographs are found downstairs in a separate, air-conditioned art gallery. Kandinsky,

Picasso, Motherwell and a number of "Op Art" pieces from the 1960s are on display.

Once outside, you really get a feel for the opulence of the place. The magnificent gardens, originally landscaped by William Bosworth in the Italian Villa style, are built in a series of terraces that drop down the hill. The view of the rolling hills, the Hudson River and the Palisades beyond is spectacular. The terraces include a stone teahouse, a statue of "Oceanus" that commands a lookout, a rose garden and a nine-hole golf course. And that's not all. There's also all those modern sculptures placed around the greenery. Some blend in beautifully. Others, like an orange cube or Calder's "Large Spiney" may take you back a bit.

Last stop on the tour is the coach and carriage house where the men can admire the 1916 Crane Simplex or the 1939 Cadillac convertible along with a number of pony carts, halters and horse stalls.

The Visitors Center at Philipsburg Manor is where you begin the reserved tour, run by *Historic Hudson Valley*. You are asked to sign in, get a "badge" and watch an introductory film. Tours are limited to 18 people at a time. So do come early - if you are not ready to board the minivan when it leaves, they will sell your seat to the "standbys". The tour takes about 2 1/2 hours and much of that is walking - including up and down stairs. As for tickets, if you can't book direct, you may be able to get on a ferry or bus tour.

Not far from Kykuit is the **Union Church of Pocantico Hills**, a community church where the Rockefeller family worshipped. The small stone structure is famous for its stained glass windows created by two modern masters. Henri Matisse designed the rose window above the altar, while the side windows and the huge Narthex panes were painted by Marc Chagall in strong colors and swirling images. Tours are conducted by *Historic Hudson Valley* also and cost $3.00 (use telephone number below). The church is located on Route 448, east of Route 9 in North Tarrytown.

HOURS: By reservation only.
ADMISSION: Adults: $18.00; Students, seniors: $16.00
LOCATION: See Philipsburg Manor listing
TELEPHONE: 914-631-8200 • Day Cruises 800-53-FERRY

HYDE PARK

For people who lived under Franklin Delano Roosevelt's administration, there is either a deep love for the man who dominated the White House from 1932 to 1945 — or an abiding hatred. As president during the great Depression and World War II Roosevelt was both blamed and praised for cataclysmic changes in American life. And Roosevelt's charming boyhood home has always been identified with the man.

Now a National Historic Site, the Hyde Park complex consists of the family home, the beautiful grounds on a high, green hill overlooking a clean Hudson River and the **Roosevelt Library and Museum**. Starting at the home, you enter from a parking lot which is lined with apple trees still bearing fruit. The white, classically proportioned country house is not overly large and can accommodate only 50 people at a time. However, there is an easy traffic flow since you do not have to wait for a tour guide to take you through. Instead, you may move about as you like, using the cassette tape recording as your guide. The cassette was recorded by Eleanor Roosevelt and gives you an interesting insight into family life in the inimitable accents of that voice. Guided tours may be available during winter months.

Upon entering the main hall, you see the heavy furnishings that characterized a country home of the 1890's. Further on, the pretty Dresden Room is brightened by the colorful floral drapes and upholstery picked out by Sara Roosevelt in 1939 shortly before the King and Queen of England visited. The whole house, in fact, shows much more the influence of Franklin's mother, Sara, than of his wife.

Upstairs, the boyhood bedroom and FDR's bedroom contain the memorabilia we expect. Favorite pictures, the leash and blanket of the scottie Fala on his own chair, and books and magazines that were scattered there in March, 1945, are still present in the room.

Next to the house is the FDR Library. The museum section contains gifts from foreign rulers, cartoons, photographs, and a passing picture of both the Depression and World War II. Special exhibits on both Franklin and Eleanor are here, plus the wooden wheelchair Roosevelt used. Outside on the quiet green lawn next to the rose garden are the graves of both FDR and Eleanor. And, in another section of the estate, **Val-Kill**, the separate residence of Eleanor, is open to viewers on a limited basis.

HOURS: Wed.-Sun. 9-5.
ADMISSION: Adults: $5.00; Seniors: $4.00; Under 17 free.
LOCATION: Hyde Park, N.Y. Take Garden State Parkway to NY
Thruway to Exit 18. Cross Mid-Hudson Bridge, then
Route 9N for 7 miles. Follow signs.
TELEPHONE: 914-229-9115

VANDERBILT MANSION

If the Roosevelt home radiates quiet wealth, the Vanderbilt Mansion exudes conspicuous consumption. A marble palace in the style of the Italian Renaissance, it is set on large estate grounds where swans paddle about in a meandering stream. Inside, the mansion's furnishings are closer to French Rococco than Italian Renaissance. The huge marble reception hall opens to both the dining room and drawing room. The dining room, which seated thirty, and the beautifully furnished drawing room were the scene of gala balls. A small side room called the Gold Room was the gathering place for guests to sip sherry before dinner. This room attracts tourists to its gold leaf decoration. The ceiling painting depicts scantily clad maidens floating in the azure sky.

If the downstairs chairs all look like thrones, then the upstairs bedrooms of Mr. and Mrs. Vanderbilt were certainly fit for a king and queen. Walls of embroidered silk and a bed with a marble gate around it are features copied from a French queen's bedroom to outfit the one Mrs. Vanderbilt used. As for Mr. Vanderbilt — he merely had a canopy with a crown above his bed and true Flemish tapestries hanging on the walls. It all goes to show what you could do if you had money in the pre-income tax days.

The mansion with its marble and finely turned Circassian walnut and the quiet, heavily treed grounds all help to recreate the splendor of a bygone era. Tours begin at the Visitors' Center where you can also buy tickets and pick up brochures and postcards. A film about the mansion is shown here. It's a short walk over to the mansion where you are allowed to inspect the opulent rooms at your own pace. Tours usually take between 30 to 45 minutes. Guided tours available off-season.

HOURS: Wed.-Sun. 9-5. Closed major holidays.
ADMISSION: Adults: $2.00; Under 17 free.
LOCATION: Use Hyde Park directions.
TELEPHONE: 914-229-9115

THE EDISON LABS

For many area schools, a trip to the Edison Labs is *de rigeur* around the 4th or 5th grade. Therefore, parents get the idea that this is strictly a children's tour. So while troops of camera-toting Japanese and Germans tramp through the facilities at West Orange, there are still local residents who have never set foot inside the laboratory where Edison worked for 44 years.

Indeed, if a visiting scientist hadn't dragged me there when we first moved to the Garden State, I never would have troubled to go. The second time around, I was under the influence of an Architectural History course, and insisted we see Glenmont, Edison's elegant Victorian home.

Actually both buildings comprise the **Edison National Historic Site**. Headquarters are on a busy commercial area of West Orange. You buy the tickets there, and make reservations for Glenmont (on days when entrance is available). Then you can begin your tour of the Labs (which takes about forty-five minutes.) Tours are by National Park Service personnel.

Among the rooms you will see is the phonograph room which displays various models of Edison's prized invention. Naturally, the group will be treated to audio effects — anything from Edison reciting "Mary Had A Little Lamb" in tinfoil to a comedy routine on an inch-thick wooden record.

Before or after the tour you can watch the first feature motion picture — "The Great Train Robbery". A few years ago this movie was shown in the **Black Maria** (a replica of the original tarpaper studio which is on display outside). But in order to accomodate the large number of tourists, the film is now shown separately, along with a movie about Edison. "The Great Train Robbery", by the way, is of interest not only because it is the first Western. This early 1900's silent picture was filmed locally, using the talents of laboratory workers and the trains of the Erie Lackawanna. (You will probably recognize the Essex County terrain, if not the old railroad cars).

The chemical labs, the machine shop and the huge junk storage bins are also part of the extensive tour. Grand finale is the golden oak library where Edison's desk, cot and 10,000 volumes still stand. Even the six-foot wall clock remains stopped at 3:27 — the time on October 18, 1931 when Edison died.

HOURS: Daily, 9-5. Tours start at 10:30. Last tour is 3:30.
ADMISSION: Adults: $2.00; Under 17 free.

GLENMONT

Tickets to Glenmont, the recently refurbished home of Edison, are sold on a first come, first served basis to visitors to the National Historic Site at the main office. Visiting days are limited, so its best to call first if your main object is to see the elegant Victorian house set on a sweeping lawn in the private development called Llewellyn Park (about 2 miles from the Labs). Tours are guided.

Glenmont is a rambling, Queen Anne style house, where Edison resided with his second wife, Minna, after he moved north from Menlo Park. Here he entertained visitors from around the world — but it is also a warm family home where his children grew up. The house is filled with carved oak woodwork, oriental rugs, wild animal skins, stained glass windows, and a large, sunny Conservatory that is worthy of an English manor house. One finds rich fabrics and tile floors, paintings and of course a gentleman's library filled with leather-bound tomes. There is a pipe-organ and a grand piano that was used both by the children and by musicians auditioning for Edison's phonograph company.

The upstairs bedrooms and sitting rooms are less ornate, obviously meant for family life although the furniture is still of the monumental variety. The tour is a pleasant glimpse not only of a famous man's home, but of an unhurried, elegant era.

HOURS: Wed.-Sun.: 11-4:00. Call first as hours may change.
ADMISSION: (For Labs and house) Adults: $2.00; Under 17 free.
LOCATION: Lewellyn Park, West Orange (Buy tickets at Labs)
TELEPHONE: 201-736-0550

HISTORIC SPEEDWELL

Every 19th Century technological breakthrough led to further inventions. And Historic Speedwell in Morristown is the scene of one of the most important American achievements. It was here that Samuel Morse and Alfred Vail spent years perfecting the electro- magnetic telegraph. And that invention gave rise to the later inventions of radio, television and more. Perhaps some inventor today will find inspiration from the exhibits here.

One thing you learn from a visit to this green and pleasant compound: you do not have to be a scientist to be an inventor. Samuel Morse was a portrait painter by profession. At the **Vail House** (the main building of the complex), you can see the portraits Morse painted of the senior Mr. and Mrs. Vail. These were painted in 1837. Although Morse did not live here, he was a frequent guest.

The original Vail money came from their Iron Works. One of the buildings is devoted to an exhibit concerning the making and molding of iron machinery and to the ironworkers themselves. The foundry was best known for its early steam engines. In fact, the first trans-Atlantic steamship was built here.

But it is at the *Factory*, originally built for cotton weaving, that you will find the most information about the telegraph. Vail and Morse held the first public demonstration of this new wonder here in 1838. An exhibit of documents, models and instruments illustrates the invention and development of the telegraph.

Historic Speedwell is situated on the old homestead of the Vail family across from a picturesque dam where a Vail factory once stood. The Vail House itself is a fine example of a comfortable mid-19th century home.

HOURS: Apr.-Oct.: Thurs., Fri.: 11:30-4; Sat., Sun.: 1-5.
ADMISSION: Adults: $3.00; Seniors: $2.00; Children 6-16: $1.00
LOCATION: Route 202 (Speedwell Ave.) at Cory Road, one mile north of Morristown Green, Morris County.
TELEPHONE: 201-540-0211

GROVER CLEVELAND BIRTHPLACE

Grover Cleveland, the only United States president to be born in New Jersey, spent his first year in this pleasant Manse. The clapboard house was built in 1832 for the pastor of the First Presbyterian Society. Two years later, Reverend Richard F. Cleveland obtained that position. Grover was born in 1837, but by the following year the pastor had retired and moved his family to Buffalo.

The house, which is a State Historic Site, therefore boasts a melange of furniture. The open hearth kitchen reflects the earlier 1830 period when life in the country was fairly simple. However, a number of later pieces from Cleveland's presidency reflect the richer, more ornate world of the 1880's. A large chair from the White House term plus several other pieces show both Cleveland's girth and his station in life.

The caretaker of the Manse is happy to act as guide and to point out the photographs, clothing, medals, sheet music, etc. that have been collected about Cleveland. A picture of Mrs. Cleveland, a beautiful young woman whom he married when she was 21 and he 49 adorns the house and the guide bubbles with anecdotes about her. No heavy history here. No talk of Pullman strikes and gold panics and oppressed workers. What you learn is good presidential gossip. Frances was Grover's ward, and she turned down his marriage proposal several times before she finally said yes. She was the youngest First Lady ever; their first baby, Ruth, became the namesake of a still popular candy bar, etc., etc.

After his second term (Adlai Stevenson was his Vice-President), Cleveland retired to Princeton where he served as lecturer and trustee. He became friends with Woodrow Wilson, then president of the university. They are both buried, incidentally, in Princeton Cemetery.

All the downstairs rooms of the "Old Manse" are open to the public and include the well-filled living room; a bedroom with high-backed bed, cradle and quilts; a den with lots of memorabilia and the earlier, pre-Victorian kitchen. The house, by the way, is set on a busy street in Caldwell and is easy to miss since it's not really very large. Free.

> **HOURS:** Wed.-Fri.: 9-12 & 1-6. Sat.: 9-12 & 1-5.; Sun.: 1-6. Call first.
> **LOCATION:** 207 Bloomfield Ave., Caldwell, Essex County.
> **TELEPHONE:** 201-226-1810

THE BALLANTINE HOUSE

One of the pleasures of visiting the Newark Museum is the presence of the Ballantine House right next door. You enter this opulent late Victorian townhouse from an interior passageway in the museum proper. And while you cannot go completely into the rooms, you can see perfectly when you enter partially. It is a marvelous job of restoration with the colors brighter and the furniture cleaner than it probably ever was in its heyday. Now that the second floor is open, you can also visit the bedrooms.

Photo: Courtesy Newark Museum

The Gilded Age in Newark is evoked by the elaborate library of the Ballantine family.

50

The Ballantines, were a Scotch family who rose from poor immigrants to wealthy beer barons within a span of two generations. Since a townhouse on Washington Park was the sure sign of success in Newark, John Ballantine commissioned this spacious, seventeen room, three-story Renaissance Revival house to be built in the mid-1880's.

In the high Victorian period, the term "interior decoration" was taken literally and every inch of space is covered, plastered, panelled, draped, ensconced or otherwise prettified. The dining room, for instance, features oak and cherry parquet floors, mahogany woodwork, a ceiling of molded papier mache panels between painted plaster beams, and walls of leather-looking paper. Add to that a brick and wood fireplace, small stained glass windows, tapestried chairs and a table sparkling with white linen and you get a scene of solid bourgeois luxury that was meant to impress the guests.

Other rooms on view include the rich, red-toned library, the delicate French-style drawing room and the somber reception room. A magnificent stained glass window with its rising sun presides over the stairwell leading to the second floor where china and silver are on view. The Ballantine House provides not only insights into Victorian highstyle living, but its legacy of manners and mores as well.

HOURS: Wed.-Sun.: 12-5.
LOCATION: (Enter through Newark Museum) 49 Washington St., Newark.
TELEPHONE: 201-596-6550

LAMBERT CASTLE

Situated high on a bluff in the Garrett Mountain Reservation overlooking Paterson, Lambert Castle is most impressive. Built by silk manufacturer Catholina Lambert in the heyday of 19th Century opulence, it appears as a Medieval castle with rounded towers and crenelated turrets — just perfect for longbow archers to repel the invading hordes.

However, it was not the invading hordes that undid Lambert, but the silk strike of 1913 together with a decline in the American silk trade. Bankruptcy loomed and many of Lambert's prize possessions — European paintings and fine furnishings — were sold to pay debtors. He retained the house, though, until his death in 1923.

The view from Lambert castle is spectacular, encompassing both the city of Paterson with its many church domes and spires and the mountains beyond. At the moment this is all you can get — the castle is closed for renovations until 1997.

The building serves as headquarters for the Passaic County Historical Society. Memorabilia about the Great Falls, famous sons, and photographs of Paterson will be part of the collection when the castle re-opens.

LOCATION: Valley Road. Garrett Mountain Reservation, Paterson, Passaic County.

TELEPHONE: 201-881-2761

RINGWOOD MANOR

If they ever film a Chekov play in New Jersey, Ringwood Manor would make a perfect setting. This rambling manor house set on a rise overlooking a small lake where ducks paddle about is a prime example of the Victorian country house. Actually the house was originally the residence of Martin Ryerson, a colonial ironmaster, and relics of the old iron forge days still dot the landscape. Short cannons and iron chains are placed about at intervals. The grounds are either well kept or dingy depending on whether the park received its funding from the State for the year.

But it is the expanded manor with a porte-cochere designed by Stanford White, that gives Ringwood its high Victorian look. As the country home first of Peter Cooper, the industrialist and philanthropist who founded not only Cooper Union but the short-lived Greenback Party as well, and then of his son-in-law Abram S. Hewitt, Ringwood became a pleasant haven filled with antiques, and cottage furniture. Approximately 30 rooms are open to the public (the house contains many more) and bedrooms with lace curtains, parlors filled with paintings, heavy oak stairways and bronze chandeliers create a pleasant ambience. The walls are also hung with mementos of the Cooper-Hewitt family: newspaper articles and cartoons on politics both national and local, for Peter Cooper ran for President when he was 85, and Hewitt was Mayor of New York.

Outside on the grassy lawn and beyond, visitors picnic or meander around the wide grounds with its gardens and playgrounds. The manor is one corner of a huge state park high in the Ramapo mountains. Each section of the park has its own toll gate and parking fee although Tuesdays are usually free in New Jersey state parks. Shepherd's Lake has a lovely swimming, canoeing and picnic area and therefore is by far the most popular area of the park, filling up early on weekends.

Another historic section of *Ringwood State Park* is: **Skylands**, a 44-room mansion in the Jacobean style that looks like an English castle. No furnishings inside but there are handsome carvings on the walls, the ceilings and the fireplace. Skylands is best known for its gardens (see Garden section). At the moment the mansion is not open to the general public except occasionally for one weekend in December.

> **HOURS:** Park — daily. MANOR HOUSE: Memorial Day — Labor Day: Wed. — Sun.: 10-4.
> **ADMISSION:** Parking fees, $3 weekend during warm weather.
> **LOCATION:** Route 17 past N.Y. State line to Sloatsburg Road
> **TELEPHONE:** 201-962-7031 or 7047

LYNDHURST

Just a few minutes south of the Tappan Zee Bridge and run by the National Trust for Historical Preservation, this Gothic "castle" was the summer home of Jay Gould. The crystal greenhouses were once the foremost indoor gardens in America although they are now empty. The house, with its turreted towers and manicured lawn, is often used in commercials and advertisements as an example of the good life.

Visitors are taken through the home by tour guides and are shown, among other things: an ornate dining room with enough carved woodwork to fill a Gothic church; the butler's pantry which reminds one of the "Upstairs, Downstairs" days when people really had butlers; and the huge drawing room with its many landscape paintings, its stained glass windows and view of the Hudson. Much of the interior is wood or plaster painted to look like stone to enhance the Medieval effect. This is not unusual in homes built in the Gothic Revival style.

The newly renovated carriage house now offers a lunchroom where you can buy light salads and sandwiches. The gift shop and a museum gallery are housed in a former garage. This will afford more time to walk around the gorgeous grounds.

HOURS: Mid-Apr.-Nov.: Tues.-Sun. 10-5 Nov.-Apr.: Weekends 10-5.
ADMISSION: Adults: $7.00; Seniors: $6.00; Students: $3.00
LOCATION: U.S. Route 9, Tarrytown, N.Y., 1/2 mile south of Tappan Zee Bridge.
TELEPHONE: 914-631-4481

SUNNYSIDE

Home of Washington Irving, America's first internationally famous author. Built in a whimsical manner to suit Irving's individual taste, the reconstructed house is a cross between the Dutch and the quaint. It is built on the banks of the Hudson with lovely grounds, including an ice house and swan ponds. At the Visitor's Center a charming film on the Legend of Sleepy Hollow is shown. Guided tours only. Because the rooms and hallways are small, the tour takes time. Sleepy Hollow Church and graveyard are nearby.

HOURS: 10-5 Daily except Tues.. Closed major holidays.
ADMISSION: Adults: $7.00; Children: $4.00; Seniors: $6.00; Under 6 free.
LOCATION: Take Tappan Zee Bridge to New York, then Route 9 south to Sunnyside Lane.
TELEPHONE: 914-591-8763

BOSCOBEL

A stately Federal mansion set on the banks of the Hudson River (it was moved 15 miles from its original location), Boscobel was begun by Morris Dyckman in 1804. Dyckman, who made his money as an arms dealer, was able to afford the best furnishings. Although he died before it was finished, his wife moved in and furnished it most elegantly. The house is completely restored and refurbished (in fact it was refurbished twice!) and reflects an authenticity of period.

A large central hall, sweeping stairway, patterned wallpaper, Duncan Phyfe furniture, china, glass, silver and a bevy of whale oil lamps reflect an era of early and gracious wealth. The wide lawns, the rose garden and the view of West Point across the river all add to the ambience of quiet gentility. Guides take you through the home, but you may peruse the outdoor scenery on your own. Tours run every twenty minutes. A small gift shop is located in a separate building.

HOURS: Daily except Tues. Closed Jan. & Feb. Tours: 9:30-5 Nov., Dec., Mar., 9:30-4 Closed major holidays.
ADMISSION: Adults: $6.00; Children 6-14: $3.00; Seniors: $5.00
LOCATION: Garrison, N.Y. on Route 9D, 8 miles north of Bear Mt. Bridge.
TELEPHONE: 914-265-3638

MACCULLOCH HALL

Unfortunately, this 1908 Federal structure has very limited public hours because the furnishings within are quite handsome. Oriental rugs throughout, huge Waterford crystal chandeliers brought over from the millionaire Twombly estate (now Fairleigh Dickinson campus), and an original portrait of Washington by Rembrandt Peale are among the eclectic collection of the mansion's last owner.

There is no attempt to furnish each room according to a specific period but you will see quality cupboards, china, and crystal of the 18th and 19th Century throughout the house.

Macculloch Hall includes two upstairs galleries. One is an area dedicated to Thomas Nast, the famous cartoonist whose vitriolic cartoons helped to topple the corrupt Boss Tweed regime. Nast was a Morristown resident (his home is practically across the street) whose drawings became classics. His depiction of Santa Claus is the one we now use as the standard and he also created the donkey and the elephant as symbols of the political parties. The Nast room includes cartoons, paintings, drawings, and awards.

The house is shown by guided tour (allow a half-an-hour at least) but you may wander through the pleasant garden by yourself. The mansion is specially decorated for Christmas and offers extended hours the first week in December.

HOURS: Thurs. & Sun. 1-4 PM. Open to groups by appointment.
ADMISSION: Adults: $3.00; Seniors & Students: $2.00
LOCATION: 45 Macculloch Ave., Morristown, Morris County (2 blocks west of South Street).
TELEPHONE: 201-538-2404

DRUMTHWACKET

On any Wednesday you can visit Drumthwacket, the Governor's Mansion in Princeton, and get a tour of the gracious Greek Revival building that has been refurbished to the hilt. The governor will not be in, of course. For two hours, this white-columned house belongs to the people who pay for its maintenance - namely New Jersey citizens.

The mansion, with its two-story high Ionic columns and wide veranda will remind many of the plantation houses of the deep south. Indeed, Charles Olden, who built it in 1835, had spent nine years in New Orleans and was impressed by southern architecture.

The entrance hallway includes several historic paintings on loan from various museums. A docent explains the history of the building as you move from room to room. Moses Taylor Pyne bought the estate from Olden's widow in 1893. Pyne named the house Drumthwacket - Celtic for "wooded hill." He added two wings. One of these includes a striking wood-panelled library. This room boasts a Gothic Revival stone fireplace mantel that would be worthy of a Dracula film.

The dining room is most impressive. The extra-long table is set with sterling silver candelabra and an ornate punchbowl - all part of the silver service from the battleship U.S.S. Jersey. The full silver service (created by Tiffany's way back when) is exhibited on special occasions. More often, gold-trimmed Lenox china with the green seal of New Jersey is used.

Across the hall in the confortably furnished living room a special exhibit of New Jersey porcelains from the studios of Cybis and Boehm may be on display. Outside, you can meander through the lovely formal terraced gardens behind the house. Free.

HOURS: Wed.: 12-2. Group tour by reservation.
LOCATION: 354 Stockton Street, Princeton.
TELEPHONE: 609-683-0057

BAINBRIDGE HOUSE

This small brick building is wedged between stores and movie houses on the well-traversed Nassau Street and stands practically opposite the iron gates of Princeton University. The one-time home of Captain William Bainbridge, a hero of the War of

1812 and a commander of the U.S.S. Constitution, it serves now as headquarters for the Princeton Historical Society. Luckily, this particular historical society keeps its house open to the public much longer than most. A typical small home of the well-to-do family of the late 18th Century, it features period furnishings, a history of Princeton, but is given over mostly to changing exhibits.

There is also a surprisingly well-stocked souvenir and book shop here. The Historical Society here also conducts tours of Princeton, which should be reserved beforehand. Anyone can join the Sunday walking tour at 2 p.m. Self-guided tour maps are also available here.

HOURS: Tues.-Sun.: 12-4. Closed Jan., Feb. except weekends.
ADMISSION: Free (donations accepted)
LOCATION: 158 Nassau Street, Princeton, Mercer County.
TELEPHONE: 609-921-6748

WILLIAM TRENT HOUSE

The founder of Trenton, so to speak, because his house and property were known as "Trent's Town", William Trent built his stately home in 1719. It was later the residence of four governors. "A genteel brick dwelling house, three stories high, with a large, handsome staircase and entry", according to an early observer, it is one of the best restorations in New Jersey. In Georgian style with 18th Century English furniture and many early American pieces. Some of the William & Mary and Queen Anne furnishings here are equal to what you would find in Colonial Williamsburg, and the old-fashioned kitchen is really worth the tour. Guided tours by knowledgeable volunteers.

HOURS: Daily 12:30-4
ADMISSION: Adults: $1.50 Children: $.50
LOCATION: 15 Market Street, Trenton.
TELEPHONE: 609-989-3027

KUSER FARM MANSION

The country home of the Kusers was built in 1882 as both a vacation home and a working farm. The family had financial interests in hotels, beer, cars and more, but are best known for their connection with 20th Century Fox. The elder Kuser had helped William Fox start his motion picture company with a $200,000 loan. The connection continued for years with the Kusers showing movies at a specially constructed screen in their dining room well into the 1960s.

While the house here is not a place of super luxury (it was meant for casual summer entertaining and family get togethers) it is one of meticulous craftmanship. Specially trained German craftsmen worked on the ornately carved mantelpieces throughout the house. Double floors, heavy woodwork, stained glass windows and a bedroom featuring a Delft tile fireplace are among the details to be noted. The 45-foot dining room features the heavily ornate table and chairs that were the hallmark of the Victorian age.

The Kuser Mansion and surrounding farm were sold to Hamilton Township in the late 1970s to be used as a public park. The outdoor area includes a gazebo and many picnic tables, and has a pleasant, quiet atmosphere. Last tour begins one half-hour before closing. Free. Special Christmas open house.

HOURS: (House) May-Oct., Thurs.-Sun.: 11-3, Feb.-Apr. & Nov.: weekend only.
LOCATION: 390 Newkirk Avenue, Hamilton Twp., Mercer County (take Kuser Road exit from 295 just before Trenton.)
TELEPHONE: 609-890-3630

WALT WHITMAN HOUSE

A narrow row house in Camden contains the rooms where the poet who sang of America lived out the last eight years of his life. Accumulations of furniture (much of it the landlord's which Whitman took over along with the house), photographs and memorabilia are here. Whitman had had a paralytic stroke and much of what is in the house was given to him by friends during this invalid period. A bathtub kept in the bedroom is typical of the many gifts his friend collected for him.

Actually, this is a rather "poor" house. Whitman spent the money collected by friends for his living quarters on an elaborate mausoleum in a Camden cemetary two miles away.

Space has been expanded by the purchase of the house next door. There is now enough room for the books, manuscripts and photographs that have piled up. (Whitman was the most photographed writer in America in his time.) A painting by Thomas Eakins, hats, locks of hair, etc. are just a portion of the memorabilia. A guide will show you around. As of this writing, the house is closed while waiting for a new curator. Free.

HOURS: By appointment
LOCATION: 330 Mickle Blvd., Camden.
TELEPHONE: 609-964-5383; 609-726-1191

CRAFTSMAN FARMS

No it's not a farm. And there usually are no craftsmen. This is the home of Gustav Stickley, a well-known furniture designer of the early 20th century. He was also the foremost American spokesman for the Arts and Crafts movement. His large, wooden, somewhat chunky furniture is often referred as "Mission" style.

Stickley also published a journal called "The Craftsman" (hence the name of the Farm) which printed his house designs. Although he was not a trained architect, his plans appealed to those who disliked the overly ornate houses of the Victorian age. Since local builders used these plans, there are many Craftsman style houses in New Jersey. They are typically two story, with large overhanging eaves, a porch supported by round, wooden columns and windows that are grouped together. When styles changed, and his furniture and house plans were no longer popular, Stickley went into bankruptcy. Craftsman Farms was saved from developers a few years ago. Nowadays, Stickley furniture is back in vogue and one of his dressers can go for $300,000.

There are 26 acres left of the original 650 acre tract. The main house - a large log cabin with a stone chimney - was intended as a clubhouse for a boy's farm. This explains the huge kitchen and the fifty foot - long living room and dining room. The home features rounded ceiling beams and hammered copper fireplace hoods and of course, Stickley furniture. Tours take about an hour and include a short walk around the sloping acreage. There is also a interesting gift shop which sells books on the Arts and Crafts Movement.

HOURS: April-Oct., Thurs.: 12-3, Sat. & Sun.: 1-4.
ADMISSION: Adults: $4.00; Students, seniors: $3.00.
LOCATION: Route 287 to Route 10 West to Powder Mill Estates. Follow signs.
TELEPHONE: 201-540-1165

PENNSBURY MANOR

Here is a complete recreation, on the original site, of the beautiful Manor House built by William Penn on the banks of the Delaware. Located 25 miles above Philadelphia in what was then a wilderness, the estate includes many outbuildings such as a bake and brew house, a smoke house, ice house and stable. Although everything was built from scratch in the 1930s, great care was taken to follow the letters and journals of Penn regarding this self-sufficient estate.

There are two striking things about Pennsbury Manor. One is the earliness of the period. The house was built in the late 17th Century (Penn lived there only from 1699 to 1701), so the furnishings reflect the heavy Jacobean hand. The tour guides look as if they came from the pages of Mother Goose with their tunics and high black hats.

The other is the surprising elegance of this Quaker household. Although nothing is lavish, still the furnishings are richer than one would expect of a Quaker leader.

As the guide points out, although William Penn was a great believer in the equality of men, he was still the Proprietor, entitled to receive an annual fee from each settler for each parcel of land sold. He had, after all, received the Charter of Pennsylvania from King Charles II. He also came from a wealthy background and apparently relished good furniture.

After a tour through the bedrooms, parlors and countingrooms of the Manor, a tour through the grounds is in order. First to the barge-landing where a handsome replica of the ornate barge that Penn used to travel down to Philadelphia is moored. (Actually it looks more like a large gondola than a modern-day flat barge.) Then there is the herb garden, the barnyard with its peacocks and hens, and the brew house where it is supposed great vats of ale were mixed and where huge ovens held the bread to be baked for the estate. A worker's house, too.

The grounds include orchards and gardens. Walnut, hawthorn and hazel trees, fruit trees and rosebushes created a little corner of England in the new wilderness of America.

HOURS: Tues.-Sat.: 9-5; Sun:12-5 Last tour at 3:30 Jan & Feb Tours at 11 & 2.
ADMISSION: Adults: $5.00; Seniors: $4.00; Students: $3.00; Under 6: Free.
LOCATION: Bordertown Road, near Levittown, Bucks County, PA.
TELEPHONE: 215-946-0400

ANDALUSIA

Nicholas Biddle was one of America's first millionaires, and the Biddle name still connotes a sense of grace, polish and "old money" in the Philadelphia area. Andalusia was the country seat of Nicholas, although the house came to him through marriage. He transformed it in 1834 from a Regency mansion to its present form — one of the outstanding examples of Greek Revival architecture in the Northeast. Indeed, its facade of startling white pillars and "Greek temple" architrave will remind you of the many antebellum Southern mansions built in the same style.

The house faces the Delaware River and its large sloping green lawn runs down to the edge of the water. On this lawn you will find both a billiard room and a Gothic "ruin". The "ruin", a crumbling tower, was built that way. This was not uncommon in the 1830s, when the romantic novels of Sir Walter Scott, plus tales of excavations in the mid-East, had Americans crazy over anything Medieval, Greek, Turkish or Egyptian.

Inside the mansion, furniture varies from splendid, polished Regency buffets to odd shaped Greek-style chairs. The music room, with its delicate pianoforte and whale oil lamps brings visions of genteel ladies offering an evening musicale to an assemblage of local gentry.

Outside again, there are extensive grounds which include tennis courts, a swimming pool, a hedge walk, a grape arbor and another huge house which is not open to visitors. Tours of Andalusia are for groups only, but one can go through with a minimum of seven people for $63.00. For groups of twenty or more there is a package called "Mansions Along the Delaware". Call Pennsbury Manor for this.

HOURS: By reserved tour only.
LOCATION: Bensalem Twp., Bucks County, PA.
TELEPHONE: 215-245-5479.

GREEN HILLS FARM

Bucks County, Pennsylvania, was a haven for writers in the 1930s. Most of the literary celebrities of that time moved on to other pastures. But Pearl S. Buck, who reached the zenith of her fame during the pre-World War II period, (she won the Nobel

Prize in 1938) remained here in her lovely country home until her death in 1963.

The stone and wood house seems to typify the Hollywood picture of a writer's country retreat: a huge floor-to-ceiling brick fireplace, great expanses of polished wood flooring, overstuffed sofas and walls lined with books. Add to this a collection of Oriental lamps and tables, screens and sculptures, and you get a picture of Pearl S. Buck, author and admirer of Chinese culture. At one point there were also nine adopted Amerasian children in the house which explains the generous dimensions and open spaces of the home.

Visits to Green Hills Farm are by guided tour only. The tour includes a look at the room where all the awards and prizes are displayed and the study where Ms. Buck wrote her works (sitting in a most uncomfortable looking straight backed Chinese chair). Outside there is a lovely old-fashioned patio, lots of green rolling hills, and a separate shop where you may purchase Oriental pieces and other souvenirs. The Pearl S. Buck Foundation, dedicated to helping Amerasian children abandoned by their fathers, is located in the big red barn not far from the house. A film about the Foundation often precedes the tour.

HOURS: Tours are given Tues.-Sat.: 10:30, 1:30 & 2:30, Sun.: 1:30 & 2:30. Mar. 1 - Dec. 31.
ADMISSION: Adults: $5.00; Seniors, students: $4.00; Under 6: Free.
LOCATION: Perkasie, PA Take 202S to 313W to town of Dublin, PA. Turn left at Maple Ave. (which becomes Dublin Road) then one mile.
TELEPHONE: 215-249-0100 or 800-220-2825

See Also: *Winterthur* (Restored and Reconstructed), *Longwood* and *Duke Gardens* (The Garden Variety) and specific homes of the prominent in the chapter on "Walking Tours".

RESTORED AND RECONSTRUCTED COLONIAL, FEDERAL & VICTORIAN VILLAGES, FARMS, MILLS & HOMES

Photo: Courtesy N.J. Travel & Tourism

In This Chapter You Will Find:

Waterloo Village, N.J.
Van Cortlandt Manor, N.Y.
Philipsburg Manor, N.Y.
Clinton Historical Museum Village, N.J.
Historic Towne of Smithville, N.J.
Wheaton Village, N.J.
East Jersey Old Towne, N.J.
Batsto Village, N.J.
Millbrook Village
Allaire Village, N.J.
Historic Cold Spring Village, N.J.
Longstreet Farm, N.J.
Fosterfields, N.J.
Howell Living History Farm, N.J.
Israel Crane House, N.J.
Miller-Cory House, N.J.
The Hermitage, N.J.
Other Historic Houses in New Jersey
Winterthur, DE
The Hagley Museum, DE
South Street Seaport, N.Y.

WATERLOO VILLAGE

The largest restoration in New Jersey, Waterloo offers homes and mills scattered along the woodsy terrain next to the Musconetcong River.

The village complex covers over 5000 acres and includes buildings ranging from a tiny 1740 duplex to a solid 1870 mansion. Since Waterloo prospered both during the Revolutionary War and the later era of the Morris Canal and Sussex Railroad, the houses reflect the Colonial, Federal and Victorian styles. When you tour the village, however, you find that most guides are dressed in the clothes of the late 18th Century working class. A blacksmith and a potter are usually on hand at their workplaces.

The speeches the guides give to school and scout groups are often the most interesting thing about a restored village. The hostess in the *Canal House*, for instance, demonstrated the wooden-knobbed weasel that used to draw the wool yarn into a skein. Every time the weasel made a full skein, it would go "pop", thus explaining the childhood song about thirty years too late for me.

A favorite for children is the gristmill where huge stones grind the corn which the guide upstairs pours between the stones. Then you troop downstairs where the waterwheel is creating a loud whoosh. Here you discover the cornmeal pouring out the spout, while another guide explains the process.

There's a lot of walking to do here — several homes, the General Store (where you can buy the clay candlesticks the potter makes), and the Canal Museum. The Methodist church looks like it's straight out of Vermont. Bring good shoes. A further walk up the hill takes you to a complete Indian village as it would have been when the first settlers came. A long house, animal skins drying, clothes, and the accoutrements of tribal life are here, together with a guide who explains the customs.

Food is available at the Picnic Pavilion or you can bring your own to eat outdoors. The quaint stine tavern serves cheese, crackers and wine when it's open.

HOURS: April-Nov.: Wed.-Sun.: 10-6; Nov.-Dec.: 10-5.
ADMISSION: Weekends: Adults: $8.00; Seniors: $7.00; Children: $6.00; Under 6 Free.
LOCATION: Byram Twp., Sussex County. Take I-80 to Route 206N. Left at Waterloo Road.
TELEPHONE: 201-347-0900

THE VAN CORTLANDT MANOR

Set on a rise overlooking both the Hudson and Croton Rivers, Van Cortlandt Manor is a prime example of the strong influence of the Dutch in the New York-New Jersey area. At one time in the late 1700s, the estate extended from the Hudson River to Connecticut. The Manor House is now one of the better colonial restorations in the area.

Tours begin at the reception center where accurately costumed guides take groups of fifteen people through several buildings. Our group stopped first at the *Ferry House*. The ferry once plied the Croton River and travelers would stop here for food, drink, and lodging. The building is not large, but travelers would sleep three or four to a bed so they all managed.

At the other end of a long brick walk, lined with rows of tulips, is the *Manor House* itself. While not as elegant as the Southern Colonial mansions, it is impressive for this area — three stories high with a two-story porch wrapped around it. A heavy Dutch door opens to the main floor where the atmosphere is one of burnished wood and quiet elegance. Delft tiles line the fireplaces. Chippendale and Queen Anne furniture fill the rooms, and English china rests in the practical Dutch cupboards whose doors could be closed at night.

The ground floor kitchen is a magnet for groups. Here the guide shows the original Dutch oven (a heavy iron kettle with a closed lid), the beehive oven in the back of the fireplace and the gridiron for baking steaks.

Van Cortlandt Manor, also includes a smokehouse, ice house, and blacksmith forge. The tours are geared for adults and schoolage children. There is also a picnic area available.

HOURS: 10-5 Daily except Tues. Closed major holidays.
ADMISSION: Adults: $8.00; Children: $3.00; Seniors: $6.00.
LOCATION: Croton-on-the-Hudson, N.Y. Take Tappan Zee Bridge to Route 9N to Croton Pond Ave., one block east to South Riverside Ave., turn right and go 1/4 mile to entrance.
TELEPHONE: 914-271-8981

PHILIPSBURG MANOR

A large farm and gristmill, a wood-planked bridge that spans a tranquil stream, an old stone manor-house and a huge modern reception center filled with exhibits are all a part of this **Historic Hudson Valley** restoration. The estate is set up as it would have been from 1680 to 1750, with authentic furnishings and authentically garbed guides. You begin with a movie about the Philipse family who once managed 90,000 acres and shipped flour and meal down the Hudson. Unfortunately, they backed the losing side during the Revolutionary War and lost their holdings as a result.

Guided tours of the manor, a demonstration of the gristmill, and a walk around the large property and through the barn are part of the outing. You can see sheep and lambs gamboling about as you traverse the property. The Visitors Center includes a large, well-stocked gift shop and a glass enclosed cafe that offers light lunches (closed on Tuesdays). This is also the embarkation point, in season, for tours of the Rockefeller estate, Kykuit.

HOURS: Daily, 10-5 - March-Dec.
ADMISSION: Adults: $7.00; Seniors: $6.00; Students: $4.00; Under 6: Free.
LOCATION: Upper Mills, North Tarrytown, N.Y. Take Tappan Zee Bridge, then Route 9N for 2 miles. Look for signs.
TELEPHONE: 914-631-3992

CLINTON HISTORICAL MUSEUM VILLAGE

An old red mill with a churning water-wheel sits by a 200-foot wide waterfall to create the picturesque environment for this museum village. In fact, the red mill is one of the most photographed structures in New Jersey. It is this mill that is the hub of the "village". The other buildings are smaller and scattered along the banks of the river. You can find a log cabin, a little red school house, a general store/post office, a blacksmith shop, a quarry with stonecrusher and an information center in the small complex.

As for the mill, the 1810 structure offers four floors of exhibits. There is a strong emphasis on the Victorian period here. The museum also runs a series of specials to attract the crowds. These include summer concerts, craft days and a harvest jubilee. Guided tours for groups are given but must be arranged in advance.

Across the river, the large stone building facing the mill houses the **Hunterdon Art Center** (closed Mondays), which is certainly worth a visit. Exhibits of prints, painting, and sculpture are always on hand. There is an entrance fee here. Take a camera along for a shot of the picturesque dam.

From the art center you can walk up the main street of the small country town of Clinton. Some nice boutiques and a fern-hung luncheon spot make for pleasant browsing.

> **HOURS:** April- Oct. 31: Tues.-Sun.: 10-4. Gift shop always open.
> **ADMISSION:** Adults: $3.00; Seniors: $2.00; Children: $1.00; Under 6 Free.
> **LOCATION:** 56 Main Street, Clinton, Hunterdon County (Off Rte. 78).
> **TELEPHONE:** 908-735-4101

HISTORIC TOWNE OF SMITHVILLE

Set around Lake Meone and only 12 miles from Atlantic City, this shopping "towne" started out as a colonial village combined with boutique shops, set among brick walkways and planted flowers. Way back in the 1970s and early 1980s, there were costumed "colonials" spinning yarn in tiny restored houses on one side of the lake, and charming shoppes on the other. Now the two sides of the lake are two entities: Smithville and the Village Greene. But hard times have hit and at this moment there are only about 35 to 40 shops and eateries in business on both sides. The old Quail Hill Inn is now a huge antique center. The Smithville Inn (the only truly historic building here and once the center of the Towne), is closed.

It is still a pleasant spot, parking is free, and in the summer there are several family attractions - such as paddle boats, miniature golf, and a train ride. And a new carousel will be installed permanently. Will this revive the place? What will happen? There was a time when visitors to Atlantic City would come here to relax, square dance at the Inne, shop and just walk around. Keep tuned.

> **HOURS:** Vary for shops. Restaurants daily for lunch and dinner.

WHEATON VILLAGE

Set around a green, with buildings styled in 1888 gingerbread, Wheaton Village is a nice, clean spot in the middle of a small industrial town called Millville about 35 miles west of Atlantic City. The village is dedicated to the glass industry that still flourishes in this corner of New Jersey and its main attraction is the **Museum of American Glass**. The museum is housed in an elegant Victorian building and includes glass items that go back to Jamestown.

Glass collectors will probably enjoy this museum with its flower-embedded paperweights, medicine bottles, cut glass and new exhibit of contemporary glass. You learn everything you ever wanted to know about bottles, Sandwich glass, cut and pressed glass. The foyer boasts the chandeliers from the old Traymore Hotel in Atlantic City and the original brass sconces from the Waldorf Astoria.

Another attraction is the glass factory where visitors can watch from a gallery above while gaffers plunge their gathering rods into the blazing furnaces and then shape them into wine glasses, bottles and paperweights. Three times a day there are "shows" which means an announcer with a mike explains just what the gaffer is doing. This is hot work and even from the gallery you can feel the intensity of the furnace. And nowadays, Wheaton Village allows visitors to make their own paperweights. For $40.00, you (and a qualified gaffer) make an individual creation. Call to reserve for this offer.

Other buildings in the Village include a craft arcade where you can see weavers, potters and printers going about their work. The craftsman's handiwork plus lots of glass vases and paperweights can be purchased in the stores that line the village green.

For kids there's a small play area, on the green, an 1876 schoolhouse to peek at and an 1880 Train Station (with a miniature train ride for an extra fee).

The General Store sells penny candy from an old-fashioned glass jar but for real food you have to go to the Country Kitchen right outside the gates. Entrance fees are for the museum, the factory and other attractions. If you just want to buy something at the glass and crafts shops there's no fee for "strolling". Special event weekends feature everything from art glass demonstrations to fire engine musters.

HOURS: Daily, 10-5 (Reduced schedule Jan.-Mar.)
ADMISSION: Adults: $6.00; Students:$3.50; Seniors: $5.50; Under 6 Free. Family Rate: $12.00. Reduced winter rates.
LOCATION: 10th & "G" Street, Millville, Cumberland County. Take Routes 47, 49 or 55.
TELEPHONE: 609-825-6800

EAST JERSEY OLDE TOWNE

A reconstructed Colonial village has been standing in Johnson Park, Piscataway, for lo, these many years. A good number of small houses are there, set on a pleasant village green meant to resemble an 18th Century settlement in the Raritan Valley. Several of the buildings have been moved from other sites. One can find a church, a farmhouse, a tavern, among others.

At the moment these houses are not open. Since the Middlesex County Cultural and Heritage Commission took over, some changes are planned. First an overhaul of the buildings to make them more habitable (heat, light, etc.) After this overhaul (which should be finished by 1996) events are planned for school groups and others. These will emphasize folk art of all cultures, not just the English colonial heritage.

The East Jersey Olde Towne Foundation will retain control of the Three Mile Run Church (a 1703 structure) that sometimes has weddings performed in it. They will also operate a gift shop. In the meantime, in spite of construction, one can walk around and peek into the houses.

LOCATION: River Road (Route 18) at Hoes Lane, Piscataway, Middlesex County.
TELEPHONE: 908-745-4489

BATSTO VILLAGE

What was once a self-contained community lies within the Wharton Tract (a huge State preserve within the section known as the Pine Barrens). Tall trees, open lowlands, lakes with clusters of campgrounds are all part of this unusual region which reminded me of the North Carolina tidelands.

As for Batsto Village itself, it was once the center of the bog iron industry in New Jersey. Later, glass was manufactured here, then lumbering and cranberry farming were tried. As you approach, you find a handsome farm surrounded by split rail fences with horses, chickens and ducks in view. The huge farmhouse has a late Victorian tower rising eight stories from its center, giving the place a "haunted mansion" look. The rooms inside are filled with the furniture of the well-to-do families that lived there, and the wall-to-wall library of James Wharton, the financier who once owned the place, is most impressive. The tour takes 45 minutes and is very comprehensive.

The first stop at Batsto is the Visitors Center. If you want the mansion tour buy your tickets immediately for they admit only 15 people at a time to this once-an-hour inspection. But there are other things to see at Batsto. A walk-through museum at the Visitors Center features old time tools and other exhibits about the region. A General Store, a barn with several animals, a large lake where fishing is allowed, a genuine sawmill, and some refurbished workers houses. During the summer these houses usually have some craftsmen inside — a weaver and a blacksmith will be at work depending on state funding. One of the homes is set up as an ironworkers house to give you some feel for the community life that existed here.

The farm with its unusual main house, surrounding barns and wide swept fields all in the middle of the untouched pine barrens has the true look of the haunting past. It also has the attraction of a horse and carriage ride which is sometimes available on summer weekends. Mansion may be closed Mon.-Wed.

HOURS: Mem. Day-Labor Day: 10-6; rest of year: 11-5. Closed major holidays.
ADMISSION: (to Mansion) Adults: $2.00; Children 6-11: $1.00.
LOCATION: Route 9 to 542 West. Or Garden State Parkway New Gretna Exit to 9S to 542.
TELEPHONE: 609-561-3262
PARKING: $3.00 weekends.

MILLBROOK VILLAGE

One of New Jersey's best kept secrets is this authentic 19th Century village set in the Kittatiny Mountains. It is run by the National Park Service as part of the Delaware Water Gap Recreation Area. On weekends, guides dressed in period costumes of the 1860-1880 era, lead tours through several houses and engage in such crafts as woodworking and blacksmithing.

The original Millbrook Village was a small enclave of houses and stores clustered around a grist mill that opened in 1832. Since the mill served grain farmers in the surrounding countryside, the town became the social and commercial center of the community. In this way it mirrored much of America's agricultural life. A hotel with taproom, a smithy, a general store and a simple white-steepled church are among the buildings that surrounded the original mill by the brook.

Millbrook reached its zenith between 1870 and 1885. The village declined after 1900 and by mid-century it was a ghost town. What you see here now is a re-creation of Millbrook at its height. A village green, busy townfolk, lovely, well-kept homes and a church within walking distance are part of the scene. It could almost be Kansas except for the mountainous terrain. Free.

HOURS: Late June — Labor Day: Wed.-Sun: 9-5. Sept., Oct.: Weekends, 9-5.
LOCATION: Sussex County. Take Route 80 west to the last exit in N.J. (Millbrook exit). Turn right, follow Old Mine Road 12 miles north.
TELEPHONE: 908-496-4458

ALLAIRE VILLAGE

Set inside the greenery of Allaire State Park, this complex was once an active workers community during the 19th century. The huge brick furnace is one left over from the bog iron days when James P. Allaire bought the ironworks in 1822 and sought to establish a sort of ideal, self-contained community. Since this was the age of Oneida settlements and Utopian communities, such a worker's paradise did not seem unusual. In fact, as long as the ironworks transformed local bog into pig iron, everything prospered. But after twenty-five years, competition from the high grade iron ore brought economic ruin to the region. The village became deserted. A well documented display on the ironworks can be found in the clean, air-conditioned Visitors Center.

Historic Allaire Village, as it is now called, is operated by a separate non-profit organization. They do not get their money from New Jersey State, which runs the park. During the warm weather weekends you will find docents, dressed in 1830s costumes, standing in the various buildings. They will talk about village life, and perhaps there will be a blacksmith or pattern maker about. You can view the church, which has a unique architectural feature - its steeple was erected on the wrong end! There's alot of hilly walking here, with a pond, a bakery, and a gift shop plus several other houses. The well-stocked gift shop is often open from Wednesday to Sunday.

If you visit during the week, the Visitors Center may not be open and the docents may not be around, but you can walk around the grounds and take pictures. On summer and fall weekends there are always lots of activities including craft and antique fairs. There are even lantern tours of the village in November and December.

While visiting Allaire Park, you're sure to want to ride the **Pine Creek Railroad**, a narrow-gauge rail line that runs a short trip for visitors on both diesel and steam locomotives. For information on this call 908-938-5524. The State Park also offers nature trails, bicycle trails and picnic areas. At the parking lot there is a concession that offers hot dogs and ice cream when it is open.

> **HOURS:** Park: 8 AM-8 PM. Village: Weekends: 10-4 May-Oct.
> **ADMISSION:** Weekends: $3.00, (Parking). Mem. Day - Labor Day.
> **LOCATION:** Allaire State Park, Monmouth County. Take Exit 98, Garden State Parkway, go 2 miles west.
> **TELEPHONE:** 908-938-2371 (Park) 908-938-2253 (Village)

HISTORIC COLD SPRING VILLAGE

A delightful little restored village has sprung up among the pine trees on a quiet stretch of road not far from the hubbub of the Wildwood motels. Cold Spring Village (not to be confused with the village of Cold Spring near Boscobel or Cold Spring Harbor in New York) has much charm. It's not so large as to be exhausting, nor so small that it might disappoint.

The buildings are set around a village green that has a mid-19th century look to it. Most of them have been moved here from elsewhere. They range from an ancient colonial to the large Grange Hall which dates back to 1897. In between, you will find a tiny 1820 octogonal house and various forms of American Colonial. Inside the various structures, you'll find a printer at his shop or an 1820s school complete with resident schoolmistriss, or a tinsmith punching holes in tin. These are for the most part docents who explain what they are doing while they work.

There are bits of country nostalgia here such as an old fashioned water pump (the water is undoubtedly from the cold spring), a small farm enclosure, and walkways made of crushed clamshells. A horse-drawn carriage, on hand the day I visited, was a big hit with the children. In the large visitors center, a Marine Museum offers displays on the whaling industry and other facts. For those who get hungry, the village also offers an ice cream store and bakery. Full meals are available at the Grange Hall where old style American fare is featured. Weekends there are often special events such as singers, contests and so forth. Two railroad stations add to the local color.

> **HOURS:** Father's Day — Labor Day: Daily 10-4. Weekends: June, Sept., Oct.
> **ADMISSION:** Adults: $3.50; Children: $1.00; Seniors: $3.00.
> **LOCATION:** 720 Route 9, Cold Spring, Cape May County. Take G.S.P. Exit 4A to Route 9S.
> **TELEPHONE:** 609-898-2300

LONGSTREET FARM

For those who want to recapture the sights and smells of an era not so long past, a visit to Longstreet Farm quite fills the bill. Although the farm is kept to the 1890 to 1900 era, the machinery here was used well into the 1920s and may bring back memories to those born on a farm. Old-fashioned combines and tractors, an apple corer, a machine that de-kernelizes corn (but only the hard corn meant for animals) and other antique contraptions are kept in a series of barns and sheds. Of course, animals are present, although not in profusion. There are lazy pigs lying in the mud, horses swatting flies, cows, chickens, and flies, flies, flies. In fact, if your children have ever asked why horses have tails,they can discover why here — they make the most efficient fly-swatters.

Open-slatted corn cribs that allow the air to circulate are on view. The milking shed is fitted out in the old way — with slots for the cow's head and buckets for hand milking. The carriage house contains a variety of buckboards. And they do have people here, too. Since Longstreet is a living historical farm, the workers dress in casual 1890s clothes as they go about their usual farm chores: feeding, seeding, plowing, milking — all in a day's work according to the season.

No guided tours are given to individuals but groups may call ahead and arrange them. The main farmhouse has tours on weekends, but the farm is open all year and follows the seasonal activities of plowing, harvesting, threshing, sheep-shearing and ice-cutting.

The farm is just one portion of the beautiful **Holmdel Park**, which provides much lovely scenery. Across the street, a sheltered picnic area offers tables and a snack bar. In a hollow below the shelter, a pond allows ducks to swim gracefully and accept breadcrusts from visitors. And beyond the pond, a cultivated arboretum presents a colorful view of flowering crabapples, rhododendrons and hundreds of shade trees. The park also provides a nature trail that winds among the beech, oak and hickory trees. Wildflowers and blueberry bushes are other plusses at this abundant county park. Free.

> **HOURS:** 10-4 daily, Sept.-May. 9-5 daily, June-Labor Day.
> **LOCATION:** Longstreet Road, off Holmdel Road. Take Garden State Arts Center Exit off GSP, follow Keyport Road, look for signs.
> **TELEPHONE:** 908-946-3758

FOSTERFIELDS

Another old-fashioned farm that dates from the turn of the century in American agriculture, Fosterfields is run by the Morris County Park Commission. The large farm has many farm implements on display and a variety of farm animals visible in various enclosures along the walkway. There are also barns and various outbuildings. The main house, **The Willows**, has been restored. It is a handsome Gothic Revival farmhouse with many original furnishings intact. Tours and cooking demonstrations are available here on specific days. Special Christmas tour, too.

On weekends, from the spring to fall season, there are demonstrations of farm tasks such as ploughing, sowing seed or threshing. Perhaps the women at the farmhouse will be washing clothes and setting them out to dry. Often, the audience is allowed to get involved.

The handsome Visitors Center has displays on farming and also offers a short film on the history of Fosterfields. Here is where you can pick up brochures and information on any of the special activities — whether it's a Fourth of July picnic or a Saturday devoted to hay-racking.

HOURS: Apr.-Oct., Wed.-Sat.: 10-5; Sun.: 1-5.
ADMISSION: Adults: $4.00; Children, Seniors: $3.00.
LOCATION: Route 510 & Kahdena Rd., Morris Twp., Morris County.
TELEPHONE: 201-326-7645

HOWELL LIVING HISTORY FARM

Yet another active farm set in the turn of the century mode. What you find here is farm life that is pre-computerized. Various stages of mechanization are on show — the reaper reaps and binds mechanically, but it does not thresh. The wheat is bound by machine but the machine is pulled by a plodding draft horse, not a yellow Caterpillar. The wagon that picks up the bound sheaves is also available for hayrides. We were lucky enough to get a hitch in this wagon — great fun if you don't have back trouble or allergies.

There's plenty of acreage at the farm and you're part of the bucolic atmosphere from the moment you leave the parking lot and walk down the dirt road to the farmhouse. On the way you pass sheep and chicks and geese and oxen — all safely behind fences, thank goodness. The farmhouse itself is a simple one. School groups are welcome here to weave burlap, make corn husk dolls, and help out in other ways. On Saturdays, a professional farmer is on hand to guide the draft horse in ploughing, sowing and reaping.

There are several Saturdays devoted to such things as a Spring Market and a Fall Festival. You might give Howell Farm a call before visiting to see if anything special is planned. Free (donations accepted).

HOURS: Tues.-Sat.: 10-4; Sun.: 12-4.
LOCATION: Howell Twp., Mercer County. Take Rt. 29 to Belle Mtn. Ski Area turnoff (Valley Rd.) then 2 miles east.
TELEPHONE: 609-737-3299

ISRAEL CRANE HOUSE

A handsome house built in the Federal period and then remodeled in the Greek Revival style, the Crane house was moved from its original site to the present location by the Montclair Historical Society. The group also trains the docents who give guided tours throughout the three-story building.

Furnishings in the Federal and Empire style are evident in the main house. Upstairs in the garret, a full schoolroom exists. (One of the Cranes did run a school here.) An authentic blackboard (which is, incidentally, a large board painted black), an old-fashioned dunce cap and the elongated desks that accommodated several children at a time are part of the set-up here. Also in the garret are a full tool collection and a mass of dried herbs.

Behind the main house is a two-story kitchen building reconstructed to resemble the 1840 kitchen that once existed. One unique feature of the Crane House is that the docents do allow you to sample the cooking. Just a tiny piece, but you can taste bread from the beehive oven, while the chicken simmers over the open hearth. Docents are quite good at explaining about the cooking utensils (such as the lazy-back which eased cooking chores for post-Colonial wives). Beyond the kitchen building is a pleasant backyard planted with flowers and herbs in the 18th Century fashion. And beyond that, the *Country Store Museum* is housed in a small building erected by Nathaniel Crane in 1820. Although the items in the store are just wooden models and are not for sale, you do get the sense of an old-fashioned post-office/store as the social center for a town. A small gift shop here offers books and mementos for sale. Special talks and classes are given periodically at the house.

HOURS: Sept.-June: Sun.:2-5, Wed.: 1-4. Group tours weekdays.
ADMISSION: Adults: $2.00; Children: $.50
LOCATION: 110 Orange Rd. (Off Bloomfield Ave.) Montclair, Essex County.
TELEPHONE: 201-744-1796

MILLER-CORY HOUSE

Every Sunday during the school season, volunteers cook, churn butter and perform seasonal tasks in and around this 1740 farmhouse. The everyday, humdrum tasks of Colonial life — from soap-making to herb-drying are emphasized here. The house, the adjacent Visitor Center, and a separate kitchen comprise a small enclave of Colonial life. In pleasant weather, wool spinners and other workers may be found outside and the separate kitchen is the scene of soup and bread making. Good idea, since there is often a line for a tour of the Miller-Cory house itself.

Guided tours of the house proper take about half-an-hour, with 15 people to each tour. Although three tours may go on simultaneously, there may be a wait on a busy fall afternoon. The tour is most thorough and includes everything from how to tighten the rope springs on a bed to how to make utensils from a cow's horn. School children and adults will find the house tour highly educational while pre-schoolers may be content to simply mosey around the grounds. They can tour the herb garden, the tool collection in the Visitor Center, or watch the outdoor volunteers at work.

HOURS: Sept.-June, Sun.: 2-5; Jan.-Mar., Sun.: 2-4.
ADMISSION: Adults: $1.00; Children: $.50.
LOCATION: 614 Mountain Ave., Westfield, Union County.
TELEPHONE: 908-232-1776

THE HERMITAGE

Known now primarily as an example of 19th century Gothic Revival architecture, the original Hermitage was a two-story brownstone erected in 1750. During the late 18th century it was owned by Lt. Colonel Prevost and his charming wife, Theodosia. At that time, it was host to James Monroe, Alexander Hamilton, General Lafayette, and Aaron Burr among others. When Colonel Prevost died, Burr wooed his widow. In 1782, Burr and Theodosia married in the parlor of the Hermitage.

Twenty-five years later Dr. Elijah Rosencrantz bought the house (which his family retained for 160 years). In 1847 the structure was remodeled into the picturesque Gothic Revival home it is today. Steep gabled roofs trimmed with carpenter's lace and diamond-paned windows give it the mid-Victorian look we often associate with Charles Dickens. In fact, one of the several programs given at the house is a performance of "The Christmas Carol".

The Hermitage owns a large collection of antique clothing (448 women's gowns alone) that includes fans, handbags, and handmade lace. There is also much original furniture, old maps, letters and photographs in the collection. The house was bequeathed to the State in 1970 by the last remaining member of the Rosencrantz family and is administered by the Friends of the Hermitage. Special events include a costume exhibit from June to September and two Craft Boutiques that last four weeks each.

> **HOURS:** Summer: Wed. & Sun. 1-4. Otherwise: Wed. & 1st & 3rd. Sun. 1-4. Special hours for craft show in fall and spring.
> **ADMISSION:** Adults: $3.00; Under 12, free.
> **LOCATION:** 335 N. Franklin Tpke., Ho-Ho-Kus, Bergen County.
> **TELEPHONE:** 201-445-8311

OTHER HISTORIC HOUSES (N.J.)

The number of historic houses in New Jersey is so large it would take an entire volume just to list them. Here are a few: (Please note that besides their regular hours, many of these sites offer special Christmas viewing hours).

COOPER MILL: An 1826 mill where you can see corn ground into meal before your eyes. Guided tours upon request. Open Fri.- Tues., 10-5, July & Aug. Weekends only May, June, Sept. & Oct. Located on Route 513, Chester, Morris County, one mile west of Rte. 206. *Telephone:* 908-879-5463.

FORCE HOUSE: Next to Memorial Field in Livingston, the 18th & 19th Century homestead of a local family. Open on 2nd & 4th Sunday of the month except summer. 366 S. Livingston Ave., Livingston, Essex County.

BELCHER-OGDEN MANSION: A well-respected restoration on a historic street in Elizabeth. Tours by appointment only. *Location:* 1046 E. Jersey Ave., Elizabeth. *Telephone:* 908-351-2500.

GREENFIELD HALL: Well-furnished, handsome Georgian building that features personal items belonging to Elizabeth Haddon, and a doll collection. Open Fri.-Sun.: 10-4. Call for library hours and guided tour. Expansion planned. *Location:* 343 King Highway, Haddonfield, Camden County. *Telephone:* 609-429-7375.

MARSHALL HOUSE: One-time home of James Marshall who discovered gold at Sutter's Mill, California, but never made any money from the find. Built in 1816. Prize possession is a friendship quilt. Headquarters Lambertville Historical Society and start off point for seasonal walking tours. *Location:* 60 Bridge Street, Lambertville, Hunterdon County. *Telephone:* 609-397-0770.

VAN-RIPER-HOPPER HOUSE: Dutch Colonial farmhouse with period furnishings, local history display, herb garden. Open Sat., Sun.: 1-4. $2.00 fee. *Location:* 533 Berdan Ave., Wayne, Passaic County. *Telephone:* 201-694-7192.

SOMERS MANSION: Oldest house in Atlantic County has unusual roof shaped like upside-down ship's hull. Local memorabilia. A State Historic Site. Tours given by Historical Society next door. *Hours:* 1st & 3rd Tues. & by appt.. *Location:* Route 52 to Shore Rd., Somers Point. *Telephone:* 609-927-2212.

ACORN HALL: Mid-Victorian home in the Italianate style with many original furnishings in its two parlours. Children's toys and gadgets. Well-kept lawn with huge oak and Victorian garden with gazebo. Open Thurs. 11-3; Sun.: 1:30-4, spring through fall only. Adults: $3.00; Children: $.50. 68 Morris Ave., Morristown, Morris County. *Telephone:* 201-267-3465.

THE OLD MONROE SCHOOLHOUSE: Hand-hewn stone schoolhouse with wooden desks, hand slates and pot-bellied stove. Picnic facilities. Open 1st Sun. June-Oct. 1-4 Adults: $1.25; Children: $1.00. *Location:* Route 44 between Hamburg and Newton, Sussex County. *Telephone:* 201-827-9402.

TOWNSHIP OF LEBANON MUSEUM: A white 1823 schoolhouse with all its desks, textbooks and inkwells in place. Reserved school tours are booked and classes taught. *Hours:* Tues., Thurs.: 9:30-5. Sat.: 1-5. Free. *Location:* Musconetcong River Road, New Hampton, Hunterdon County. *Telephone:* 908-537-6464.

BARCLAY FARMSTEAD: Federal period Quaker farmhouse furnished with 19th century pieces. Interprets life of the period. Free. *Hours:* Tues. - Fri.: 9-4. *Location:* Barclay Lane, Cherry Hill, Camden County. *Telephone:* 609-795-6225.

PROPRIETARY HOUSE: New Jersey's last Royal Governor, William Franklin, lived in this well-to-do residence. Tours by appointment only. *Location:* 149 Kearny Ave., Perth Amboy. *Telephone:* 908-826-5527.

DR. WILLIAM ROBINSON PLANTATION: Restored 1690 farmhouse with artifacts, maps and pictures in its museum section. Guided tours by costumed docents. *Hours:* April-Dec., 1st Sunday of month 1-4. *Location:* 593 Madison Hill Road, Clark, Union County. *Telephone:* 908-381-3081.

WINTERTHUR

The *creme de la creme* when it comes to American decorative arts, Winterthur is Henri DuPont's version of hundreds of restored homes rolled into one. The main mansion contains 175 rooms, each one decorated in a pre-1860 style. In many cases the rooms are more than merely decorated — whole dining rooms, kitchens, etc. (including walls, ceilngs and fireplaces) were transported panel by panel and placed inside the mansion. Several style periods are shown: Seventeenth Century, William and Mary, Queen Anne, Chippendale, Federal, Empire and Victorian.

Each piece is documented, so that the Duncan Phyfe room, for instance, had its architectural elements removed from a specific house in New York where Phyfe furniture was used. You can find a striking plantation dining room removed in its entirety from a South Carlina home, a New England kitchen, a Shaker bedroom, a New York parlour, and a flying staircase copied from the Montmorenci estate in North Carolina. One oft-photographed room features authentic 18th Century Chinese wallpaper that covers both the walls and the ceilings.

There are more than rooms at Winterthur. The Cobblestone Court, right inside the building, looks like a movie set for an 18th Century film. This courtyard features the facades of four different buildings, including The Red Lion Inn and a typical Connecticut home.

The one-hour *Introductory Tour* includes some of the best rooms. The *Reserved Tour* is two hours long and includes many upstairs rooms and the cobblestone courtyard. *The Yuletide Tour*, also very popular, features some of the top rooms, dressed for Christmas. There are new galleries which are museum-like, with much descriptive material. These allow self-guided tours.

81

Besides the museums, there are extensive gardens at Winterthur — sixty acres of greenery, dotted with woods and copses. During spring, flowering displays include azaleas and dogwoods. A special tram takes you through the gardens. The main Visitors Center (where you get the garden tram and tickets) offers a luncheon buffet and a marvelous book and gift shop. Also here are the free maps and brochures you will need for your tour. And for those who want to do some serious shopping, there are rugs and chairs and china for sale at the Gallery and Plant Shop, a luxurious little building located across from to the main house.

For lovers of 18th Century architecture and furnishings this is the premier place to visit. Only a multi-millionaire could lavish this attention to detail on his "collection".

HOURS: Mon.-Sat.: 9:30-5. Sun.: 12-5. Closed major holidays.
ADMISSION: $13.00 (one-hour tour)
LOCATION: NJ Turnpike to 295 & Delaware Mem. Bridge, then north on 195 to Route 52 (Exit 7). Left on 52 to Winterthur.
TELEPHONE: 800-448-3883

HAGLEY MUSEUM

Another DuPont complex and a huge one at that. The acreage includes homes, offices, barns and the black powder apparatus of the original gunpowder mills that was the foundation of the DuPont fortune. The "museum" section offers exhibits that trace industrial development throughout the 19th Century. From there you take a small bus to visit the other sections such as the original DuPont home. The bus goes through a steep wooded area along the banks of the Brandywine River, passing machine shops, roller mills and other stops of interest.

At the original DuPont residence, called *"Eleutherian Mills"* you find a handsome Georgian structure surrounded by gardens. Nearby is the office where the company began. It still contains the old desks and ledgers. There are guided tours at both these places, but you are free to roam around the gardens, the barn (which contains both a Conestoga wagon and antique carriages and cars) and the cooper's workshop.

Also on the premises, along the bus stops, are an early schoolhouse where children of the workers could learn their ABCs and a worker's home that now houses a good coffee shop. A picnic area and several vending machines are on the grounds also, while the gift shop is near the Visitors Center.

HOURS: Apr.-Dec.: Daily 9:30-4:30. Jan.-Mar.: Reduced.
ADMISSION: Adults: $9.75; Seniors, students: $7.50; Children 6-14: $3.50; Under 6 free. Family rate: $26.50
LOCATION: Greenville, Delaware, off Route 141
TELEPHONE: 302-658-2400

SOUTH STREET SEAPORT

Boston has its Quincy Market. Baltimore has its Inner Harbor. It was only a matter of time before New York jumped on the bandwagon and restored its own quaint seaport area. The South Street Seaport was years in the making. But now there is enough holiday atmosphere about the place to make it one of New York's most popular tourist spots. Busloads of New Jerseyans come in every day to walk the broad plazas, shop, eat, and vie for elbow space with Wall Street executives.

The "museum" (as it is called) is actually the entire restoration of several blocks around New York's earliest seaport. Schermerhorn Row, Water Street, Fulton Street and South Street boast some of the few remaining Federal style townhouses to be found in the big city. These gracious rowhouses have been beautifully restored and now house shops and restaurants. At the water's edge there are several ships available for touring. Tours of The *Wavertree*, a sailing ship under restoration, the lightship *Ambrose*, and the 4-masted barque, The *Peking*, can be fascinating with the right docent. The talks really give you a feeling for the hard work, danger and close quarters of the old ships.

A more fanciful view of the sea may be obtained from a ride on the *Seaport Liberty Cruise Line*, a Circle Line that offers a one-hour, bay area version of its standard cruise for about the same money. In warm weather you can also book a two-hour sail on the schooner *Pioneer*.

Ship tours and rides cost extra, of course, as does entrance to the formal exhibit galleries, the Children's Center and the guided tour of the historic area. Tickets may be purchased at the Pier 16 ticketbooth or the Museum Visitor Center.

But the main attraction is the food and shops. Unfortunately, many of the early quaint shops are being replaced by high class chains one can find elsewhere. The Fulton Market now purveys ethnic fast food for the most part—sushi, empanadas, moussaka, etc. Pier 17 is like a Jersey Mall escept for its balconies, which let you observe either the street scene or the passing boats.

There are some well known seafood restaurants around, such as **Sloppy Louie's**, but its the open air cafes with their wide plazas that seem to be most popular. Since car traffic is prohibited in certain areas during the day, one can actually sit here and relax without breathing auto exhaust.

There are wide open walking spaces here and the plaza next to Pier 17 attracts street performers and musicians. On a sunny day, with the wind off the river, it is New York as we would like it to be. No cars, no muggers, (no place to buy an aspirin or a Band-Aid or a box of tissues either, should you need them) but after all, you can't expect everything.

HOURS: Daily for shops and restaurants.
ADMISSION: (Museum): Adults: $6.00; Seniors: $5.00; Students: $4.00; Children: $3.00. Boatride and combination tickets extra.
LOCATION: Fulton & South Sts. just off FDR Drive, NYC.
TELEPHONE: (Museum): 212-748-8600

See Also: *Pennsbury Manor* and *Historic Speedwell* (Homes of the Rich and Famous), *Jockey Hollow/Wick Farm* (Where Washington Slept, Ate and Fought), *New Jersey Historical Museums* (Museums of All Kinds) and such tours as *Bordentown* and *Mt. Holly* in the "Walking Tours" chapter.

MUSEUMS OF ALL KINDS

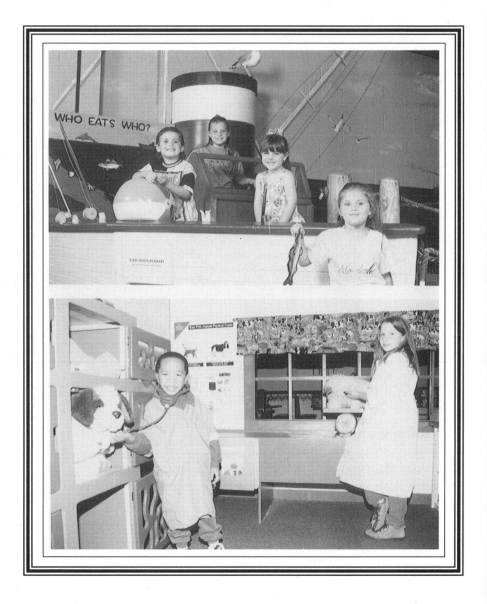

Photo: Courtesy Garden State Discovery Museum

In This Chapter You Will Find:

New Jersey — Art & Science Museums

Liberty Science Center, New Jersey State Museum, Newark Museum, Montclair Art Museum, Morris Museum, Bergen Museum, Monmouth Museum, Other Museums of Art and Science.

New Jersey — Specialty Museums

NJ Children's Museum, Garden State Discovery Museum, Franklin Mineral Museum, The Golf House, NJ State Police Museum, Doll Castle Doll Museum, Aviation Hall of Fame, Campbell Museum, Edison Memorial Tower and Museum, other NJ Specialty Museums.

New Jersey —Historical Museums

Museum of Early Trades and Crafts, Schoolhouse Museum, Ocean County Historical Museum, Hopewell Museum, Ocean City Historical Museum, Spy House Museum, Cape May Historical Museum, New Jersey Historical Society, Monmouth County Historical Association, Camden County Historical Society, Paterson Museum, American Labor Museum.

New York Museums

Metropolitan Museum of Art, American Museum of Natural History, The Cloisters, The Frick Collection, Museum of Modern Art, Forbes Galleries.

Pennsylvania Museums

Franklin Institute, Please Touch Museum, Philadelphia Museum of Art, Museum of American Art, Rosenbach Museum and Library, The Mercer Mile, Brandywine River Museum.

LIBERTY SCIENCE CENTER

Perhaps you've seen the gleaming white building with its campanile style tower and spherical hump as you pass Exit 14B on the Turnpike. That's the new science and technology museum in the forefront of the interactive, get-the-kids-to-like science centers. Set in the middle of Liberty State Park, the modern building is surrounded by grasslands and a large car park.

As you enter the building, the first thing that strikes your eye is the aluminum Hoberman Sphere which expands and contracts as it hangs in the 90 foot atrium in the center of the building. This fascinating ball lets you know you have come to a place where technology is king.

Exhibits are housed on the four levels that circle the atrium. There are three distinct areas: Environment, Health and Invention. This covers everything from fish tanks on the top floor to pink-toed tarantulas over at the bug zoo, to the playful doodads on the bottom floor.

Some of the star attractions are: 1. A virtual reality basketball game where you play "hoops" against a video "pro". 2. A large touch tunnel where children navigate a pitch-black maze using only their tactile senses. 3. A mini-wall for rock climbing.

Down on the Invention Floor there are plenty of goodies including: a remote-controlled racetrack; a sound booth where you can mix high-tech electronics to compose music; and the Discovery Room where guests can build their own structures assisted by staff members.

Guests can also check the weather station on the outside deck and get a view of the harbor and the Statue of Liberty from the 170 foot tower.

As for the Kodak Omni theater - it's housed in a geodesic dome (which helps give the Science Center its unique appearance). It features an eight-story curved screen and seating for 400 people. Movies produced in the Omnimax format are twice as large as feature films and use a six-channel sound system. This gives an all-surrounding feel to the films (and vertigo to some). These nature films are popular - best to reserve for weekend seatings.

Even the gift shop is colorful — it includes models of the giant cockroaches and a photo imaging system. The cafeteria offers ordinary fast food but a beautiful view. And the special 3-D shows in the theater are fun - even if they do cost extra.

HOURS: Daily: 9:30-5:30
ADMISSION: Adults: $9.00; Omni: $7.00; Combo: $13.00. Student/
Senior: $8.00, $6.00, $11.00; Children (5-12): $6.00,
$5.00, $9.00.
LOCATION: Exit 14B, NJ Turnpike, turn left. Follow Liberty State
Park signs, take Burma Road to Center.
TELEPHONE: 201-200-1000

NEW JERSEY STATE MUSEUM

It stands in Trenton, pristine and white against the backdrop of the Delaware River, the very model of a modern, well-kept museum. There is no admission charge. The separate Museum Theater, just adjacent, offers a well-proportioned stage and comfortable seating for movies and live performances. The Planetarium, housed in its own section, seats 150 people. The restrooms are clean, well maintained and plentiful. The State Museum at Trenton seems to have everything — except enough visitors. Nowadays, there are many weekend specials to attract customers.

Set up as a family museum, with exhibits to interest both children and adults, the museum offers a balance between the art and science sections. On the upper floors, several galleries of paintings and decorative arts, which range from 17th century urns to 20th century cubist canvasses, bring a wide dimension to the Jersey collection. The natural science section offers an excellent collection of stuffed animals posed within their natural habitats. Another large display is devoted to life around the seashore with relief dioramas depicting the chain of tidal life from worms to higher life. There are also full exhibits on insects, minerals and the solar system. The first floor is devoted to changing exhibits of art and sculpture.

As for the **planetarium**, which costs extra, shows are given two or three times on weekends and also during summer. Check for appropriate children's ages. The seats are comfortable and the simulated sky has great depth once the stars get moving around. Laser concerts are scheduled on some Friday and Saturday nights and are highly popular with teenagers. There is a gift shop outside the planetarium with lots of science items. Another gift shop upstairs has a larger selection.

For people living within easy driving distance of the museum, it is a bargain not to be missed. For those farther away, it is a worthwhile stop when you are in the area. Parking is a problem on weekdays, so try for a weekend visit. Free.

HOURS: Tues.-Sat. 9-4:45. Sun. 12-5.
LOCATION: 205 West State Street, Trenton. Use Route 29 along Delaware River or Route 1 into State Street.
TELEPHONE: 609-292-6464, 609-292-6308

✵ THE NEWARK MUSEUM

A few years ago, the Newark Museum was expanded. Now it is not only twice its previous size, it has also been completely redesigned so that it is open, airy, convenient - a first class museum that is worth every penny that was put into it. There is room to show off the collection - American paintings, Tibetan statues, African masks, - plus plenty of space for the special exhibits that come and go. The center court is open for light lunches and teas. The well designed corridors make for easy walking.

The Asian Galleries on the third floor include not only the museum's fine Tibetan collection but Indian, Chinese and Korean treasures as well. Here, as in the other galleries, the exhibits are well mounted and the explanatory material easy to read. The second floor includes both 19th Century American art and lots of contemporary painting.

In another wing of the second floor is the completely revamped Junior Gallery and mini-zoo. The terrariums and aquariums found here are a far cry from the strange funnel-like enclosures once used for small animals. Nearby is the Native American Gallery with its large collection of costumes and artifacts. And of course there is a program hall for all the school classes that come to the museum.

It may be a little confusing at first, moving from one wing to another, but floor plan guides are available. The renovated 50 seat **Dreyfuss Planetarium** is on the left hand side of the garden entrance. This facility offers sky shows to the general public on weekends and holidays. The museum also includes a pleasant garden complete with a lifelike sculpture of George Segal's Tollhouse. A tiny one-room schoolhouse that dates back to 1784 and a Fire Museum are also part of the garden scene.

There are two museum shops - one for kids, one for adults. And attended parking is available in the adjacent parking lot, corner of Central & University Avenues. Have your parking ticket stamped at the Information Desk. The Ballantine House which has been completely refurbished (q.v.) is next door. You enter through the museum. Free. Planetarium fee.

> **HOURS:** 12-5 Wed.-Sun., except major holidays.
> **LOCATION:** 49 Washington St., Newark (facing Washington Park)
> **TELEPHONE:** 201-596-6550. Planetarium: 201-596-6609

THE MONTCLAIR ART MUSEUM

A true art museum nestled in a town that was once an artists' center, the Montclair Museum reflects a high level of community support. Built in 1912, this is not somebody's leftover mansion but a solid, stone neo-Classical edifice dedicated to the showing of painting and sculpture. The major collection is of American paintings covering a period of three centuries. Many familiar names — Edward Hopper, Mary Cassatt, George Inness — are represented here, along with a host of other American artists. Although there are many paintings in the permanent collection, they are used as part of the constantly changing exhibits which are usually themed for a certain point of view.

A permanent Indian collection is of interest to the kids. Costumes and artifacts go beyond New Jersey's Lenni Lenape — the Plains and Southwest Indians are given equal treatment here with good displays of Sioux and Navajo dress.

This is quite an active museum what with lecture series, morning coffee hours, gallery talks. There is a small gift shop on the first floor.

> **HOURS:** Tues.-Sat. 11-5; Sun. 1-5. Summer: Wed.-Sun. 12-5. Closed major holidays.
> **ADMISSION:** Adults $4.00; seniors & students $3.00; under 12 free. Free Sat.: 11-2.
> **LOCATION:** Bloomfield Ave. & South Mountain Ave., Montclair, Essex County.
> **TELEPHONE:** 201-746-5555

THE MORRIS MUSEUM

On rainy days, empty weekends or just any day, there's nothing like a quick trip to a local bastion of culture to uplift the spirit, educate, and get the kids out of the house all in one fell swoop. The Morris Museum of Arts and Sciences is one of these dependable bastions. Housed in a lovely old mansion surrounded by great trees, it is small enough not to be to exhausting to young children. It is also varied enough to appeal to children of all ages, plus their parents. Science and technology exhibits have included displays on computers, sound waves and fibers.

There is also a rock and mineral exhibit. (This one comes complete with a dark room for viewing fluorescent rocks.) The natural sciences are represented by glass-encased exhibits of stuffed animals in their natural environments, plus a live zoo downstairs. The children usually trek down to this room with its lazy alligator and turtles safely inside glass cases. And since it is called a museum of arts and sciences, there is always at least one art exhibit on display that is changed every few months. Major expansion allows for extra space for shows and traveling exhibits. Some, like the recent Star-Trek exhibit, take over almost the whole first floor, and cost an extra fee.

Social Sciences are found on the second floor. Here, 3rd, 4th and 5th graders can see graphic examples of their studies of both North American Indian and colonial life. Besides the colonial kitchen and everything you'd ever want to know about the Lenni Lenape Indians, the second floor also offers a special "touch and feel" room for two-to-seven year olds.

Other popular exhibits are the model railroad and the tiny dinosaur room. And last, but not least, is the Gift Shop with an interesting range of gifts. The museum also includes a comfortable 300 seat theater which is the scene of many special events and shows.

HOURS: Mon.-Sat. 10-5; Sun. 1-5.
ADMISSION: Adults $4.00; seniors and children $2.00
LOCATION: Route 287 to Exit 36 to Columbia Tpke to 6 Normandy Heights Rd., Morristown, Morris County
TELEPHONE: 201-538-0454

THE BERGEN MUSEUM

Here is another local museum that offers both the arts and sciences, with a nice balance between the adult and children's exhibits. Although much of the gallery area in this private institution is given over to changing exhibits, the permanent collection includes the Hackensack Mastodon and the newer Dwarskill Mastodon and several other natural history displays.

For children there is the Nature Room which displays snakes, frogs and fishtanks. And of course, there is the inevitable Indian collection of artifacts. Changing exhibits include photographs, invitational paintings and technological displays. And there is always some children's activity offered on Saturdays. The museum is located (or should I say, hidden) in the right wing of the Bergen County Community Services Building, a huge brick building in the typically bureaucratic style of architecture.

HOURS: Tues. - Sat.: 10-5: Sun.: 1-5.
ADMISSION: Adults: $2.50; Children, Seniors: $1.00
LOCATION: Corner of E. Ridgewood and Fairview Aves. Paramus, Bergen County
TELEPHONE: 201-265-1248

THE MONMOUTH MUSEUM

This handsome, modern building, set in the middle of a community college campus, offers two distinct sections. One is for adults, and the other, an enlarged wing, is devoted to children. Each section offers a single exhibit devoted to a specific theme. The exhibit in the children's wing is changed every two years. One concerned America's westward expansion and included everything from frying pans to wagon wheels to desert snakes, all with a touch and feel emphasis. Another show had to do with fossils and dinosaurs and again, the single theme took up the entire space of the wing.

Meanwhile the art galleries in the main section are changed more often. The exhibit I saw depicted seaside life in the late Victorian era, complete with wooden carousel and turn of the century costumes. Very well done. There was a good balance between the written information, the old photographs and newspapers and the costumed mannequins.

The children's section is quite popular with school groups. For that reason the Becker Children's Wing is open to the public only from 2:00 to 4:30 p.m. weekdays during the school year. Regular hours apply weekends. As for individuals, it's quite a nice place to visit, but call first to make sure an exhibit is on, since it takes many weeks to change from one complete theme to another. And be aware, that although the Monmouth Museum is located inside a public college campus, it is a private institution and is not free.

HOURS: Tues. - Sat. 10-4:30. Sun. 1-5. (Adults)
ADMISSION: Adults: $3.00; Children, Seniors, Students: $2.50
DIRECTIONS: Exit 109, Garden State Parkway, then west on Newman Springs Road (Route 520) to entrance of Brookdale Community College, Lincroft, Monmouth County.
TELEPHONE: 908-747-2266.

OTHER N.J. MUSEUMS OF ART AND SCIENCE

JERSEY CITY MUSEUM: Located on the top floor of the Jersey City main library, the museum is a combination of rotating exhibits of contemporary art (usually one-person shows) and a permanent gallery of 19th Century paintings and furnishings. Free. *Hours:* Wed.: 10:30-8, Tues. - Sat.: 10:30-5. No Sat. in summer. *Location:* 472 Jersey Ave., Jersey City. *Telephone:* 201-547-4514.

RUTGERS GEOLOGY MUSEUM: A super-large room ringed by a balcony comprises this science museum located on the second floor of the Geology Hall on the Rutgers campus. A reconstructed mastodon, charts of geological periods, small fossils, mineral display, etc. Interesting lectures and demonstrations for school groups. The small gift shop has minerals for sale at reasonable prices. Free. *Hours:* Mon.: 1-4; Tues.-Fri.: 9-12, Sept.-June. Call for summer hours. *Location:* George and Somerset Sts., College Ave. Campus, Rutgers, New Brunswick. *Telephone:* 908-932-7243.

JANE VOORHEES ZIMMERLI ART MUSEUM: Housed in modern Voorhees Hall, on the Rutgers campus, the art gallery includes a permanent collection of American artists with many well-known names, such as Winslow Homer, among the exhibits. Prints, sculpture and changing displays. Free. *Hours:* Weekdays except Mon.: 10-4:30; Weekends: 12-5. *Location:* Voorhees Hall, Hamilton St., College Ave. Campus, Rutgers Univ., New Brunswick. *Telephone:* 908-932-7237.

PRINCETON ART MUSEUM: Mentioned in the section on Princeton but worth another mention here since it is one of the nicest art museums in New Jersey. Recently expanded and now beautifully laid out; modern, well-lit, and with a collection that encompasses European and Oriental art as well as American. Free. *Hours:* Tues.-Sat.: 10-5; Sun.: 1-5. *Location:* Princeton Campus, Nassau St. & Witherspoon, Princeton, Mercer County. *Telephone:* 609-258-3788.

NOYES MUSEUM: A striking modern museum set on the edge of a wildlife refuge which specializes in changing exhibits of contemporary painting and sculpture. A well-mounted collection of duck decoys is also on display. The building overlooks a lilypad lake and is quite pleasant. *Hours:* Wed.-Sun., 11-4. *Admission:* Adults: $3.00; Seniors: $1.50; Children: $.50; Free on Fridays. *Location:* Lily Lake Road, Oceanville, Atlantic County. *Telephone:* 609-652-8848.

MIDDLESEX COUNTY MUSEUM: Set in a handsomely restored 1741 Georgian mansion (known first as Ivy Hall and then as the Cornelius Low House) the museum offers changing exhibits of art, local history and special themes. A one-theme exhibit often takes up the entire house. Entrance is most easily attained through the Busch Campus of Rutgers University. Free. *Hours:* Tues.-Fri., Sun.: 1-4. *Location:* 1225 River Road, Piscataway. *Telephone:* 908-745-4177.

TRENTON CITY MUSEUM: Housed in the Victorian Italianate building known as Ellarslie, the museum offers a combination of changing art exhibits and a permanent collection of local historical material. Also exhibits of Trenton's porcelain sculptors such as Boehm and Cybis. Ellarslie is set inside of Trenton's Cadwalader Park, which was designed by Frederick Law Olmstead. Free. *Hours:* Tues.-Sat.: 11-3; Sun.: 2-4. *Location:* Cadwalader Park, Parkside Ave., Trenton. *Telephone:* 609-989-3632.

New Jersey Specialty Museums

NEW JERSEY CHILDREN'S MUSEUM

This fairly new museum is dedicated to the proposition that children learn through play and experience. Set in a reconditioned industrial building in Paramus with 15,000 square feet of space, the museum is 100 percent hands-on. Children from 3 to 8 can touch, climb, put on clothes, and play-act to their hearts content.

The walls are brightly painted, the floor is carpeted, and at first it may remind you of a giant nursery school. But the exhibits are for more expansive than what you would find at your local pre-school. There is a real Hughes 269 helicopter, for instance. It has been simplified so that a child can climb inside and pretend to fly. There is a genuine backhoe with a hardhat to match. And most popular of all - the fire engine that comes complete with firehose and a bell.

There are forty interactive exhibits. These include a fantasy castle, a prehistoric cave where kids can scribble their own "cave paintings" on a blackboard, and a garage where they can repair a jeep. The huge space is divided into sections devoted to dance, music, architecture, medicine and so forth. The "office" has real computers and adding machines; and the piz-zeria has the kids busy for hours.

The museum is not meant as a drop off spot. Parents or teachers must supervise the children and accompany them but they are welcome to join in the play. There are assistants around to help. Children under one, free. No strollers and no food allowed.

HOURS: Daily 9-5 (until 8 on Fridays)
ADMISSION: $7.00
LOCATION: 599 Industrial Ave., Paramus (behind Route 17 "Toys R Us".)
TELEPHONE: 201-262-5151.

GARDEN STATE DISCOVERY MUSEUM

Talk about synchronicity! When it comes to hands-on, interactive, educational, colorful museums that are geared specifically for children under ten, New Jersey has gone from none to two in the last few years. And that's not counting all those play areas and "Discovery Zones" that are popping up all over. Like The Children's Museum in Paramus, this place owes much to early interactive museums like "Please Touch" in Philadelphia. In fact the co-directors worked at the Franklin Institute for many years.

The Garden State Discovery Museum serves the southern part of the state. The two women who run it have filled the 15,000 square foot center with painted murals on the walls and a number of interesting and innovative exhibits. The theme is New Jersey, so included is a Jersey diner complete with chrome and red vinyl seats and a kitchen where kids can whip up plastic hamburgers, a farm market, and a "Down the shore" exhibit where kids fish off a boat or send rubber ducks down a stream.

Other areas include a rock-climbing wall and the one-hundred seat theater where the kids can put on costumes and play. A flowered Volkswagen "bug", a house construction complete with gravel pit and junk musical instruments are also on hand. The museum directors have wisely included a snack area (with cafe tables) where you can eat your own sandwiches and augment them with vending machine items. There are also kiddie-size picnic tables outside and a good sized gift shop inside. Geared for 2 to 10 year olds - and parents must accompany. Luckily there's a family membership available.

HOURS: Tues.-Sun. 9:30-5:30. Til 8:30 p.m. Thurs. in summer.
ADMISSION: $6.50; Seniors: $5.50; Under 18 mos. free.
DIRECTIONS: 16 N. Springdale Road, Cherry Hill, Camden County, not far from NJ Tpke Exit 4. Call for directions.
TELEPHONE: 609-424-1233

FRANKLIN MINERAL MUSEUM

New Jersey is both the zinc mining and fluorescent rock capital of the world. While this may not be on the same level as a financial or entertainment capital, it does provide one mecca for rock-hounds — Franklin Borough in Sussex County. Here, you will find both the Franklin Mineral Museum and the Sterling Hill mine (check separate listing).

Children seem to have a fascination with rocks — as any mother who has ever dumped odd-sized stones out of her darling's pockets can attest. At the Franklin Mineral Museum you can dig for rocks with pick and shovel at the adjacent Buckwheat Dump. The museum itself is divided into several sections: a fluorescent rock display, a general exhibit on zinc and other minerals, and a replica of an actual mine. An additional room features dinosaur footprints, fossils and Indian artifacts.

Once you enter the small building you are ushered into a long, narrow room, you face a row of gray, ordinary rocks of varying sizes behind a glass case. The guide flicks off the lights, and lo and behold — the rocks turn into an extraordinary array of shining colors. Green, purple, blue luminous rocks, many with unusual patterns, glow behind the glass while the guide explains their names and properties. The guide flicks on the light and it's all over. The rocks are back to their old pedestrian form.

Next is a tour of the mine replica. The plaster labyrinth we entered was not so much scary as claustrophobic. Once the tours are over, one can visit the gift shop in the main lobby where you'll find a good selection of rocks, gemstones and necklaces at non-inflated prices.

But for many, the highlight of the trip is the chance to go prospecting in the rock dump at the back of the museum, although chances of finding a true specimen are slim. You must bring your own equipment — pickaxes, hammers, shovels plus a bag to carry your specimens. School age children must be accompanied by an adult until they are fourteen.

> **HOURS:** Mon.-Sat.: 10-4; Sun.: 12:30-4:30. Closed Dec. 1-Mar. 1. Tours take about one hour.
>
> **ADMISSION:** Adults: $4.00; Children: $2.00. Same rate applies for dump.
>
> **DIRECTIONS:** Route 80 to Route 15 Sparta, then Route 517 to Franklin then one mile north on 23. Museum is on Evans St.
>
> **TELEPHONE:** 201-827-3481

THE GOLF HOUSE

Set among the posh country estates of Far Hills, the Golf House includes a stately house, museum and the working headquarters of the United States Golf Association. A circular driveway leads you up to the white portico where you might almost expect a butler to take your bags. However, you simply park in the adjoining lot and enter the massive doors. In the front lobby you will find a combination information stand and gift shop. You can pick up brochures and proceed around the mansion from there.

There are two floors of exhibit space and among the most popular rooms are those with hands-on displays. You can practice putting, take a video quiz, trace the history of the game and compare the swings of various players. There is even a golf video game which you can play (using joysticks). If you like it well enough you can buy a copy at the gift shop.

Other exhibits include a history of the game itself, plus rooms devoted to golfing costumes, golf clubs, and the evolution of the golf ball. There is even a whole exhibit devoted to turf and how to keep the greens well maintained. Other exhibits include pictures and information on golf greats (such as Bob Jones). Some of the well-prized momentos are the golf clubs of presidents Wilson, Franklin Roosevelt and of course, Eisenhower. Also on view is the Moon Club used by Alan Shepard to play on the lunar surface.

The house contains a magnificent flying staircase, paintings and sculpture and a library of 8000 volumes. You can also visit the interesting Technical Center (behind the main house) where they test golf balls (with a machine called "Iron Byron") and other paraphenalia. Free.

HOURS: Mon. - Fri. 9-5; Weekends: 10-4. Closed holidays.
LOCATION: Route 512, east of Route 202, Far Hills, Somerset County
TELEPHONE: 908-234-2300

NEW JERSEY STATE POLICE MUSEUM

For mystery buffs or history buffs, the exhibits in this two-million dollar edifice offer information about the role of the State Police as well as insights into crime detection. In fact you'll feel like Sherlock Holmes just trying to locate the place — the museum is inside the grounds of the New Jersey State Police Headquarters and directional signs are scant.

The museum buildings include a refurbished log cabin that once was the dormitory for State Troopers. It now houses a 1930 Buick touring car, and other exhibits of transportation used early on. You learn that the State Police only began in 1921 and that Colonel H. Norman Schwarzkopf (father of Stormin' Norman) was the first Superintendent.

The main building is full of state of the art interactive exhibits and easy to read posters. The 911 exhibit, for instance, lets the viewer decide whether to send an incoming call to the police, fire or medical emergency unit. There are microscopes that let you examine your own thumb prints.

Most interesting of all the "interactives" is the exhibit called "Scene of the Crime". Through a glass window you see a murder scene. A man is lying on the floor of a kitchen in a pool of blood. Flour is spilled on the counter. Is the dead man the owner of the premises, or is he an intruder? He was shot but where is the murder weapon? An overhead video walks you through the preliminary investigation and the procedures for collecting and pre-serving evidence.

But the "piece de resistance" of the museum is its exhibit on the Lindbergh case. The kidnapping of the baby son of Charles and Anne Lindbergh took place in 1932 from an estate just out-side of Hopewell. The State Police played a major role in the investigation and some of the evidence used to convict Bruno Hauptmann of the crime is on display. You can see the baby sleeping suit that was sent by the kidnapper to the Lindberghs, along with a ransom note. Reward posters, pictures and memo-rabilia of the "trial of the century" which took place in Flemington in 1935 are here. Free.

HOURS: Monday - Saturday, 10 AM - 4 PM
LOCATION: Located on Route 175 (River Road) West Trenton (near Exit 1 on Route 95).
TELEPHONE: 609-882-2000 Ext. 6400

DOLL CASTLE DOLL MUSEUM

No, this is not a collection of doll princesses set inside a lifesize doll castle. Rather, it is a museum run by the editors of Doll Castle News (a magazine devoted to information for and by doll collectors), and is housed upstairs over the printing office. Over 2000 dolls and stuffed animals are on display, plus miniatures, dollhouses and such. The collection includes corn husk, cloth and soft-sculpture dolls as well as the traditional kind. The em-phasis is not so much on antique dolls as on the variety of 20th Century creations. The museum is meant for both children and doll enthusiasts (and according to the owner here, doll collecting is the second most popular hobby in the United States).

HOURS: June - Oct.: Wed., Thurs., Fri.: 10-4 and by appt.
ADMISSION: Adults: $2.25; Children $.50.
LOCATION: 37 Belvidere Ave., Washington, Warren County.
TELEPHONE: 909-689-7042

AVIATION HALL OF FAME

Aviation achievements from balloon voyages in 1850 Perth Amboy to modern day flights are commemorated in this interesting museum which is actually in two separate sections. One section is located on top of the stairs at the old Teterboro Airport Control Tower where views of the runway and a short film on aviation history await. Most of all, you can listen in to pilot-control tower conversation over the radio. They even offer birthday parties up here for those who love the atmosphere. Kids can use fake telephones to make believe they are bringing in the aircraft.

The larger museum section is on the other side of the airfield. Here you will find a house filled with aviation memorabilia and displays (which include a small, hands-on helicopter.) Outside, in the back, you can climb aboard an old-fashioned propeller plane, and see how the folks in the Forties and Fifties used to ride. (At least the seats were wider then — and only two across!).

For those who remember when a Sunday afternoon outing with the kids was a jaunt to the airport, and for Air Force veterans, this is a fun place to visit. But it's best to call first, since much of the work force here is volunteer, and there may be unexpected closings.

> **HOURS:** 10-4 Tues.-Sun. in summer. Weekends or by appt. rest of year.
> **ADMISSION:** Adults: $3.00; Children: $2.00; Seniors: $2.00.
> **LOCATION:** Atlantic Aviation Hangar, Teterboro Airport, off Route 46, Bergen County. Look for sign.
> **TELEPHONE:** 201-288-6344

CAMPBELL MUSEUM

For America's biggest soup company what else but a collection of soup tureens, bowls and ladles? However, since the decoration of tureens was considered high art in the 17th and 18th centuries, the collection here is quite dazzling. Porcelain, silver, pewter — the most extensive collection in the world is found here and includes pieces used by European royalty. Because part of the collection always travels, what is shown will vary. However, such stellar pieces as a huge silver tureen crafted into a warship (from Catherine the Great's table) makes a visit here well worth the trip. You will also find cows, boar's heads, rabbits, and chickens fashioned in clay and used for serving soup. A movie depicting how tureens are fashioned is shown in the Visitor Center, by appointment. Light snacks are often served. And during the Christmas period, a display of antique toys is on view. The museum, by the way, is housed next to the Campbell Administration building which is easily accessible from Route 30. Free.

HOURS: Mon. - Fri. 9-4:30. Closed holidays.
LOCATION: Campbell Place, Camden.
TELEPHONE: 609-342-6440.

EDISON MEMORIAL TOWER AND MUSEUM

The tower is shaped like an electric light with a bulb on top and commemorates the site of Edison's Menlo Park laboratory, birthplace of the incandescent bulb. The original laboratory was moved to Greenfield, Michigan, by Henry Ford for his Americana Museum, but there is a small museum here with lightbulbs, phonographs, and other mementos of Edison's achievement. Free.

HOURS: Wed. - Fri.: 12:30-4; Sat., Sun.: 12:30-4:30.
LOCATION: Christie St., Menlo Park, (off Rte. 27) in Edison State Park, Middlesex County.
TELEPHONE: 908-549-3299

OTHER N.J. SPECIALTY MUSEUMS

WHIPPANY RAILWAY MUSEUM: Set in an old boxcar of Erie Lackawanna vintage, the museum includes a model railroad set, lots of lanterns, badges, posters and other memorabilia. Open weekends in warm weather. Once in a while there's a special train ride from here. Small fee. *Telephone:* 201-887-8177 for hours. *Location:* Depot yard, Route 10 and Whippany Road, Whippany, Morris County.

AFRICAN ART MUSEUM: Run by the S.M.A. Fathers and set inside a church complex, this museum highlights West African art and artifacts. Masks, beadwork, sculpture, religious symbols from Ghana, Mali, etc. Tours for school groups. Free. *Location:* 23 Bliss Ave., Tenafly, Bergen County. Call for hours. *Telephone:* 201-567-0450.

AFRO-AMERICAN HISTORICAL AND CULTURAL MUSEUM: Concentrates on Afro-American experience in America. Exhibits on Civil Rights movement, athletes, black dolls, quilts, typical kitchen, African artifacts. Over 4000 square feet on 2nd floor of Greenville Library. Free. *Location:* 1841 Kennedy Blvd., Jersey City. *Hours:* Mon.-Sat.: 10-5. Closed Sat. in summer. *Telephone:* 201-547-5262.

BARNEGAT BAY DECOY AND BAYMAN'S MUSEUM: Dedicated to the carved duck decoys that this region is famous for - plus other wood carvings which are all on display. Also exhibits on oystering, clamming, and the work of maintaining the boats, nets, etc. of the baymen whose families still live in the region. *Hours:* Wed.-Sun.: 10-4:30. *Location:* 137 W. Main St. (Route 9), Tuckerton, Ocean County. *Telephone:* 609-296-8868.

HIRAM BLAUVELT WILDLIFE MUSEUM: First art museum to concentrate on wildlife and sporting art exclusively. Also includes prehistoric and extinct specimens of birds and animals. Housed in mansion. Free. *Location:* 705 Kinderkamack Road, Oradell, Essex County. *Hours:* Tues.-Thurs.: 10-4. *Telephone:* 201-261-0012.

HUNGARIAN HERITAGE CENTER: Used as a meeting place for programs and activities for Hungarian-Americans, the center includes 10,000 feet of exhibition space. Folk art, and immigrant life plus special exhibitions by Hungarian artists are featured here. *Hours:* Tues.-Sat.: 11-4. *Location:* 300 Somerset St., New Brunswick. *Telephone:* 908-846-5777.

NEW JERSEY MUSEUM OF AGRICULTURE: Early farming equipment, 17th century trading post, tractors, buggys, kitchen work, plus displays of land-clearing, etc. This is a large museum with everything from egg laying to cow milking carefully depicted. *Hours:* Wed.-Sat.: 10-5; Sun.: 12-5. *Admission:* Adults: $3.00; Children: $1.00. *Location:* Off Route 1 and College Farm Road, Cook College, New Brunswick. *Telephone:* 908-249-2077.

THE STONE MUSEUM: Located inside a landscape establishment, the museum is a collection of stones, meteorites, fossils and fluorescent rocks and some displays. Outside there are stone terraces and walkways around a man-made lake. It's a cross between a store and a museum, but there is no pressure to buy, and you are welcome to spend as much time as you wish. Free. *Hours:* March 15 - mid-Dec., Daily 8-5; Sun., 10-5. *Location:* 608 Englishtown Road (Route 613) Monmouth County. *Telephone:* 908-521-2232.

VOLLENDAM WINDMILL AND MUSEUM: Inside this replica of an authentic 60 foot high Dutch windmill is a small museum which includes tools and millstones. Set way out in a rustic area of the state, the seven story structure boasts sail arms that are 68 feet long. Around Christmas time there is also a Charlie Brown Christmas Treet Farm. *Hours:* May 1 - Sept. 30: Weekends: 12-4:30. *Admission:* Adults: $2.50; Age 6-18: $1.00. *Location:* 231 Adamic Hill Road, near Milford, off Route 519, Hunterdon County. *Telephone:* 908-995-4365.

New Jersey: Historical Museums

MUSEUM OF EARLY TRADES AND CRAFTS

Created to preserve the life and times of early settlers, this small museum encompasses thirty-eight years of collecting and research. Diaries, ledgers, advertisements, broadsides, and newspapers were scoured for details of everyday life in the Colonies — most particularly, the New Jersey colony. The exhibit on brooms, for instance, is based on the business of one particular broommaker in Florham Park. He started out with one broommaking machine, used local cattails for the brush, and did business as a sideline to farming. Later, as times prospered, the broommaker had several employees and a full time business. This information and much more is imparted by the docents who greet each visitor at the door.

For the first generation of settlers, home meant a one-room shack with a dirt floor. Furniture was made from the wood of surrounding trees. You ate what you grew or bartered. Mother was the family doctor and every household had an herb garden.

Major exhibits of the museum change every few months but each one takes a particular trade or craft and follows it through three generations. The exhibit I encountered emphasized shoes. Shoes were made by the father of the family in the first generation. Cobblers came in later. Leather was taken from the hides of cows that were slaughtered for food. Shoes which were made at night by candlelight had neither right nor left feet. Both were exactly the same. Just imagine — a colonial mother didn't have to stand there in the morning and repeat, "No, the left shoe goes on the left foot," as I do.

Besides the changing exhibits, there is a permanent room set up as a colonial kitchen. The museum also contains a complete set of tools for the 34 trades that existed in New Jersey at the time of the Revolution. Although the museum is small, the lectures are so comprehensive that you should plan to spend at least an hour here. Special demonstrations on Saturdays.

HOURS: Tues.- Sat.: 10-4; Sun.: 2-5. Closed major holidays.
ADMISSION: Adults: $2.00 Children: $1.00
LOCATION: Main Street (Route 124) and Green Village Road, Madison, Morris County
TELEPHONE: 201-377-2982

SCHOOLHOUSE MUSEUM

Although this historical museum is set inside an 1873 schoolhouse, only one section of the vast paraphenalia collected here is devoted to the little old schoolroom. Besides the teacher's platform, desks, maps and schoolbooks, there is also a colonial and Victorian kitchen and sections set up as typical rooms of the 19th Century. Over 3,000 items are jammed into the one huge room — everything from bobbin lace to beaver hats. Upstairs, the attic has even more with lots of 19th Century dresses, firemen's uniforms, etc. Memorabilia of the church, early Dutch settlers and local celebrities (including a well-known actor), tools and harness and more are all to be found in this well-stocked museum. Free. (Donations accepted).

HOURS: May - Oct.: Sun. 2:30-4:30. Groups by appt.
LOCATION: 650 East Glen Ave. right off Route 17, Ridgewood, Bergen County.
TELEPHONE: 201-447-3242

OCEAN COUNTY HISTORICAL MUSEUM

Basically a historic house with rooms set up in comfortable 19th Century fashion. A music-library room, and a well-set dining room set the tone. The Victorian kitchen is of particular interest since it is chock full of useful gadgets that have since been deemed non-essential. A gizmo for softening corks had the curators mystified until a tourist told them what it was.

Upstairs a child's bedroom is all set up and a small school-house impresses the youngsters. Downstairs, in the basement, there are museum-type memorabilia including pictures of Lakehurst during the age of dirigibles. In the main house there are now changing exhibits. A new wing is dedicated to Ocean County industries such as cranberry production and glass making.

HOURS: Tues. and Thurs.: 1-3; Sat.: 10-1
ADMISSION: $2.00 (donations)
LOCATION: 26 Hadley Ave., Toms River, Ocean County
TELEPHONE: 908-341-1880

HOPEWELL MUSEUM

Again, a combination historic house/museum with rooms done up in particular periods. The house itself is Victorian, but the rooms display Colonial, Empire and Victorian furnishings. An 1880 organ and a Joseph Bonaparte sideboard are prized posses-sions here. In the back of the mansion, an addition houses a large Indian collection and a great many costumed mannequins. The costumes include ballgowns, wedding dresses and other fin-ery worn in the 19th Century. Upstairs there are even more deco-rated rooms since this house is much larger inside than it seems from the exterior. Guided tour. Free. (Donations accepted).

HOURS: Mon., Wed., Sat.: 2-5
LOCATION: 28 East Broad St. (Route 518) Hopewell, Mercer County
TELEPHONE: 609-466-0103

OCEAN CITY HISTORICAL MUSEUM

Life in the 1890's is graphically depicted in this small historical museum which is now housed in the Community Cultural
Center along with the library and art museum. Mannequins in
costumes and photos hark back to the heyday of the Jersey shore
when Victorian families headed for Ocean City, the quiet and
sober neighbor of Atlantic City. Indian artifacts and mementos of
the wreck of the Sindia are all here. Free.

> **HOURS:** Mon.-Fri.: 10-4; Sat.: 1-4. Closed holidays, Winter:
> Tues.-Sat.: 1-4.
> **LOCATION:** 1735 Simpson Ave., Ocean City, Cape May County.
> **TELEPHONE:** 609-399-1801.

SPY HOUSE MUSEUM

A combination of historic site and two museums make up this
unusual complex by the seashore. One section is a cottage erected
in 1663 and called "The Spy House" because it was a favorite
meeting place of Revolutionary War spies. The Shoal Harbor
Marine Museum and the Penelope Stout Museum of Crafts of
Man comprise the rest of the complex. You can find lobster pots,
eeling equipment, and a variety of furniture in this tripart museum. Many special weekend events, from colonial baking to
military encampments, are planned from spring to fall.

> **HOURS:** Sat., Sun.: 2-4.
> **ADMISSION:** Donation
> **LOCATION:** 119 Port Monmouth Rd., Port Monmouth. (Take Exit
> 117 off Garden State Parkway to Route 36E to Port
> Monmouth.)
> **TELEPHONE:** 908-787-1807

CAPE MAY COUNTY HISTORICAL MUSEUM

Housed in a well-preserved 18th Century home, the museum
includes an 1820 dining room all set up, a children's room with
antique toys, and much glassware and china. Across the yard the
well stocked barn features harpoons from Cape May's whaling
past, Indian artifacts and farm implements. Here also is the huge
glass prism top to the old Cape May lighthouse. Visits are by

guided tour and take about an hour. The adjacent Genealogy Room is of interest to many historians because of the number of Mayflower descendents in the Cape May area. There is also a small gift shop in the museum proper.

HOURS: Summer: Mon. - Sat., 10-4; Spring & Fall: Tues. - Sat., 10-4. Dec. - Mar. Sat. only
ADMISSION: Adults $2.00; Under 12 $.50.
LOCATION: 504 Route 9, Cape May Courthouse
TELEPHONE: 609-465-3535

NEW JERSEY HISTORICAL SOCIETY

One of the most extensive collections of books, manuscripts and other material about the Garden State is found in the library of this 4-story building and museum of this historical society. The museum consists of rooms set up with colonial, federal and Victorian furnishings, and smaller rooms relating to specific interests such as music and printing. Artifacts of everyday life, plus rotating exhibits on quiltmaking, shipbuilding, etc. are featured here.

The newest wrinkle is the addition of an interactive exhibit at the Kids Center. Covering the periods of the 1750s, 1850s, 1950s and the present, the exhibit allows kids to try on clothes, use a telephone switchboard or a telegraph. The Society is planning to move to a new building close to the Performing Arts Center which should make it more accessible to the public.

HOURS: Wed.-Fri., 3rd Sat.: 10-4
ADMISSION: $2.00
LOCATION: 230 Broadway, Newark.
TELEPHONE: 201-483-3939

MONMOUTH COUNTY HISTORICAL ASSOCIATION

Another combination of museum and society headquarters is housed in a handsome, 3-story Georgian colonial not far from the scene of the battle of Monmouth. Impressive collections of mahogany furniture, old china, glassware and paintings furnish the historical rooms of the "mansion" (it was actually built in 1931). You can also find specialty rooms devoted to dolls, old boxes, and so forth, plus an attic filled with bicycles, pony carts, and other leftovers from the 18th and 19th centuries. A new "hands-on experience" allows children to try on period clothes. The Association also administers several historic houses in Monmouth County.

HOURS: Tues. - Sat.: 10-4; Sun.: 1-4.
ADMISSION: Adults: $2.00; Children: $1.00; Seniors: $1.50.
LOCATION: 70 Court St., Freehold.
TELEPHONE: 908-462-1466

CAMDEN COUNTY HISTORICAL SOCIETY

Three sections include: a museum with early American glass, fire-fighting equipment, military artifacts and the tools of early handicrafts set up in "shops" of cobblers, carpenters, coopers, etc.; a library with 18,000 books and pamphlets, manuscripts and newspapers; and Pomona Hall, an excellent example of early Georgian architecture furnished in both 18th and 19th Century fashion. Pomona Hall is a separate house, connected by a breeze-way to the museum section. The guided tour will take you through many well-furnished rooms.

HOURS: Tues. & Thurs.: 12:30-4:30; Sun.: 1-5. Closed Aug. & major holidays.
ADMISSION: Adults: $2.00; Seniors: $1.00; under 12 free.
LOCATION: Park Blvd. & Euclid Ave., Camden.
TELEPHONE: 609-964-3333.

THE PATERSON MUSEUM

Located a block and a half from Paterson's Great Falls, in the one-time factory building of the Rogers Locomotive Company, the Paterson Museum takes up the huge first floor of the imposing red brick building. The museum contains a fascinating compilation of photographs, factory machines, old posters and early inventions. Among other things, you'll find the great wheels that spun silk thread and ribbons, model trains for children, a mock-up of the Botto House (q.v.) and reminders of the Colt factory. Although primarily a historical museum, there are other exhibits including a mineral exhibit.

Paterson seems to be the only community in New Jersey that does not equate the historical with the quaint. The great spinning machines, and the metal shell of the first submarine all testify to the fact that the dominant thrust of the 19th Century was the Industrial Revolution. The Rogers locomotive that stands outside the building was the Iron Horse that opened up the plains.

HOURS: Tues.- Fri.: 10-4:00: Sat., Sun.: 12:30-4:30. Closed holidays.
ADMISSION: Adults: $2.00; Children free.
LOCATION: 2 Market St., Paterson, Passaic County.
TELEPHONE: 201-881-3874

AMERICAN LABOR MUSEUM (BOTTO HOUSE)

A combination historic house/museum with an emphasis, for a change, on the working class. This family home of an Italian immigrant worker became a rallying place for striking union members during the 1913 Paterson Silk strike. Since Haledon had a Socialist mayor at the time, and Paterson itself had banned group assemblies, workers gathered here to hear the likes of John Reed and Big Bill Hayward during the bitter strike.

The Botto House is a sturdy, well-built wooden structure smack-dab in the center of a middle-income neighborhood in a suburb of Paterson. Although it was once modernized, it has been transformed back into its earlier self. In fact, the nice new kitchen floor was ripped up and replaced by those dull linoleum sheets of 1903 vintage. Ah, history. The guide will show you how the family lived in the old days. Vegetables were grown in the garden, rabbits and chickens were kept for food, canned goods went into the root cellar and nothing was thrown away. The outdoor garden is kept much as it was at the time when Italian immigrants lived here and worked in the nearby mills.

Aside from the homey artifacts, the museum section of the Botto House is devoted to pictures and displays about the early American labor movement. These include photographs of the unsafe and unsanitary working conditions in turn-of-the century factories, the 1913 silk strike, and many changing exhibits. As both a museum and a historic home, the Botto House offers a nice change from the usual historical fare in New Jersey.

HOURS: Wed. - Sat.: 1-4.
ADMISSION: Adults: $1.50; Children under 12, free.
LOCATION: 83 Norwood St., Haledon, Passaic County. Call for directions.
TELEPHONE: 201-595-7953.

OTHER NEW JERSEY HISTORICAL MUSEUMS

There are dozens of other small historical museums dotted about the state. These reflect the past highlights of a particular region, as do many of the ones mentioned in this chapter, and are no less important. However limitations of time and space make it impossible to visit or even list the many historical museums available. Since these museums are usually of local interest they are often mentioned in local newspapers and special events are always written up. Readers interested in history should also check the listings of historic houses in this book. They are very similar in scope and content to the historical museums and may be found in such chapters as *"Where Washington Ate, Fought and Slept"*, *"Homes of the Rich and Famous"*, *"Walking Tours"* and *"Restored Villages, Mills, Farms and Homes."*

New York Museums

METROPOLITAN MUSEUM OF ART

This huge Palladian building that covers several blocks of New York's Fifth Avenue is still the Grande Dame of museums this side of the Atlantic. It is the repository of a European culture wafted to our shores by millionaires whose art collections were donated for reasons of either generosity or tax exemptions. At one time the Museum was so old-Europe centered that it admitted neither American nor "Modern" art. However, all that has changed.

With the American Wing you get a museum and a half at the Met. The "wing" is, in fact, equal to most medium-sized museums. The three floors encompass American furniture and decorative arts, recreated 17th and 18th Century rooms, paintings and sculpture. To view it chronologically you must take an elevator and start at the top with the William and Mary chairs, descend through the restored rooms, the many paintings of George Washington (including the original "Crossing the Delaware"), pass the Frederic Remington sculptures and end up on the first floor with large well-lit canvasses by Whistler and John Singer Sargeant. To get back to the main museum you cross the *piece de resistance:* the Englehard Garden Court. This immense courtyard contains purple willowed Tiffany screens, Louis Sullivan stairs and a wonderful 1900s ambience.

But to begin at the beginning — when you first enter the Metropolitan's huge marble lobby you may feel as if you've entered Grand Central Station by mistake. Milling crowds, a central information booth, several ticket booths, coat-check areas, signs for the restaurant and rest-rooms, a bookshop and a jewelry counter doing booming business — this is a museum? Well, one traditional feature of the Museum is that from the front lobby it's Greeks to the left, Egyptians to the right and Europeans upstairs.

If you are with young children you might as well go for the mummies and the Temple of Dendur. Great stone sarcophagi and ancient sphinxes have a fascination for children that roomsful of paintings simply don't. The Medieval armor on the first floor is another child's favorite.

The second floor houses the European paintings which start with the Medieval period. From there you wander through Italian and Northern Renaissance, Dutch Masters, English portraits and French landscapes.

There are so many rooms to see — a Renaissance patio and a medieval tapestry hall, rooms devoted to gilded musical instruments and whole wings devoted to modern art, New Guinea artifacts and costume design.

For the exhausted, there's always lunch where you can wait on line for cafeteria food, or sit in elegance at the center restaurant and pay New York prices for a plate of chicken salad. (Reserve for the restaurant at the Information Booth when you arrive.) They are both in a large marble hall and the din of two hundred people and clanking silver can become a bit much. But it's a unique place and both children and little old ladies like it.

HOURS: Tues.-Thurs., Sun.: 9:30-5:15; Fri., Sat.: 9:30-8:45.
ADMISSION: Suggested donation: Adults: $7.00; Students, seniors: $3.50. Children under 12, free.
LOCATION: Fifth Ave. between 81sth and 84th Sts., N.Y.C.
TELEPHONE: 212-879-5500; 535-7710

AMERICAN MUSEUM
OF NATURAL HISTORY

Although this huge building dates back to the 19th Century the insides have been spiffed up and modernized. Special lighting and piped in music enhance many of the displays. And most recently, the dinosaurs (or at least their bones) have been revamped. Videos, interactive computers, and some surprises are on hand at the Hall of Dinosaurs. The brontosaurus is out (he has a new name and a longer tail) and the other dinos look more like those loping lizards in Jurassic Park than the towering bones of yore.

Part of the museum is dedicated to Anthropology with special halls recreating life, costumes, tools and instruments of the American Indian, the Asian people, Pacific people and so forth. Great stone heads from Mexico, the smell of the South American jungle, tribal music from Africa are all included. And then there are all those dioramas with mannequins depicting the different types of cave men.

Three floors of stuffed cheetahs and elks and elephants are part of the permanent exhibit here. And the Gem and Mineral collection has a sparkling setting where huge sections of quartz and amethyst glow behind modernistic lucite cases in a darkened room. For kids, the giant blue whale and stuffed penguins are always popular.

The Information Desk not only has floor plans (a must in this two-section museum) but the free "highlights" tour leaves from here also. For those who want to rest their feet and see something overwhelming at the same time there is the Naturemax theater (extra price) where a 40 foot screen full of volcanos or waterfalls gives an almost 3-dimensional effect.

As for eating, first you find the basement (and you practically have to be a member of the Explorer's Club to accomplish that) and then you decide between a fast food eatery and a trendy little glass-enclosed restaurant where you can eat sun-dried tomatoes and wonder when the heck this museum became chic.

The **Hayden Planetarium** is right next door but you can gain entrance through the museum proper — although you must pay a hefty separate fee. The planetarium is one of the largest in the country and runs both regular star shows and specials for children. There are also Laser concerts here, a lunar landscape, and a nice big meteor chunk to inspect.

HOURS: Daily: 10-5:45 (Wed., Fri., Sat. til 9).
ADMISSION: (Suggested) Adults: $6.00; Children: $3.00. Planetarium: Adults: $5.00; Children: $3.00; Seniors: $4.00.
LOCATION: Central Park West and 79th St., New York.
TELEPHONE: 212-769-5100; Planetarium: 212-769-5900.

THE CLOISTERS

High on a tree-covered bluff just minutes from the bustling streets of Manhattan's Washington Heights, there stands a world apart. The Cloisters, a museum built in the style of a 14th Century monastery, displays the art and architecture of the Middle Ages in a setting completely devoted to that single age. Unlike its mother museum (for the Cloisters is a part of the Metropolitan Museum of Art) which tries to cover the span of art from antiquity to the 20th Century, this monastic replica covers only the 12th to 15th Centuries in Europe. But the Cloisters includes both religious and secular art and geographical variety. The red tile roof and campanile of the building reflect the style of a Southern European monastery. But inside you will find the actual stones of a Romanesque Chapel, and a Gothic hall complete with arched ceiling and flying buttresses.

The Cloisters gets its name from the covered walkway surrounding an enclosed garden that was typical of the Medieval monastery. The main cloister at the museum is the one on the first floor, but there are several other cloisters downstairs which one can walk through. Of particular interest to gardeners is the herb garden here. Two hundred species of plants grown in the Middle Ages sprout among the espalier trees and arcades of a Cistercian cloister.

Every museum has its star attractions and certainly one of the stellar crowd-pleasers at the Cloisters is the *Hall of the Unicorn Tapestries*. Remarkable in their color, preservation and realism, these four panels tell a story which you read by moving from one to the other (they are not hung in consecutive order). The story of the hunt, killing and resurrection of the Unicorn shows the life of the Medieval aristocracy as well as the symbolism of the age. The *"Belle Heures of the Duc de Berry"* and the *Chalice of Antioch* are two other attractions in the downstairs treasury.

Of course no visit to a museum is complete without a stop at the gift shop. Here you can find books, records of medieval music, posters, jewelry and replicas of statues and artworks.

113

Since the Cloisters is built on a bluff overlooking the Hudson, be sure to drink in the view of Fort Tryon Park and the wild Palisades across the river in New Jersey. John D. Rockefeller Jr. paid for it all — the Cloisters, the park and the view, when he donated the whole shebang in 1938.

HOURS: Tues.-Sun. 9:30-5:15. Nov.-Feb.: 9:30-4:45.
ADMISSION: Suggested donation: Adults: $7.00; Seniors, students: $3.50. Includes admission to the Met. Museum.
DIRECTIONS: George Washington Bridge to Henry Hudson Parkway North. Take first exit off Parkway to Fort Tryon Park. Follow signs.
TELEPHONE: 212-923-3700

THE FRICK COLLECTION

This little jewel of a museum, housed in the former mansion of the coke and steel magnate is a must for art lovers. The European paintings and furniture display a heavy emphasis on both the Renaissance and Eighteenth Century. The Fragonard Room with panels painted for Madame Du Barry and the Boucher Room with panels commissioned by Madame de Pompadour have the appropriate French furniture and ambience to take you back to the reigns of the various Louises. Medieval paintings, enamels, Rembrandts and lots of 18th Century British portraits and landscapes abound.

Since this was once a home, the paintings are hung much as they would have been in the days of opulence. Gainsborough ladies and Turner landscapes decorate the comfortable halls, and a lovely inner courtyard provides the sort of atrium for rest and contemplation cultured people once thought necessary. There is also a lecture hall for free talks.

Only the first floor is open, but this is a formidable collection, so allow at least an hour to browse through. Children under ten are not admitted and those under 16 must be accompanied by adults — they are serious about art in this place.

HOURS: Tues.-Sat.: 10-6; Sun.: 1-6.
ADMISSION: Adults: $5.00. Students, Seniors: $3.00.
LOCATION: One East 70th St. (At Fifth Ave.) N.Y.C.
TELEPHONE: 212-288-0700

MUSEUM OF MODERN ART

The remodeled MOMA opened in 1984. It may look more like an airport terminal than a museum, with its walls of glass and escalators, but it reclaimed its crown as arbiter of taste for the modern world. The collection ranges from Henri Rousseau and early Impressionists to the latest works. A leader in the collecting of photographs and films as art, the museum has also a section on industrial design which lets us all know what is good design and what isn't. An ice cream scoop featured here becomes the ice cream scoop to use. The Industrial Design section is on the top floor and features a helicopter hanging from the ceiling. And in the basement there are two movie theaters. Outside there is still the famous sculpture garden, but the cafeteria is now a huge indoor space featuring very ordinary food. The popular museum shop is located across the street.

HOURS: Sat. - Tues.: 11-6; Thurs. & Fri.: 12-8:30; closed Wed.
ADMISSION: Adults: $8.00; Students, Seniors: $5.00. Children with adult, free.
LOCATION: 11 West 53rd St. (between 5th & 6th Aves.), N.Y.C.
TELEPHONE: 212-708-9480.

FORBES GALLERIES

Since Malcolm Forbes was one of New Jersey's most colorful residents, many Jerseyans enjoy a peek at the toys of this fabulous millionaire and his family. And toys they are - literally. For in one of the sections of this museum you will find 12,000 toy soldiers set up in dioramas or vignettes that include Indians circling cowboys, jousting knights, marching bands and so on.

In another section, called *"Ships Ahoy"*, there are 500 toy boats on display. These are intricately wrought boats done in all sorts of materials. You will also see the glass panels from the grand salon of the old ocean liner, *The Normandie* along with other art deco designs.

Other galleries include *Presidential Papers* (with documents emphasizing the personal side of the presidents) and a Trophy Room. One room is reserved for rotating exhibits often of "objects de luxe". And of course, since the Forbes collection is famous for them, you do get to see twelve of the jewelled Easter Eggs and other ornaments created by the Imperial jeweller, Faberge, for the Russian Czars.

The galleries are housed inside the Forbes Magazine building in Greenwich Village. Admission is free but entry is limited to 900 people per day except for Thursdays which is reserved for groups.

HOURS: Tues., Wed., Fri., Sat.: 10-4.
LOCATION: 62 Fifth Ave. at 12th St., N.Y.C.
TELEPHONE: 212-206-5548

Pennsylvania Museums

THE FRANKLIN INSTITUTE

The venerable Franklin Institute was always a pioneer in hands-on exhibits. Now it has designed a soaring modern hi-tech addition to the original classical building. Architecturally it's like going from the 18th to the 21st century. As for exhibits - they range from the old hands-on favorites to new Disney World style contraptions. The museum now has four main sections: The Science Center, Futures Center, the Fels Planetarium and the Omniverse Theater. In addition there are computer terminals in the halls that can answer your questions about what is where. What you will find is:

The Science Center: This is the original museum which still has many of its popular exhibits. There's the 36 times life-size heart you (or at least a child) can walk through. And the steam locomotive in the basement that chugs along for ten feet every hour. And the giant lever you can pull down and swing on. And the T-33 Air Force jet trainer you can "fly" plus lots of other exhibits on physics, printing, and such.

The Fels Planetarium: The 340 seat planetarium remains from the old days, but it is now outfitted with a state-of-the-art Digistar projection system which gives viewers a three-dimensional feel to their star-gazing.

The Futures Center: This brave new world is divided into several permanent exhibits with names like FutureSpace, FutureEarth, and FutureComputers. Here you will find such things as a fiberglass model of a human cell one million times its actual size; a computer that let's you "age" yourself so you know what you'll look like twenty years from now; a model of a NASA space station; a ten foot globe with fibre-optic lights to show population growth shifts; a man-made forest and a host of other futuristic displays involving cyberspace and such.

The Omniverse Theater: There are 350 large reclining seats arranged in steeply angled rows. Above and around you is the movie screen, 79 feet across and four stories high — a hemispheric dome. Lots of loudspeakers to project the sound all over. This is the place for nature films that roar and soar. Since seating is limited it's best to reserve a seat.

The museum now has underground parking and three restaurants, a huge atrium for resting and an outdoor science park. Expect to spend at least four hours here.

> **HOURS:** Daily. Science Center: 9:30-5. Futures Center: Same except open to 9 pm Wed. - Sat.
> **ADMISSION:** Science & Future Centers: Adults: $9.50; Children, Seniors: $8.50. Separate prices for Omniverse, planetarium or combination tickets.
> **LOCATION:** 20th Street and Benjamin Franklin Parkway, Philadelphia
> **TELEPHONE:** 215-448-1200

PLEASE TOUCH MUSEUM

When visiting Philadelphia with younger children, this place is sure to hit the spot. One of the first hands-on, interactive museums to cater specifically to children under eight, it is also one of the most copied. Starting out in 1976, the museum has changed address several times. But it is now permanently ensconced in a multi-floored space right in the center of the city's museum district. In fact it is directly across from The Franklin Institute which caters to the school age child (and grownups).

Since this is an urban museum, one display is set up to recreate a city's bus system - there's even the front of a bus on the floor. But there's also an outdoors "set" for boats that go down a river, and the standard kitchen and fruit market areas where kids can recreate grownup activities. A unique stop is the Russian nursery school, for an introduction to other cultures. Another exhibit is based on Maurice Sendak's most popular books: "Where the Wild Things Are", "In the Night Kitchen" and others. A giant bed, a giant mixing bowl, lots of pots and pans for creating a rumpus, and other scenes from the book are translated into play activities.

The newly opened **Science Park**, (summer 1995) a joint venture with the Franklin Institute, is a family centered, outdoor park with such interactive "elements" as a sky bike, Jumping Fountain, Bubbling Volcano and so forth (beginning to sound like Sesame Place, doesn't it?). Admission to the park is free with admission to either museum.

HOURS: Daily, July 1 - Labor Day: 9-6; Rest of year: 9-4:30.
ADMISSION: Adults, children: $6.50; Seniors: $5.00. Under one, free.
LOCATION: 210 21st St. (Across from Franklin Institute), Philadelphia.
TELEPHONE: 215-963-0424

PHILADELPHIA MUSEUM OF ART

It is a Greek temple that surveys the town and the river from an imposing height, with a magnificent flight of steps leading up to its classical columns. The steps, in fact, are as famous as the museum ever since Sylvester Stallone ran up them in the movie, "Rocky".

But inside the pillared entrance (you can avoid most of the steps by parking in the back parking lot), one of the best collections of art in North America awaits. Galleries of European art include the Johnson Collection on the first floor, which is heavy in Renaissance paintings. Twentieth Century art comes next and includes Marcel DuChamps' famous "Nude Descending A Staircase." The variety of the museum is evidenced by the fact that there is a medieval cloister, an Indian temple, a Chinese palace hall and a Japanese teahouse all within these portals.

The kids will find the collection of armor, which includes swords, lances, maces, chain-mail and breastplates, to be fascinating. And one whole section, devoted to Americana, includes period rooms filled with Philadelphia style bonnet-and-scroll top bureaus, secretaries and chests. There is plenty of early silverware, also.

Tours are offered by volunteer guides at no extra cost. They leave on the hour, from 10 AM to 3 PM and originate in the West Entrance Hall. Downstairs, there is a pleasant restaurant and gift shop.

HOURS: Tues. - Sun.: 10-5; Wed. to 8:45. Closed legal holidays.
ADMISSION: Adults: $7.00; Seniors, Students: $4.00. Under 5 free. Free on Sunday until 1 PM.
LOCATION: Benjamin Franklin Parkway & 26th St., Philadelphia
TELEPHONE: 215-763-8100

MUSEUM OF AMERICAN ART

This is the new name for the old Pennsylvania Academy of Fine Art, one of the earliest art museums in the country. It is housed in an ornate Victorian building created by architect Frank Furness. It is as striking an edifice as you will find anywhere. Inside, a glass domed ceiling, carved walls, Gothic arches, and ornamental bronze railings recreate the atmosphere of 1876 when this structure went up in time for the Philadelphia Centennial. A teaching institute as well as a museum, the Academy was originally founded by Charles Willson Peale and was home to Thomas Eakins and Mary Cassatt.

The permanent collection is dominated by American artists — Peale and Gilbert Stuart and others. Benjamin West's well-known "William Penn's Treaty with the Indians" hangs in the rotunda. A number of portraits of George Washington (it was not unusual for an artist to copy the same work over and over again in those days) hang in the rotunda also. However the collection also emphasizes contemporary artists on the American scene.

The Academy is situated in Philadelphia's Center City, close to the grandiose City Hall. A small cafe and museum shop are available on the first floor.

HOURS: Tues. - Sat.: 10-5; Sun.: 11-5. Closed major holidays.
ADMISSION: Adults: $5.00; Seniors: $3.00; Students: $2.00. Free on Sat. 10-1.
LOCATION: North Broad and Cherry Streets, Philadelphia
TELEPHONE: 215-972-7600, 972-7633

ROSENBACH MUSEUM AND LIBRARY

Located two blocks south of Rittenhouse Square in a lovely section of Philadelphia, this townhouse was once the home of rare book collectors. The books and furnishings of the Rosenbach brothers are at once a paean to the good life and a paradise for collectors. Since one brother searched for antiques while the other concentrated on books, the home is a treasure trove of decorative arts. At the same time it is an important research library.

There are 130,000 manuscripts and 30,000 rare books which range from medieval illuminated manuscripts to letters written by George Washington and Abraham Lincoln stored here. Lewis Carroll's own edition of Alice in Wonderland and the manuscript of James Joyce's Ulysses together with hundreds of first editions are shelved in what is essentially still a home with beautiful and delicate furniture.

The dining room where the brothers entertained wealthy guests features an Empire style table, Venetian Grand Canal scenes, Chippendale chairs and a delicate glass chandelier. A painting of Fanny Kemble by Thomas Sully and a scrolled fireplace adorn the cozy parlor. Some of the upstairs rooms are more museum-like with displays of special exhibits in glass cases and there is a room devoted to the illustrations of Maurice Sendak. Up here you will also find the personal library of Dr. Rosenbach.

Although the Rosenbach brothers lived in this house only from 1950 to 1952, when they were both old, the house and collection seem to come out of some turn-of-the-century novel by Henry James. It seems incredible that this cultured, even dandified atmosphere existed in the post-World War II period. Yet it's all here — oriental carpets and Herman Melville's bookcase (stacked with first editions of "The White Whale"), 17th Century gold chests and delicate French parlors. The museum is a must for collectors, librarians, art historians and anyone who wants pointers on how to live with class. Not for children, but senior high school and college students are welcome. Since the tour takes over an hour, allow sufficient time.

HOURS: Tues. - Sun.: 11-4. Closed holidays. Closed August.
ADMISSION: Adults: $3.50. Students, Seniors: $2.50
LOCATION: 2010 Delancey Place, Philadelphia
TELEPHONE: 215-732-1600

THE MERCER MILE

Three unusual museums in Doylestown are the legacy of Henry Chapman Mercer (1856-1930) a businessman, ceramicist, archaeologist, and according to many, an eccentric. The highly individual creations are known collectively as the Mercer Mile since they are within close distance of one another. They consist of:

THE MERCER MUSEUM: A sprawling, turreted structure of reinforced concrete, the museum houses a vast collection of America's pre-Industrial tools and crafts. Mercer was one of the first to collect early Americana (although everyone seems to be doing it now). He collected with the eye of an archaeologist, and all the minutae of everday life — from kitchen utensils to hatmaking machines — are revealed here. Small objects are exhibited in rooms by craft (e.g., the evolution of buttermaking) while larger objects are left free-standing or are suspended. Visitors often gasp when they step into the main section of the museum and find Conestoga wagons, harpoons and whaling skiffs suspended from the ceiling. Six floors of exhibits surround the central hall. Gallows, hearses, prisoners docks and the kitchen sink — it's all here. A library of early Americana is also on the premises.

HOURS: Mon. - Sat., 10-5; Sun.: 12-5; Tues. until 9.
ADMISSION: Adults: $5.00; Seniors: $4.50; Students: $1.50
LOCATION: Green & Ashland Sts., Doylestown (Take Rte. 202 or Rte. 611 to Ashland St.)
TELEPHONE: 215-345-0210

FONTHILL MUSEUM: The home of Mercer, it looks like a Spanish fantasy set on the quiet Pennsylvania landscape. Filled with the colorful Moravian tiles from his factory, the home has arches and winding stairways and uneven rooms and beautiful views. Guided tours only. Reservations required. *Hours:* Daily 10-5; Sun.: 12-5. *Admission:* Adults: $5.00, Seniors: $4.50, Students: $1.50 *Location:* E. Court St. off Rte. 313, Doylestown. *Telephone:* 215-348-9461

MORAVIAN POTTERY AND TILE WORKS: A short walk from Fonthill, the Tile Works shows the machinery and raw materials of the tile making process (workers are not always present) and also houses a gift shop where these unusual tiles may be bought. Tours leave on the hour and half hour. *Hours:* Daily 10-4:45. *Admission:* Adults: $2.50, Seniors: $2.00, Students: $1.00. *Location:* E. Court St. off Rte. 313. *Telephone:* 215-345-6722.

THE BRANDYWINE RIVER MUSEUM

From the front it's a century old grist mill; from the back it's a strikingly modern glass tower overlooking the Brandywine River, and altogether it is a most pleasant museum where the setting and structure are almost as interesting as the paintings within.

Inside the stone and glass structure, the atmosphere belongs to the Brandywine River artists (a group that formed around Howard Pyle and N.C. Wyeth) and to Wyeth's talented progeny, particularly Andrew and his son Jamie. Both Pyle and N.C. Wyeth were famous illustrators and many an older edition of "Treasure Island" or "King Arthur" contain their realistic action pictures. Although storybook illustrators have never reached the heights of adulation that "purer" artists enjoy, nevertheless they are among the most respected painters in America.

Howard Pyle began a summer teaching center in the Brandywine Valley in 1898. The artists from this center include Maxfield Parrish, Peter Hurd, George Weymouth, and, of course, N.C. Wyeth. But it is Andrew Wyeth, whose painting "Christina's World" is world famous, who holds the compelling interests for viewers in this museum. The strong emotional impact of his many canvasses dominates the collection here. You can also find a small number of Jamie's paintings in the permanent collection plus special exhibits which emphasize one or the other of the Brandywine artists.

After viewing the exhibits, you can lunch at the cafeteria where you can look down on the meandering river and wildflower garden below. This lovely preserve is part of the Brandywine Conservancy, which keeps 5,000 acres in a state of nature — a most poetic place that seems to attract strollers, readers and young romantics.

As for children, there is a special Christmas display intended for them which runs throughout the month of December. It includes model trains, porcelain dolls and decorated Christmas trees.

HOURS: Daily except Christmas, 9:30-4:30
ADMISSION: Adults: $5.00; Seniors, students: $2.50; under 6 free.
LOCATION: On Route U.S. 1, Chadds Ford, Pa.
TELEPHONE: 610-388-2700

See Also: Museums that are part of a larger entity are mentioned under the title of the larger attraction — e.g., *The Museum of American Glass* (Wheaton Village), *West Point Museum* (West Point). New Jersey planetariums that are not part of a museum are listed in a separate chapter entitled, "Other Outings."

THE CLASSICS

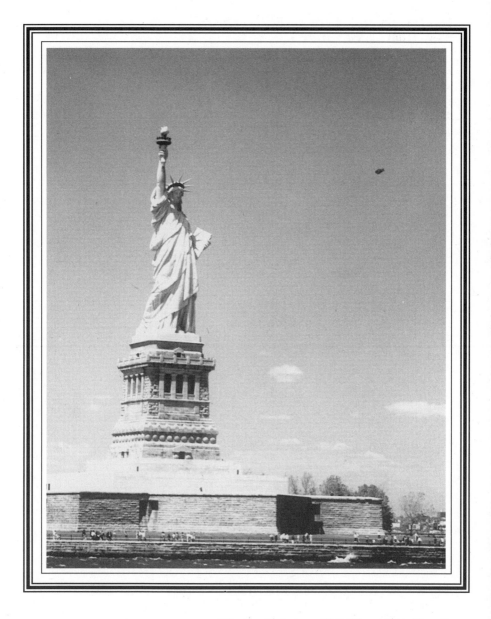

Photo: Courtesy N.J. Travel & Tourism

In This Chapter You Will Find:

United Nations Headquarters, N.Y.
The Statue of Liberty
Ellis Island
World Trade Center, N.Y.
Empire State Building, N.Y.
Circle Line Tour, N.Y.
West Point, N.Y.
Independence Mall, Philadelphia, PA

UNITED NATIONS HEADQUARTERS

The first thing you notice as you approach the United Nations complex is the line of colorful flags half-circling the entrance. All member nation flags are flown at the same height —only the UN flag is unfurled higher. The next thing you notice as you step through the iron gates is that this place is clean! No old newspapers, candy wrappers or soda cans litter the area. The United Nations may not police the world, but they sure know how to police the grounds!

Outside sculpture includes a gigantic abstract object next to the circular fountain and a Japanese Peace Bell ensconced in a pagoda. If you visit in the spring be sure to check out the gardens which are in back of the buildings. Daffodils and cherry trees bloom in early spring while the rose garden with its twenty varieties of tea roses blossoms later.

Tours of the UN are still popular although nowadays you must enter the building through an airport-type security system. The tours combine a short history of the aims and activities of the United Nations itself with a description of the art and architecture you pass along the tour route. Here you will find out about the behind the scenes work of UNESCO, WHO and other specialized agencies. Many photographs of their work decorate the walls.

The number of chambers you enter during the tour depends on whether the various Councils are meeting or not. The General Assembly, which is usually open, is a huge hall with high domed ceiling and more than 2,000 seats. The slatted back walls are interspersed with banks of windowed booths where translators, photographers and TV people sit. This is the hall most often seen on television when a world-shaking meeting takes place.

The other chambers were designed by Norwegian, Swedish and Danish architects and their furnishings were donated by those countries. They all display the vertical and horizontal lines and rich wood grains we associate with "Danish Modern." In fact the whole complex has a definite Scandinavian look. A human thirst for color is seen in the gifts of other countries: a colorful tapestry from Senegal, the blue stained glass windows of Chagall and a crimson Peruvian cermonial mantle.

The tour ends in the Public Concourse where you can proceed to the bookstore, gift shops and postal counter (a mecca for stamp collectors). Handicraft items from around the world, flags, dolls of all nations are priced reasonably, but no better than anywhere else. The bargain is the fact that there is no sales tax anywhere in the UN complex! For hamburgers and french fries there's a good coffee shop here. It is also possible to eat in the reasonably priced and elegant Delegates Dining Room, for a delicious buffet.

> **HOURS:** Daily: 9:15-4:45
> **ADMISSION:** Free. For tours — Adults: $6.50, Students & seniors: $4.50. grade school children: $3.50. Children under 5 not admitted on tours.
> **LOCATION:** 1st Ave. between 45th & 46th St., N.Y.C.
> **TELEPHONE:** 212-963-7713

STATUE OF LIBERTY

Don't wait until your Aunt Mabel comes to visit — go see this icon of American freedom for yourself. New Jersey residents can embark from Liberty State Park for the short ride over. Once aboard the Circle Line Ferry, (which stops first at Ellis Island) you get a view from all angles of the glistening Lady as the boat turns to make port. As you disembark, the first building you see is the gift and souvenir shop. Here you can stock up on mugs, pennants and postcards.

Liberty lsland is larger than you might expect. On its 12 1/2 acres, there are administration buildings, a snack shop, a pleasant tree-shaded picnic area and esplanades rimming the island. Here you can savor the view of Manhattan's towers plus the wide expanse of the harbor with its bustling boats. Or take a close-up picture of the "Lady With The Lamp".

Inside, there are lines for the pedestal, for those who want to walk to the crown, and sometimes even for the museum. The museum, just a short walk up a flight of stairs within the main lobby, is devoted to the building and restoration of the statue itself. It includes an incredible amount of displays and information. There are architectural mock-ups, and an audio-visual section. The museum that was devoted to American immigration has been transferred to Ellis Island, which now rivals the statue in appeal.

As for those who actually walk the 22 stories up to the crown — expect your calves to hurt for the next week. This is not for the frail or short- of-breath. You must walk all the way up since the elevator now goes only to the pedestal (where there is no access to the crown). Kids enjoy the hike just to prove they can do it. For adults, the view from the fourth floor is just fine.

Both as a visit to a national shrine and as a pleasant day's outing on the water between two great ports, a trip to the Statue of Liberty is a must. Best to go in the spring and fall before the out-of-towners arrive.

HOURS: 9-5 Daily.
FERRY SCHEDULE: (Liberty State Park) Daily 9:30-3:45 schedule may be expanded in summer, shortened in winter. (Battery Park, N.Y.) Daily every half hour.
ADMISSION: Free for statue. Ferry fee is: Adults: $7.00; Under 17: $3.00. Seniors: $5.00.
LOCATION: To reach Liberty State Park take the N.J. Turnpike to exit 14B. Parking fee: $4.00.
TELEPHONE: (Circle Line) 201-435-9499. (Liberty State Park) 201-915- 3400. (Liberty Island) 212-363-3267.

ELLIS ISLAND

If a visit to the Statue of Liberty is inspiring, a visit to its neighbor, Ellis Island, is absolutely fascinating. Since you get both islands for the same ferry price, it is best to allow enough time to explore both - up to five hours, if you stop at all the exhibits.

For Ellis Island is the basic museum which commemorates the peopling of America, not only those who set foot on this particular island (for that is only one section) but the story from the beginning, with emphasis on the late 19th and early 20th century. A movie, shown in two theaters, recounts the experience of those who left troubled homelands to take the sea voyage to the new land. First it was in wooden ships that took six weeks to make the voyage and left everyone sick. Later it was the steamship lines who filled up their steerage section with poor immigrants. If the immigrants were turned back because of sickness or other reasons, the steamship company had to pay for the return passage.

Earlier immigration sites, greed, corruption, and the one-day processing of thousands of people are all covered in the movie as well as the displays. But there is also an amassing of hundreds of trunks, shawls, tickets, flyers and other mementos of the immigrant experience. Newspaper cartoons depict the rising tide of intolerance against the newcomers which finally culminated in a restrictive law in 1924 which ended the mass migration. Ellis Island was closed in 1954. In its newly refurbished state it is a wonderful learning experience, and an emotional one as well for anyone who descended from all those Germans, Greeks, Italians, Jews, Irish, Turks, Jamaicans and others who first came to these shores.

HOURS, ETC.: Check Statue of Liberty entry.
TELEPHONE: (Circle Line) 201-435-9499; (Ellis Island) 212-363-3204

WORLD TRADE CENTER

The highest skyscraper in New York offers the best view of the metropolis, the river, New Jersey and Brooklyn. On a clear day the 360 degree view is terrific. You buy tickets on the mezzanine floor and then take a special elevator that whisks you up to the 100th floor in a few seconds. Once there, you can sit at the various windows and drink in the panorama of the bay, the city and the provinces beyond. Conveniently, the outlines and names of landmarks are traced on the glass at every viewpoint, so you know what you are looking at.

There are also exhibits on the inner walls, a souvenir shop and a snack bar (featuring the world's most indifferent employees). For those who like to go outside, there's a rooftop promenade several flights up which is open when the wind is not too strong.

It has taken some time for people to get over the shock of the 1993 bombing, and strict security is enforced at the entrance to WTC. However, there are now plans afoot to create more exhibits at the observatory level.

HOURS: 9:30 AM - 9:30 PM daily.
ADMISSION: Adults: $6.00; Children: $3.00; Senior Citizens: $3.50; Under 6 free.
LOCATION: 2 World Trade Center Plaza, N.Y.C. Take PATH direct from Hoboken or Jersey City.
TELEPHONE: 212-435-7397

THE EMPIRE STATE BUILDING

It must be the movie, "Sleepless in Seattle", or the image of King Kong — this 1932 building, once the tallest (but not the cleanest) in the world, has come back into vogue. The 86th floor observatory has both an enclosed area and an open promenade. High powered binoculars are available for a fee. Here you will also find the snack bars, vending machine and souvenir counter. The view to the west offers New Jersey and the Hudson, to the north you get Central Park and beyond, while the east gives you the UN building and Queens.

While the observation windows here may not be as wide as the World Trade Center, you are closer to the heart of Manhattan from this vantage point. There's an observatory on the 102nd floor included in the same ticket. This one is enclosed. And you can find the *"Guinness World Book of Records"* Museum in the basement of the Empire State Building where, for a separate fee, you can see all sort of oddities.

HOURS: 9:30 AM - 11:30 PM daily.
ADMISSION: Adults: $4.00; Seniors, Children: $2.00
LOCATION: 34th Street & 5th Avenue, N.Y.C.
TELEPHONE: 212-736-3100

THE CIRCLE LINE TOUR

A standard tourist attraction since it started in the post World War II era, this boat ride takes three hours and covers 35 miles. Basically, you circle Manhattan island in a three-floor "yacht" (which doesn't look much different than a three-floor ferry) which has both open and closed areas and long benches for seating. From the 42nd Street pier the boat heads southward on the Hudson, gaining views of both New York and New Jersey. Passing the Statue of Liberty, the ride continues around the tip of Manhattan then up the East River, around the Harlem River as far as Spuyten Duyvil and then back to home base. An announcer points out the monuments, skyscrapers, bridges and churches, offering anecdotes on the more interesting ones and lots of facts and figures.

You can get a nice river breeze on this one and Manhattan never looks better than from a distance. Best news for Jersey people is that the boat now leaves from Hoboken pier (directly adjacent to the railroad station) twice a day in warm weather. What's more the price is less from here!

(For other cruises in the New Jersey area see "Excursion Boats" in the last chapter.)

HOURS: Sailings vary by season.
ADMISSION: Adults: $18.00; Children under 12: $9.00.
LOCATION: Pier 83, Foot of West 42nd St., N.Y.C.
TELEPHONE: 212-563-3200; 201-795-0500

WEST POINT

West Point has a beautiful view of the Hudson, grey Collegiate Gothic buildings that rise from rocky inclines, parades of cadets on Saturday mornings and football games in the fall. Many people begin their tour at the Visitor's Center, which is two blocks outside of the actual gates of the Point.

The center has displays, a movie about army life, and a busy gift shop. It is also the point of departure for bus tours which leave regularly during the warm weather for a 50 minute tour of the campus. The narrated tour stops at the magnificent Gothic chapel where all those spiffy weddings take place, the old chapel, at various monuments and at scenic views. If you don't want to wait for a bus tour, you can park within the campus and walk around yourself. There are benches where you can picnic, and the Thayer Hotel, which is on campus, has restaurants open to the public.

Several blocks outside the main campus is the new **West Point Museum**, with three floors of exhibits, models, mock-ups and memorabilia. The decisive battles of the world are recreated here by tiny toy figures set in fighting position behind glass. A full explanation of each battle and its significance is printed below the display. The Dark Ages began because the Roman infantry could not hold out against the Gothic cavalry. The Modern Age began when guns replaced swords, and technology replaced prowess. An interesting place with a particular point of view. Lots of armor and costumes around. The West Point trivia is fascinating also. Did you know James Whistler dropped out because he couldn't pass chemistry? His watercolors are great, though, and those of Ulysses S. Grant aren't bad either.

If you're visiting with your family you may find the kids are most fascinated by the clean-cut cadets who are unerringly polite and meticulously dressed. Hikers will like the hilly terrain and outstanding view. Free. Fee for bus tour.

HOURS: Visitor Center: Daily 9-4:45; Museum: 10:30-4:15.
LOCATION: Palisades Pkwy to 9WN to Highland Falls, N.Y.
TELEPHONE: 914-938-2638

INDEPENDENCE MALL, PHILADEPHIA

If the Bicentennial did nothing else, at least it got the city of Philadelphia to spruce up its historic area, to revamp or rebuild everything and turn Independence Mall into a first-class tourist attraction. The National Park Service administers many of the historic buildings, although the city and private organizations operate quite a few also.

First stop should be the great big, brick **Visitor Center** at Chestnut and 3rd Street. Here you can pick up a clearly marked map of the historic areas. A thirty-minute film is shown here about once an hour, which will give you the necessary background for your tour. Special exhibits are also on view here.

If you have children with you, certainly stop to see **Franklin Court** (at Chestnut and 4th Street). This complex includes a very interesting underground museum. As you descend a winding ramp you pass many displays of Benjamin Franklin's inventions, furniture, etc. At the bottom area there is an unusual show. A miniature model of the 1776 Continental Congress rises up, and taped voices discuss the adoption of the Declaration of Independence. Then the model sinks down again. Over to one side a bank of telephone receivers stands. Here you dial a particular number to hear what various famous people such as Mark Twain or John Adams had to say about Franklin — a lively way to impart history.

Next, it's on to the grassy mall (bounded by Chestnut, Walnut, 5th and 6th Streets) where **Independence Hall** and the **Liberty Bell** await. The bell is in its own glass pavilion. The line is usually not too long since it doesn't take that long to get a look and take a picture. The bell is huge, of course, and looks just like you would expect it to.

131

Independence Hall is shown by a Department of Interior guide, so there may be a wait, but there's a separate room where you can sit down and hear a preliminary talk. The Hall is most impressive, although not very large by today's standards. You can see the inkstand used by the signers of the Declaration of Independence, benches, etc. The guide gives a very full explanation of the events surrounding the adoption of the Declaration. Other buildings in the historical park include Carpenter's Hall, the Army-Navy Museum, Old City Hall and several other sites of important goings on. The U.S. Mint, right nearby, is also a fascinating visit both for coin collectors and history buffs.

Since it's only a few blocks away, most tourists walk over to the **Betsy Ross House** at 239 Arch Street, which is open daily (except Monday). This small building with its narrow staircase is always so crowded that you only have time to glimpse the mannequins who represent Betsy and other colonials. In fact, the small house is almost overpowered by the adjacent gift shop. Here you can stock up on Liberty Bells, facsimiles of the Declaration of Independence, and of course the 13-star flag which Betsy is reputed to have sewn. (*Telephone:* 215-627- 5343).

HOURS: Some buildings may be closed in winter. 9-5 Daily.
ADMISSION: Free
TELEPHONE: (Visitor Center) 215-597-8975.

THEME PARKS,
AMUSEMENT PARKS,
BOARDWALK AMUSEMENTS

Photo: Courtesy Dorney Park

133

In This Chapter You Will Find:

Six Flags/Great Adventure, NJ
Hersheypark, PA
Action Park, NJ
Dorney Park- Wildwater Kingdom, PA
Sesame Place, PA
Land of Make Believe, NJ
Gingerbread Castle, NJ
Boardwalk Amusements, NJ
  Keansburg
  Point Pleasant
  Seaside Heights
  Beach Haven
  Atlantic City
  Ocean City
  Wildwood

Other Amusement Parks
  Bowcraft
  Clementon Lake Park
  Fairy Tale Forest
  Storybook Land
  Wild West City
  Shawnee Place

SIX FLAGS GREAT ADVENTURE

It's **Six Flags** Great Adventure and its under the Warner Brothers umbrella. That means more movie themes (Batman and The Right Stuff) more cartoon characters (Bugs Bunny & co.) and less of the small amusement park type rides that parents could always opt for when the lines on the big rides seemed daunting.

So what do we have now at this 1100 acre spot that shares a theme park with a drive-through safari? (See Zoo chapter for the safari). Well, they're trying harder to section the park into real themes. The section of the park that always had a western theme (the great Teepee for gifts, the wooden fort structure for the sky-ride and Runaway Train, the Ranch House style restaurant) is now called Frontier Adventures.

On the other end of the park, several water rides have been bunched together and are called "Adventure Rivers". The decor simulates Asia and Africa but veteran parkgoers will recognize "Roaring Rapids" (the one where you sit in a tube-bottomed boat and bounce down the river) as one of these rides. Actually "Adventure Rivers" is an attempt to provide a sort of half-way water park. You are in a boat, so you do not touch the water as you would on a waterslide. On the other hand you do get completely soaked. What to wear? Most people opt for a bathing suit with clothes over it.

For kids (54 inches and under) it is simpler. Koala Canyon is a kid's lagoon with spouting water, slides and play areas. They definitely need bathing suits for this one. There are outdoor showers for everyone - but no indoor changing rooms with showers.

The Batman Forever stunt show promises to be as successful as its predecessor. The Batman Ride, a complicated upside down roller coaster with decor from the Batman movies is still a big attraction.

The center of the park with its giant Ferris Wheel, old-fashioned carousel, lakeside bandstand and Yum-Yum palace still has the original look of an 1890s amusement park. The children's section, called Bugs Bunny Land, has a mixture of traditional kiddie rides and interactive style playports. Warner Brothers cartoon characters walk around this area.

With an extended season (the park may open up as early as April school vacation week and then weekends until May) Great Adventure is betting less on the water rides than on the totality of rides and shows. For those who hate stomach turning rides there are still variety shows, high divers (the dolphins have been axed) a racing boat show and fireworks on weekends. Friday and Saturday nights, rock and country bands are on hand.

As for food — don't expect gourmet fare. Veteran visitors bring picnics in their coolers and just tailgate it in the parking lot. (You are not allowed to bring food inside the park except to the designated picnic area near the Safari section). Bring along towels and dry clothes for the long drive home. Lockers available.

HOURS: Early Apr.-mid June: call first. Last week of June-Labor Day: 10-10. Safari opens 9 AM. Open weekends, Sept., Oct.

ADMISSION: Adult: $34.00 (Combination Park-Safari ticket). Under 54": $22.95. Seniors: 1/2 price. Under 3 free. Parking and tax extra.

LOCATION: Jackson Twp., Ocean County. Take NJ Tpke to Exit 7A, then 195 to Exit 16.

TELEPHONE: 908-928-2000 / 928-1821

HERSHEY PARK

When the urge to get away for a two or three-day vacation (complete with amusement park for the kiddies) combines with an urge to avoid the crowds at the seashore, one place to consider is Hershey, Pennsylvania. Set in the green and rolling hills of the Pennsylvania Dutch dairy country, the town that gave birth to the great American chocolate bar offers a theme park, a zoo and several resorts for an overnight stay. Since it is situated a bit of a drive over the New Jersey border, many travelers find it more convenient to sleep over and spend one day at Hersheypark, one day exploring the countryside.

As for Hersheypark, itself. It's a theme park very much like Great Adventure, but smaller. There are several open theaters where parents can rest their feet and enjoy entertainment while the kids try the Fender Bender for the fourth time. A single admission price pays for all the rides and shows although of course they get you for the extras. The crowds here are well behaved and there is little problem of anyone ducking ahead in line.

You enter Hersheypark through *Tudor Square*, a small Elizabethan enclave of shops and restaurants. Then it's on to the *Rhineland* with its many rides. Here you will find the kiddie rides, a giant carousel, a two-armed Ferris Wheel and some inbetweeners. The next area, *Der Deutschplatz*, is dedicated to Hershey's Pennsylvania Dutch milieu and includes a crafts barn featuring local talent.

An aquatheater featuring dolphin and human diving acts, an amphitheater for the song-and-dance shows and two small theaters for puppet shows and children's comic shows all offer alternatives to rides. For the strong stomachs there are several roller coasters including one that splashes down in water.

There is a good, medium-sized zoo covering eleven acres on one side of the park, which gives something to those who hate rides. The Kissing Tower, a gentle space needle, offers a nice view and is something different for mothers with young children. Monorails, skyrides, and antique auto rides make this park well suited to families with kids under ten, although there are enough scary rides to please the teenagers and young adults. And the park includes such interactive features as a "ball crawl" and a cargo net climb.

Outside the park, and absolutely free, is Hershey's **"Chocolate World,"** a simulated factory tour in the Disney style. There you ride in automated cars past scenes of dairy farms, African cocoa tree plantations, and assembly belts full of kisses and chocolate bars. The whole time you are wafted past rivers of milk and glowing roasters the smell of chocolate assails your nostrils. To extend the season, Hershey features Candy Lane from mid-November through December. It combines sections of Hersheypark, Chocolate World and shopping.

For those who have time, a visit to the town itself, the nearby rose gardens (separate listing in this book) and **The Hershey Museum** are all pleasant excursions.

> **HOURS:** Late May - Labor Day: 10:30 - 10:00. Weekends and shortened hours, May & Sept.
>
> **ADMISSION:** Adults: $24.95; Children 3-8: $15.95; Seniors: $15.95; 2 and under free.
>
> **LOCATION:** Route 322, Pennsylvania, approachable from either 283 off The Pennsylvania Turnpike or Route 83 off 81.
>
> **TELEPHONE:** HersheyPark: 717-534-3900; Visitor Center: 1-800-HERSHEY

ACTION PARK

Over the years, Action Park has burgeoned from a summer stop that offered go-kart rides into a multi-million dollar creation. They have an Alpine Slide (that's a low, wheeled cart you maneuver down a fiberglass chute), speed boats, paddle boats, scenic sky ride (that's the ski lift left over from winter), bumper boats and a complete children's section. But it is the large variety of water slides and rides that brings the teenagers and young adults out here in droves. The terrain is steep and craggy and the water slides are for the most part built up against the mountain. There are rubber tube rides that twist and turn, straight slides that jackknife you into the water, closed chute rides and the Tarzan water hole where you just jump in from a swinging rope. Scrapes and bruises are not unusual from some of these rides. A tidal wave pool is comparatively tame except when it gets overcrowded.

As for the race cars and speedboats — driver's licenses are required for these. Because each person takes a long time the waiting lines move at the pace of a turtle. There are also, surprisingly, some tame areas, such as miniature golf, a sky ride and shops. However, the major thrust of the park is thrills and ever more thrills.

There is also the Bungee jump. You jump from a permanent steel tower placed on one side of the park. Another innovation is a reverse bungee, *The Human Slingshot*, where you sit in a chair and bounce upwards. Obviously for those who like a little risk with their pleasure.

The park appeals primarily to teenagers and young adults. Obviously, the time to visit here is during the week when access to the rides is easier. There's usually waiting lines for everything — although on hot days you can probably get onto the non-water rides rather easily.

Recently they've added some shows — a magic show for kiddies, and "gladiator" competitions for young adults. Saturdays, there may be name performers on hand.

Lockers and changing rooms are available for those who bring swimming gear. Luckily they have added a sandy beach where parents can sit and lounge (and even order a drink).

HOURS: Mid-June to Labor Day — Daily. Call for Spring & Fall hours.
ADMISSION: All day ticket: Adults: $27.00, Weekends: $28.00; Children: $18.00. Under 4 free.

DORNEY PARK & WILDWATER KINGDOM

This is basically a double-personality park. On one side is Dorney Park, a standard old-fashioned amusement center (it's been around since 1884) which features carousels, cyclones, glass houses, train rides and a large, new rollercoaster.

The new owners are spiffing up Dorney Park with a steam railroad, a drench everybody-in-sight boatride called White Water Landing and a Berenstain Bears area for kids.

On the other side of Dorney Park — and separated from it by a large parking lot — is Wildwater Kingdom. This is a highly popular waterpark which offers water slides in all sorts of variations. You will find looping, speeding, inner tube and kiddie water slides here. Newer and taller water rides include the Pepsi Aquablast. The giant wave pool (which manufactures artificial waves every ten minutes) has two sections: one for those who ride plastic surfboards and mattresses and one for those who stand and jump. Don't expect to be able to swim in all this mass of bodies. But the park does provide plastic sun chairs and lounges so that parents can sit and sun while their offspring surf and slide. Locker rooms and showers are available, as are surfboard rentals.

There is a special section for young children in each park - Dorney has a "tot spot". Wildwater Kingdom has Lollipop Lagoon, a large wading pool interspersed with water-umbrellas and a "submarine" with play elements. The park is located just beyond Allentown and is no further away than other major parks for many New Jerseyans. Picnicking is no longer allowed inside the gates. Parking is extra.

HOURS: Daily 10-10 Full Season. Shorter hours April-mid-June & Sept.
ADMISSION: Combination ticket: Adults: $22.95; Children Age 4 to 48" & Seniors: $4.95.
LOCATION: 3830 Dorney Park Road, Allentown, PA. Take Route 78 past Allentown, to Exit 16B.
TELEPHONE: 610-398-7955

SESAME PLACE PLAYPARK

When Sesame Place first opened it was the first activity park devoted directly to the younger set. Children from three to thirteen were supposed to stretch their minds and muscles in a series of innovative "play concepts" like swimming in thousands of plastic balls and climbing up cargo netting. While these activities still exist, the park is now more commercially oriented with enough grown-up water rides to interest Dad, Mom and older siblings in the day's entertainment. In fact, here, as in many other amusement parks, the water rides have swept away the competition.

For those who like it slow, there is Big Bird's Rambling River, a level waterway for rubber tubing (both parents and children can enjoy this). The Rubber Duckey ride is for small fry who want to take a tube ride with a little roll to it. The larger water rides are exactly like the ones at the Jersey shore or Action Park - metal structures where you chute down on a cushion of water - using either your backside or a mat. Some twist and turn, some are partially enclosed and some are straight down - you end up in a small pool of water all the same. The lines are long but they move in an orderly fashion and the park personnel make sure you don't bump into your neighbor. For those who are scared of water rides (and many young children are), there is a simple fountain in the center of the park where everybody can just jump around and get wet. In another section, a tropical island allows kids to squirt water guns and play steel drums.

There are lockers available for a fee (you have to get on line immediately if you want to grab one) and changing rooms (which can get pretty messy, so wear your bathing suit when you come).

What if you hate water? Well, there's the Bouncing mattress, a slippery mountain climb, the plastic ballroom, and giant punching bags. As for shows, one features bird and animal acts. Another large stage offers a song-and dance revue starring Bert and Ernie. The most innovative show is called "make-your-own movie" and it takes place in a small auditorium. Selected audience members coordinate their movements to a blue screen above. Later you see them and the whole audience in a rollicking adventure movie.

For diversion there is an Alphabet parade featuring costumed characters. And there are numerous picture taking opportunities. There are two eateries, but since plenty of picnic tables are available, why bother standing in line for food?

When is the best time to visit Sesame Place? Because season tickets are bought by nearby families and daycare busses come in droves on weekdays, this place is often overcrowded. Early morning and late afternoon are suggested. Bring food, towels, and sun-tan lotion.

HOURS: 9:30-8 June-August; Shorter hours May, June, Sept. Weekends only Mid-Sept.-mid-Oct.
ADMISSION: $21.95; Seniors: $18.55; 2 and under, free. Parking $5.00.
DIRECTIONS: Route 1 South through Trenton to Oxford Valley Mall, Langhorne, PA. Turn right at New Oxford Valley Road just before Mall.
TELEPHONE: 215-757-1100

LAND OF MAKE BELIEVE

For years this was a simple, down home amusement park, set in rural Warren County, next to Jenny Jump State Park. It catered to children from 3 to 9 at a time when most parks were geared to teenagers. There were a few mechanical rides and a miniature train ride. Also such simple attractions as a talking Scarecrow, a haunted house with a few scary exhibits, and an old fashioned hayride. A barn devoted to Christmas with a genuine Santa inside was always a big drawing card here.

Now it's doubled in size. The new "Pirate's Cove" section is clean and modern and makes the rest of the park look tacky in comparison. The Cove is actually a 12,250 square foot wading pool, surrounded by a large concrete deck. Inside the pool is a life-size pirate ship complete with water-slides and cannons that shoot water. The new Blackbeard's River offers simple tube rides for both parents and kids. And there are lounge chairs and benches around the pool. Lockers and changing areas are available. Hamburger stand, gift shop and picnic areas too. And for a change — free parking.

HOURS: Weekends from Memorial Day. Mid-June to Labor Day: 10-5; Sundays: 10-6. Sundays only after Labor Day.
ADMISSION: Adults: $9.50; Children 2-12: $12.50; 18 mos.-24 mos.: $8.50.
LOCATION: Route 80 to Exit 12. Two mi. to Hope, N.J. Follow signs.
TELEPHONE: 908-459-5100.

GINGERBREAD CASTLE

This fanciful castle, with its stone turret and colorfully painted ornamentation was probably quite an attraction when it first opened in 1928. There were statues of giant spiders and witches and a humpty-dumpty who sat on a wall. All this was created by a stage designer. With a proper tour guide and a little imagination it probably made a nice family outing. Years later, generations brought up on television and electronically controlled rides found the Castle pale stuff and so the place eventually closed.

Now re-opened, the main castle remains the same, but there is now more going on outside the castle walls. As part of the ticket price you get a small show featuring the guides dressed in storybook costumes. This takes place on a small outdoor platform and children are asked to be part of the play. Afterwards there are picture taking opportunities and of course the tour of the spooky castle itself. For young children.

Hours are limited since this place makes more money as a dance club at night.

HOURS: Late June-Labor Day, Weekends: 10:30-5.
ADMISSION: $6.50 Under 2 free; Seniors: $5.50.
LOCATION: Rte. 80 to Rte. 23N to Hamburg, Sussex County.
TELEPHONE: 201-827-1617

BOARDWALK AMUSEMENTS

There are small arcades, video game rooms and miniature golf places at any number of Jersey shore resorts. However, you can find the larger amusement centers at the following towns. They are located on the beach so just keep driving until you hit the ocean. Don't expect cleanliness or good restroom facilities at these places. However, the larger amusement piers have become more sophisticated over the years. They have increased the size of their rides so there are now huge roller-coasters, full pirate ships and taller rides than ever. And on certain days they offer a set price for all rides if you buy for six hours.

And now some boardwalks offer waterparks that are as big as anything you'd find at a theme park (although they may be more compacted to save space.) What's more they have plenty of lifeguards about. You'll find the lazy river ride for kids (and timid adults), slides that are partially enclosed (to give you a scarier feeling) slides with mats and slides where the only cushion on the water is your backside.

KEANSBURG: An older area that had its heyday back in the 1940s. This is where Ralph Kramden was always going to take Alice in "The Honeymooners." The boardwalk runs about 4 or 5 blocks long and includes 30 kiddie rides, 15 adult rides, a pool, and a water slide. Concessions and arcade. *Directions:* G.S.P. to Exit 117, then Route 36E.

POINT PLEASANT: Jenkinson's amusement center with rides geared for children, and early teenagers although there are a number of adult rides present. Indoor arcade and miniature golf. Less variety than some of the larger amusement areas but the atmosphere is not as honky-tonk. Fishing pier, cafeteria and Jenkinson's Aquarium available. *Directions:* G.S.P. Exit 98-S or 90N.

SEASIDE HEIGHTS: New Jersey's version of Coney Island. One of the largest of the boardwalk amusement centers, with solid amusements and concessions along the boardwalk and at the both the Fun & Casino piers. Many larger rides are here such as a big Ferris Wheel and the Pirate Ship besides the usual assortment of Trabants and Red Barons. **Water Works** is a complete condensed version of a waterpark on the square block opposite **Casino Pier** (800 Ocean Terr.). Everything from easy tube rides to the "adult" twisting waterslides.The indoor arcades, such as Coin Castle include a carousel, air hockey games and food stands along with the usual Skeeball and machine games. Rides active even during the day. A popular teenage hangout. *Directions:* G.S.P. Exit 82 to Highway 37E. Go through Toms River to bridge, follow signs.

BEACH HAVEN: Catering to families vacationing on Long Beach Island is a small cluster of amusements. **Thundering Surf/ Settler's Hill** - a combination of curliqued water slides and fancy miniature golf takes up one square block at 8th and Bay, while **Fantasy Island** a block away at 7th offers kiddie rides, arcades, and more golf.

ATLANTIC CITY: As mentioned before, the Steel Pier now offers both rides and thrill shows. And the **Tivoli Pier**, a six-story amusement center built inside of the TropWorld hotel, offers boardwalk style amusements. And you can still find many arcades and T-shirt stands on the boardwalk.

OCEAN CITY: Along the boardwalk at this family resort there is the music pier with popular concerts. Amusements can be found at the indoor/outdoor **Gillians Wonderland Pier** (6th St.) which includes a ferris wheel and other rides. **Playland** (at 10th St.) also offers arcade games and rides. **Gillian's Island** includes a small water park with kid-sized rides plus a lush miniature golf. The boardwalk here also offers a movie theater, karoake parlor, and lots of ice cream and beach stores stands.

WILDWOOD: The amusement section of the boardwalk goes on for miles and there are several separate piers. The piers vary in solidity of their wood planking (one is actually concrete) and their prices, but the rides are very similar. The usual lineup is a crazy house, a few kiddie rides and the popular adult rides such as Flying Bobsleds, Tilt-A-Whirl, Trabant, etc. Roller coasters, and sack slides are specials at several piers. And both the boardwalk and the piers boast an endless number of concessions, games and food stands.

Some piers - like Hunts and the Fun Pier, have shrunk or disappeared or changed name and direction. But **Nickel's midway Pier** is still taking in money on the land side of the boardwalk. As for **Morey's Pier** and **Mariner's Landing** (Morey owns both) - they have grown like Godzilla. They now offer huge looping coasters and other major attractions. Here again, the waterslide craze has taken over. Both offer a complete waterpark which is tacked on to the end of the pier. All manner of straight and looping slides and tube rides for a set price (either full day or 2-hours) plus a view of the beach. The piers are situated at 25th St. & Schellenger Ave. respectively, on the boardwalk.. *Directions:* G.S.P. Exit 4.

OTHER AMUSEMENT PARKS

BOWCRAFT AMUSEMENT PARK: A small park set down plunk amidst the hurly-burly of Route 22, it is open all year round although many rides are not available in winter. Paddle boats, a train ride, miniature golf and several kiddie rides make this a popular place for the under-ten set. Go-karts, baseball batting, Tilt-A-Whirl, Scrambler and auto-cars bring out the teenagers and the dating groups. And the arcade area keeps video game buffs busy all year round. The usual dirty, carny atmosphere here at the rides and the tent arcade, but it's very convenient for people in the area and you don't have to battle the beach traffic to get there. *Season:* Winter: Arcade only. Warm weather: full park. *Location:* Route 22, Scotch Plains, Union County. *Telephone:* 908-233-0675.

CLEMENTON LAKE PARK: Set on 40 acres about eight miles east of Camden, this amusement park has been operating for years now. Rides include an old- fashioned carousel, an antique roller-coaster and a small size showboat. New rides include a log flume and a pirate ship. Playport area for kids, plus traditional kiddie rides. The modern section includes a 13 acre waterpark called Splashworld, with separate entry or combination tickets available. *Hours:* Mid- May -Late June: Weekends only, 12-8. July — Labor Day: Daily, except Monday, 12-10 PM. *Admission:* $16.95 combo or $12.95 each park. *Location:* Route 534 off Routes 30 or 42, Clementon, Camden County *Telephone:* 609-783-0263.

FAIRY TALE FOREST: Old-fashioned style kiddie park set in a wooded area in northern Jersey reminiscent of the Black Forest. Molded storybook characters, such as Goldilocks and the Three Bears, inhabit little houses where the children can look in. The animated toy circus is for viewing but kids can use the carousel and miniature train ride. Picnic facilities. *Hours:* Mid-June-Labor Day: Tues.-Sun.: 10-5. Weekends only, spring and fall. Admission: Adults: $8.00; Children: $6.50; under 2 free. *Location:* Route 23, Oak Ridge, Passaic County. *Telephone:* 201-697-5656.

STORYBOOK LAND: Another children's park with small structures in the shape of The Gingerbread House, The Old Woman's Shoe, Noah's Ark, etc. The petting zoo, miniature train ride, antique car ride, and other attractions are included in the price. Christmas light display in December. Picnic area, snack bar. Ten miles west of Atlantic City. *Hours:* Mid-May-early Sept.: 11-5:30. Shorter hours spring & fall. *Admission:* $9.50 (under 1, free). *Location:* Routes 40 & 322, Black Horse Pike, Cardiff, Atlantic County. *Telephone:* 609-641-7847.

WILD WEST CITY: This northern New Jersey version of a western "Dodge City" complete with Marshal, cowboys, shootouts and a posse of kids is still going strong. You watch cowboy "acts", take stagecoach and train rides, visit the saloon for eats and a show, buy stuff. Pony rides available. Picnicking allowed. *Hours:*

Daily, mid-June to Labor Day, weekends in spring and fall. *Admission:* Adults: $6.40; Kids: $5.90. *Location:* Route 206, Netcong, Sussex County. *Telephone:* 201-347-8900.

SHAWNEE PLACE: Children's "active play" park in style of Sesame Place, only much smaller. Convenient to Poconos area vacationers (it's at the Shawnee Ski Area). Includes simple water slides, playport, wading pool, plastic ball "swim", magic show. Pony rides and video games extra. Snack bar and evening restaurant. *Hours:* Mem. Day - Labor Day: Daily, 10-5. Sept. - wknds. *Admission:* $10.00; under 40": free. Non-participant: $5.00. *Location:* Off Rte. 209, Shawnee, Poconos, PA. *Telephone:* 717-421-7231.

PLEASE NOTE: Many amusement park announced prices nowadays do not include state tax as they did in the past. Season tickets may be available at many of these parks.

ZOOS, AQUARIUMS,
NATURE CENTERS
WILDLIFE REFUGES

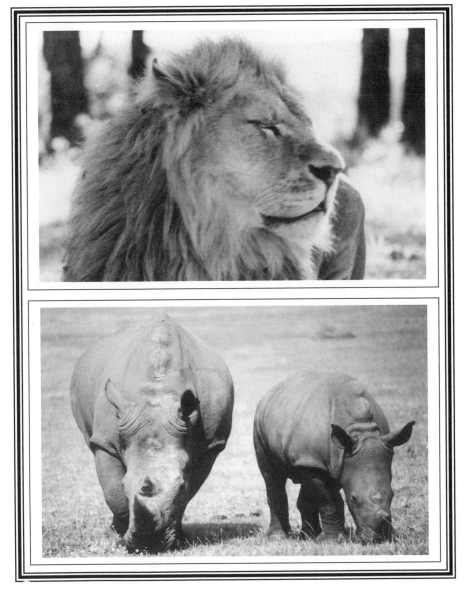

Photo: Courtesy Six Flags/Great Adventure

In This Chapter You Will Find:

The Bronx Zoo, NY
Six Flags/Great Adventure Safari, NJ
The Philadelphia Zoo, PA
Turtle Back Zoo, NJ
Cape May County Zoo, NJ
Staten Island Zoo, NY
Scotch Plains Zoo, NJ
Space Farms Zoo, NJ
Other Small Zoos, NJ
New Jersey State Aquarium
New York Aquarium, NY
Pequest Trout Hatchery, NJ
Wildlife Refuges, NJ
  The Great Swamp
  Brigantine National Wildlife Refuge
  Wetlands Institute
  Stone Harbor Bird Sanctuary
  Marine Mammal Stranding Center
Nature Centers, NJ

THE BRONX ZOO

While the smaller zoos of New Jersey are fine for younger children, once the kids have reached third grade it's time to take them to the largest urban zoo in America. Not necessarily the best (that honor belongs to the San Diego Zoo according to most experts) but the largest. Actually, the Bronx Zoo is in a period of transition. While there are still the old zoo houses, for the most part open sections allow the animals to roam free while visitors watch them from across moats. And **"Jungle World,"** an indoor home for tropical Asian wildlife, combines a natural habitat with controlled climate for the best of both worlds.

Since there are over 5 miles of terrain to cover and over 3,600 animals to see, it's a lot easier to take either the skyride or the monorail (or both) when they are in season. These may cost extra. The open sections are divided geographically as follows: **Wild Asia**: Open only in warm weather. A 40 acre habitat where elephants, rhinos, deer and antelope roam free. Visitors view them from the glassed-in monorail, "The Bengali Express." **Africa**: Lions, gazelles, antelopes, zebras and gnus roam the grassy slopes. You can view them from surrounding walkways and bridges or from the slow-moving Skyfari ride. **South America**: A smaller section devoted to anteaters and such. There is a wildfowl pond nearby where you can enjoy the aquatic birds at their colorful best. **North America**: An extensive section that includes a walk-in Wolf Wood (no, they don't bite you), polar bears, and lots of bison and bull elk.

Certain special houses offer the best this zoo or any other can come up with. First is *"The World of Darkness."* A top-notch display of bats, owls, and other nocturnal animals. Special lights allow you to watch the racoons, porcupines and bush babies cavort on the forest floor. They think it's night because the zoo has reversed the light cycles. It's a world of strange creatures with glittering eyes, and to top it all, there are special bat-flying demonstrations twice a day.

The *"World of Birds"* is housed in an ultra-modern concrete cylindrical building. Here you will find three floors of birds in a unique setting. Trees vault up the three stories while a variety of birds perch on the first, second and third story branches. Other special houses include the Penguin, Aquatic Bird, the extensive Reptile House and a new Zoo Center.

The *Children's Zoo* offers a host of fun things especially for kids under ten. Giant rope "spider webs" to climb, snail "shells" to ride in, and prairie dog burrows to explore practically turn this into an educational amusement park. The cost is extra but well worth it. You could spend almost an hour here alone. Another kids' favorite is the elephant and camel ride section (open warm weather only), and of course the *Bengali Express* with its narrated safari ride is always popular.

If you don't bring a sandwich (and there are plenty of tables if you do), there is a cafeteria open all year round. Warm weather opens the snack stands, the Pub and the zoobar.

HOURS: Daily, 10-5, Weekends: 10-5:30 PM. (Winter: 10 AM - 4:30 PM.)
ADMISSION: Adults: $6.75; Children 2-12 and Seniors: $2.00. Parking fee. Wed. free.
LOCATION: George Washington Bridge to Cross Country Expressway east to exit 4B, Bronx River Parkway North. Take exit marked "Bronx Zoo" then left to Bronxdale parking field.
TELEPHONE: 718-367-1010.

THE SAFARI AT SIX FLAGS

The largest safari outside of Africa takes about an hour to drive through and covers six miles and six continents. Some animals, such as camels, elk in heat, jealous giraffes and short-tempered rhinos can get almost too close for comfort. The brochure warns that you should keep car windows closed at all times so take an airconditioned car if you're visiting on a 90-degree day.

The road through the Safari is three lanes wide and you may travel at your own speed. Each area is separated from the other by wire fences so you must wait for the guards to open the gates between one habitat and another. Surprisingly, the warning signs to keep windows closed are apparent only in the dangerous cat sections. I noticed a number of cars with open windows and people who nuzzled deer and fed popcorn to camels. Camels, in fact, seem like the beggars of Great Adventure — they sidle up to the cars in the motheaten rags of their summer skin looking for handouts.

In the African Plains section you can watch herds of elephants eat and socialize. And nothing can make you feel smaller than to sit knee-high to a giraffe as he nudges up against your car — unless it's sitting between two giraffes who are having a love-spat and using your car as a barrier zone. The animals have right- of-way here, and if you get in real trouble honk for a Safari guard. One rhino did take particular exception to our blue station wagon. He looked suspiciously as if he were going to charge and sure enough a guard did wave us on quickly.

The Australian section is unique. Kangaroos, wallabies, walla-roos and the flightless emu strut, waddle and bound on the hilly terrain. The kangaroos are much smaller than I had imagined. They move about on all fours and since their front legs are so much shorter than those powerful hind-quarters, they look for all the world like lopsided dogs with giant tails. In a new section, the Bengal tiger has its own Indian pavillion.

For those with metal-topped cars the ride through monkey territory is always of interest. These curious simians will scamper all over your car, check on the occupants, pull on the hood ornament, knock your grillwork and then pass on to the next car.

An air-conditioned bus ride through the whole park is an alternative to driving your own car, but it costs extra for each rider.

HOURS:	9-5 Daily, late June - mid-Sept. Weekends April, May, Oct.
ADMISSION ETC.:	See Six Flags/Great Adventure entry.

THE PHILADELPHIA ZOO

This is America's oldest zoo and like the Bronx Zoo, it offers a combination of old fashioned zoo houses filled with caged animals and modern landscaped animal "habitats". The most interesting of the latter is *The World of Primates*. Orangutans, gibbons and gorillas live here and you can actually see a gorilla family sitting on the grass outside the building. And the new **Carnivore Kingdom** features natural habitats for our predatory friends. The rare white lion is the zoo's newest star.

The Treehouse - a special exhibit for children - allows kids to climb into a ficus tree, ride on a caterpillar and explore a river, a marsh, a meadow and other environmental features. One can smell the rainforest, hear the birds chirping, feel the skin of various animals and generally have a good time at this popular hands-on exhibit housed in a separate building.

Besides the lions, tigers, bears and hooved animals one would expect at a major zoo, you can also find Australia's gift to the world - kangaroos and wallabies, - plus a Rare Animal House filled with some unusual varieties of monkeys and other species.

During summer a "Birds of Prey" show on an open stage has hawks, eagles and such demonstrate their prowess during free flight. Camel rides and elephant pictures are available April through September. Other features are a monorail ride around the premises and a baby animal nursery where you can watch the newborns frolic. The zoo covers 42 acres, which makes it large, but not impossible to cover in one day. There are several nice picnic areas, plus two major eateries. It is inside the huge Fairmount Park which also includes many of Philadelphia's museums and historic houses.

HOURS: Weekdays: 9:30-4:45; Weekends: 9:30-5:45.
ADMISSION: 12 & up: $8.50; Seniors, children 2-11: $6.50
LOCATION: 34th & Girard (Use Girard Ave. Exit of Route 76).
TELEPHONE: 215-243-1100

THE TURTLE BACK ZOO

Fifteen years ago, Turtle Back was probably the best zoo in northern New Jersey. There were seven hundred animals, and fanciful settings such as a large wedge of cheese to house rodents and a large piggy bank for the pigs. Well, a loss of funds plus a change in direction has left this zoo in limbo. Most of the cute settings are gone, the number of animals is down, and the place looks disheveled. A new director hopes to turn things around.

There are still many of the hooved animals, especially various types of deer and llama. A few of the large cats, such as a cougar and a bobcat, remain. The seal pond, has been taken over by penguins. The bat cave is no more. The petting zoo is not around at the moment.

The zoo is built on hilly terrain, so you do get a good hike, but most of the exhibits are rather sad looking. The only new and worthwhile exhibit, and one that reflects the "naturalistic" philosophy, is the wolf woods. Here you can look through a plastic shield and see a pack of wolves at work and play.

The fast food and gift concessions are open sporadically. The miniature train ride, which takes you on a nice ride through the

South Mountain Reservation woods was running Friday, Saturday and Sunday at last report. We hope Essex County, which runs this facility, upgrades it soon.

The educational center presents lectures on animals to individuals and classes.

HOURS: Mon.-Sat.: 10-5; Sunday: 10:30-6. Winter: Weekends.
ADMISSION: Adults: $6.00; Children, Seniors $2.50. Under 2 free.
LOCATION: 560 Northfield Ave., West Orange (behind South Mountain Arena), Essex County.
TELEPHONE: 201-731-5800

CAPE MAY COUNTY ZOO

Cape May County has poured a lot of money into this park which once offered just a few scrawny cages. Now the landscape artists have been out in force, and the various animal enclosures are arranged along meandering paths with pleasant foliage all about. Some of the enclosures simulate the natural terrain of the animals. Others, particularly those for the big cats, are the traditional cement floor cages. But the zoo is within a park filled with the tall scrub pine and sandy soil of the region, so the general effect is of seeing animals within a natural environment. The giraffe, for instance, actually eats the leaves from a real tree.

Among the 120 species of animals here, you will find zebras, llamas, tigers, jaguars, bears, spider monkeys and a lion. The white-maned tamarin was the most unusual specie I saw there. Quite a variety of birds are on hand also, including cockatoos, toucans, a myna bird, peacocks, eagles and barnyard fowl.

This is one of the best looking zoos in New Jersey. Further expansion is planned. Outside the zoo, there is a childrens playground, a picnic area and a number of concession carts for those who didn't bring lunch. All in all, a very pleasant outing. Still free, but during tourist season, there's a man at the park entrance taking "donations". A few dollars should do it, and it's well worth it.

HOURS: Daily, 9-4:30 weather permitting
LOCATION: Route 9 & Crest Haven Road, Cape May Court House.
TELEPHONE: 609-465-5271 or 465-9210

STATEN ISLAND ZOO

This square-block, city zoo is of interest for three reasons: 1) it is convenient to those within easy driving distance of the Goethals Bridge, 2) it is primarily an indoor zoo, so it is available during the winter, 3) it is reasonable priced.

The big collection here is the snakes. Since snakes take up little room (experts assure us that snakes like those little glass cubicles where zoo-keepers put them), it is possible to crowd an amazing variety of them into one large zoo-house. The biggest rattlesnake collection in the world resides here, along with cobras, pythons, cottonmouths, a krait, an asp — you ask for it, they got it. Since reptiles are not very active you may find two — or is it three, or one? — pythons curled around one another with head and tail indistinguishable. At the end of the room a family of alligators remind you there's more to the reptile class than just snakes.

The zoo is unusual in that it also sports a small aquarium. Coral fish, sea anemones, and piranhas are among the colorful and dangerous fish floating behind glass. There are even a few small sharks. A separate tropical area includes new and roomy homes for monkeys, and white-topped tamarins. A large bat exhibit allows you to watch the bats sleeping upside down or flying through their "cave".

A pleasant children's center includes a farm and petting zoo with lambs, pigs, oxen, geese and other animals who nibble rye krisp through the fencing. Altogether, a pretty place with trees, benches, picnic tables and snack bar. There are no hooved animals here, by the way — there is no space.

HOURS: 10-4:45 Daily. Closed major holidays.
ADMISSION: Adults: $3.00; Children & Seniors: $2.00; Wednesday afternoon: Donation.
LOCATION: 614 Broadway, Staten Island. Take 278 E to Slossen Ave., Exit. Left on Slossen then right on Martling.
TELEPHONE: 718-442-3100

SCOTCH PLAINS ZOO

This private zoo, formerly called *Terry Lou*, has been a New Jersey fixture for many years. It doesn't look like much from the outside — and don't expect to find the lush environmental settings that are featured in large zoos. The walkways and installations need work.

But for a small, suburban zoo there is a surprising variety of animals. For instance, a pygmy hippo, lions and tigers, giraffes, bison and llamas all reside here. Indoors you will find chimpanzees, some ringtail lemurs and a few frisky monkeys.

Because cages at the zoo are mesh (a heavy Cyclone fence type) you can get a closer look at these animals than at many other zoos. The main outside area features mammals with an adjacent section for birds and alligators. Large animal crackers are available, and the mesh cages allow you to feed llamas, deer, etc. without fear of fingerbite.

The complete area of the Scotch Plains Zoo runs about one square city block. It should take about one hour to see it all. The zoo recently changed management. We hope things shape up here.

> **HOURS:** Weekdays: 10-5; Weekends: 10-6. Closed winter.
> **ADMISSION:** Adults: $6.00; Children 1-12: $3.00; Under one year free.
> **LOCATION:** 1451 Raritan Road (corner of Terrill) Scotch Plains, Union County
> **TELEPHONE:** 908-322-7180

SPACE FARMS ZOO

Another private zoo, this one in a completely rural area that closely approximates the natural surroundings of many of the animals housed there. The trip takes you well into the mountains of northern Sussex County, past farms of Herefords and horses grazing peacefully among the green hills.

The zoo is set up for family outings with many picnic tables, swing sets and slides for the youngsters. There is plenty of space at Space Farms (although the name derives from the family that runs it.) One hundred acres are devoted to rather simple cages of grizzly bears, lions, tigers, hyenas, monkeys, etc. plus several buildings filled with antique cars, sleighs and other collections. A large pond at the center of the acreage allows ducks and geese to paddle about, while pens of yak, llamas, buffalo and goats dot the surrounding hill.

Bears include grizzlies, polar bears and the rare Hokkaido bear from Japan. Although the bear cages seemed smaller than those at public zoos, Mr. Space assured me the bears inside were happy. At any rate, Space Farms has a high reproduction rate for animals in captivity. Maybe it's the fresh air, or the diet of fresh meat, or the natural smell that emanates from the bear cages — but there were plenty of cubs rollicking around on the day I visited.

The entrance building to the property includes a *Museum of Americana* (everything from Indian arrowheads to old clocks), a snack shop and a gift shop. And on the hills to the left of the zoo there are more museums with collections of old buggies, cars and everything but the kitchen sink. Between the animals, the museums, the swings and the slides you can make a day of it. Picnic lunches allowed.

HOURS: Daily 9-5, May 1 - Oct. 31.
ADMISSION: Adults: $7.95; Children 3-12: $3.50 plus tax.
LOCATION: Beemerville, Sussex County. Take Rte. 80 to Rte. 15N, then right to 565N. Follow signs.
TELEPHONE: 201-875-5800

OTHER SMALL ZOOS (NEW JERSEY)

There are a number of small zoos tucked away in local city and county parks that are pleasant to visit when you are in the vicinity. Among them are:

VAN SAUN PARK ZOO: A recently expanded zoo with an aviary, lots of farm animals, some larger cats and a miniature train ride. Recent additions have expanded the quality and quantity of the animals to include some exotic species. All this is set in a large county park with lots of picnic tables and a duck pond. *Location:* Forest Ave. (off Route 4), River Edge, Bergen County. *Telephone:* 201-262-3771. Fee on summer weekends.

COHANSIC PARK: Good sized city zoo set inside an 1100 acre park that borders the river in Bridgeton. Over 200 animals including lion, bears, wolves and zebras. The park also includes picnic areas, nature trails, lots more. Location: City Park, Bridgeton (Routes 49 and 77) Cumberland County. *Telephone:* 609-455-3230.

POPCORN PARK: A 7-acre licensed zoo that caters strictly to injured, abandoned and unwanted wildlife. One section houses rescued animals such as Lacey the Lion, another includes the kennels of abandoned pets waiting for adoption. The facility is run by the Associated Humane Society. *Admission:* Adults: $2.25; Children, Seniors: $1.25. *Hours:* Daily 1-5. *Location:* Humane Way and Lacey Road, Forked River, Ocean County. *Telephone:* 609-693-1900.

NEW JERSEY STATE AQUARIUM

When the new State Aquarium first opened a few years ago, it was so politically correct it verged on boredom. There were sharks in the 760,000 gallon Open Ocean tank and lots of other brown and gray fish. There were harbor seals outside and a regular feeding time. But aside from a show in the auditorium involving questions and answers between some deep sea "divers" and the audience there wasn't much entertainment value.

Now things have gotten more interesting. The harbor seals have learned to catch frisbees and do other "learning behaviors" — in fact, they now rate a 250 seat outside auditorium. Since there are no whales, dolphins or sea lions at the aquarium, the harbor seals have inherited star status here.

Meanwhile, the huge concrete aquarium building has been completely renovated. A four million dollar project called *Ocean Base Atlantic* has transformed the entire first floor into a high-tech station with stops in exotic locations. Laser lights, a motorized mobile of fish and the model of a "submersible" float overhead. You can visit the Shark Zone with its exhibits of massive Megalodon jaws and a touch tank. Then there's the CORAL station where you "visit" a Caribbean Beach, a shipwreck, and so forth. Lots of colorful fish, spiny lobsters, bright hamlets at the Rainbow Reef. And when you finally come upon the Deep Atlantic, you get the full impact of the massive open tank.

Upstairs, there are a number of interactive exhibits. The cafeteria features a promenade deck with a great view of Philadelphia. And a riverbus shuttles back and forth between Camden and the recently overhauled Penns Landing which has several new attractions.

HOURS: Daily 9:30-5:30 Mar. 16 - Sept. 15. Otherwise: Wed.-Sun.: 10-5.

Harbor seal and human eye each other at the New Jersey State Aquarium.

ADMISSION: Adults: $9.95; Students/seniors: $8.45; children 2-11: $6.95

LOCATION: 1 Riverside Drive and Mickle Boulevard, Camden (take 676 to Mickle Blvd. exit). Parking garage across street.

TELEPHONE: 609-365-3300; 800-616-JAWS.

THE NEW YORK AQUARIUM

It's in Brooklyn, of course, and you can get there easily (since getting lost in Brooklyn is even more traumatic than getting lost in Manhattan). Since the aquarium is right smack in the middle of Coney Island, many people prefer visiting in the spring or fall to avoid getting caught up in the hurly burly of boardwalk amusements.

This concrete aquarium is home to whales, sharks, seals, penguins and a variety of tropical fish. The whales swim around lazily in the big tank — what you see is mostly their underbellies, and the sharks, most of which are rather small, have a building all to themselves. For many, it's the yellow tangs and sturgeon fish and other strange and beautiful denizens of the deep that make a trip to the aquarium worthwhile.

In warm weather a training show takes place in an outside arena. A dolphin jumps up and learns to take a fish from the trainer. Since they are just learning this can sometimes look more like amateur night than Broadway. However, in this age of acute sensibilities to dolphin rights, it's rare to see such a show at all!

For northern New Jerseyans this is the only decent-sized aquarium within easy driving distance. It does have real whales and real sharks and penguins and an area where children can handle starfish and other creatures of the sea. And the newly installed indoor sections include lavish displays for penguins, walruses and other aquatic creatures. A full waterfall was running when I last visited. There is a nice souvenir stand by the way, a cafeteria, and a nice view of the beach and ocean. No children under 16 unless accompanied by an adult.

HOURS: 10-5 daily. 10-6 weekends. Shorter winter hours.
ADMISSION: Adults: $6.35; Children & Seniors: $3.00.

LOCATION: 8th Street and Surf Ave., Brooklyn. Take the Verrazano Bridge to the Belt Parkway (direction of JFK Airport) and stay on until 8th Street exit. There is a sign for the Aquarium. Parking fee.
TELEPHONE: 718-265-3474

PEQUEST TROUT HATCHERY

This sparkling new concrete building complex has three purposes. One is to raise the trout that are later thrown into the state park lakes to become some lucky fisherman's catch. The second is to introduce youngsters to proper fishing techniques and to educate them in wildlife conservation. The third is to manage this huge acreage and the wildlife that lives therein (including the birds whose chirping is amplified in the main building).

The Visitor Center includes a large room with many hands-on exhibits. There are also charts, displays, and a tankful of adult trout so that even those who do not fish can get a look at these ugly fellows. In another room a continuous movie shows how the fish are bred, fed and finally transported by truck to be dumped in fresh water streams. Finally you can go outside to see the ponds where the young fish are. A look into a glass sided building will allow you to see the tiny fingerlings.

This a popular place for school and scout groups, because during a group tour the kids often get to wield a fishing rod. There are also special Saturday classes on fishing techniques. You can buy fishing and hunting permits here plus the special trout stamps which help to fund this state center. Free.

HOURS: (General public) Fri.-Sun. 10-4.
LOCATION: Pequest Road, Oxford, Warren County (off Rte 46).
TELEPHONE: 908-637-4125

THE GREAT SWAMP

The remains of a glacial pocket, the Swamp serves as both a refuge for animals and a 5,800-acre barrier to suburban development. It was saved some years ago from the fate of airport development by a group of conservationists and donated to the Federal Government which now administers it. The area is a combination of marshes, grassland, swamp woodland and hardwood ridges. There are some stands of mountain laurel and rhododendron but a botanical wonderland it's not.

Actually, there are sections that look like a great locale for a movie called "The Creature From the Black Lagoon." Tall, leafless trees, crackling twigs, swampy underbrush — well, it's a swamp after all. Not smelly like the Okefenokee, and not deep, but still a swamp. Wooden boardwalks have been built in several observation areas so that families can traverse the wetlands and observe whatever wildlife is around. Mostly it's small — woodchucks, muskrats, frogs — and there are deer and fox, too, though they tend to stay in the interior. There are blinds for picture taking. Swamp officials recommend visits in the early morning or late afternoon. Sunday afternoon the wildlife won't come out because there are too many people around.

The Swamp consists of two-thirds wilderness and one-third management area. There are several hiking trails in dry areas but picnicking is verboten. Observation centers in Basking Ridge and Chatham Twp. (see "Nature Centers"). Old sneakers or waterproof shoes are recommended. Insect repellent in the evening. Free.

HOURS: Dawn until dusk. So. Blvd. closed summers.
LOCATION: Headquarters at Point Pleasant Road, Basking Ridge. Also Nature Centers run by Morris and Somerset Counties. Read Nature Center section.
TELEPHONE: 201-635-6629; 201-425-1222.

FORSYTHE NATIONAL WILDLIFE REFUGE

Formerly called the Brigantine Division, it is only eleven miles from Atlantic City but it's a world of immense quiet and peace. There are over 20,000 acres of grassy tidal marsh interspersed with tidal bays and channels with some brush upland area that support deer, fox and other small animals here. But the main area of the refuge is for the protection of waterfowl that use the Atlantic Flyway in their travels from Canada to Florida. Many birds (up to 150,000) winter completely in New Jersey now.

The snow goose, Canada goose, brant and black duck are among the many birds who stop here. The refuge offers a calendar of wildlife events — e.g., November 1-10: 100,000 ducks, geese and brant; June 20th: Canada goose round-up.

A self-guided tour of eight miles by car or foot circuits the waterfowl impoundments. Hundreds of birds are here no matter what time of year you visit. The vistas are flat and beyond the muddy marshes where the birds feed you can see the towers of Atlantic City. There are places where you can stop your car to take pictures (and even eat lunch, they say) but the insect population is heavy here also. Free.

HOURS: Daylight except during hazardous conditions.
LOCATION: U.S. 9, one mile east of Oceanville, Atlantic County.
TELEPHONE: 609-652-1665

WETLANDS INSTITUTE

Set in the middle of a 6,000 acre publicly owned tract of salt marsh, not far from the beach at Stone Harbor, this attractive cedar shake building includes classrooms, an exhibit hall and six research laboratories. There is a large separate room which houses a touch museum for children and other exhibits. A saltwater aquarium and a large book and gift shop are also on hand. There is also an observation tower which provides a view of the surrounding wetlands (and an occasional osprey nest). Periodic guided tours of the marsh, plus a number of lectures and ecology classes are available. Of course, individuals can use the boardwalk trail anytime during visiting hours.

Once a year the Institute operates the *"Wings 'N Water Festival"* a popular weekend fest in September that includes special events in all the local towns. Wooden duck carving, seafood dinners, and open houses are included.

HOURS: Daily; 9-4:30; Sun.: 1-4. Closed Sun. & Mon. in Winter and 2 wks. Christmas.
ADMISSION: Adults: $3.00; Children: $1.00.
LOCATION: Stone Harbor Blvd., Stone Harbor, Cape May County.
TELEPHONE: 609-368-1211.

STONE HARBOR BIRD SANCTUARY

A 21 acre sanctuary that was for years home to snowy egrets, brown ibis and herons. There are sidewalk pay binoculars to watch their flight at dawn and dusk. Their nesting time is May to October. However, in recent years, the birds have not been showing up much.

LOCATION: 3rd Ave. between 111th & 116th St. Stone Harbor, Cape May County.

MARINE MAMMAL STRANDING CENTER

Devised mainly as a rescue outfit, the center includes an education area and tiny museum. There are exhibits on conservation, lots of books and T-shirts for sale, and a large fish tank where you examine the fish through magnifying glasses. Don't expect to find dolphins or whales here — the garage sized pool can't hold them. Harbor seals and sea turtles, maybe.

LOCATION: 3625 Brigantine Blvd., Brigantine (north of Atlantic City).
HOURS: Summer hours are 11-5, some weekends thereafter.
TELEPHONE: 609-266-0538

NATURE CENTERS

So what's a nature center? Not knowing, I expected to find a log cabin in the woods where a grizzled old codger showed his bird nest collection and talked about owls. Actually the centers are a lot more sophisticated than that. What I found were modern buildings filled with classrooms, auditoriums, displays, professional staff and a host of activities, particularly on weekends. Of course the buildings are just the center of the nature area, which also has trails, wildflowers, birds, and small animals. Weekend programs may cover such diverse activities as maple-sugaring, ski instruction, movies, lectures on backpacking, bird walks, trail walks, etc. Lectures for school groups and movies for families are staple fare. Courses usually cost a small fee while guided walks and rambles are free. And naturally, one may visit these centers and walk the trails without participating in the structured programs at all.

Not all the centers are big and beautiful but they all serve their communities well. In many cases, the displays are equal to what you would find in a small museum of natural history. Here are some of New Jersey's nature centers:

LORIMAR NATURE CENTER: 790 Ewing Ave., Franklin Lakes, Bergen County. *Telephone:* 201-891-1211. Run by the Audubon Society. There is a Living Museum and a demonstration farm besides the nature program and field trips. Nature trails open every day while the Visitors' Center is available.

FLAT ROCK BROOK NATURE CENTER: 443 Van Nostrand Ave., Englewood, Bergen County. *Telephone:* 201-567-1265. Solar-heated building, 150 acres of forest with trails, brook. Various weekend activities, tree identification, classes for schoolchildren, local artists' show. Run by self-supporting environmental organization. Open daily.

BERGEN COUNTY WILDLIFE CENTER: Crescent Ave., Wyckoff. *Telephone:* 201-891-5571. A little of everything here — wildlife, daffodil preserve, waterfowl pond, nature trail, garden. At the Center, museum programs and films. Open daily except for legal holidays.

HARTSHORN ARBORETUM AND BIRD SANCTUARY: Forest Drive, Short Hills, Essex County. *Telephone:* 201-376-3587. Plant and wildlife museum. Classes in basket-weaving, plant propagation, dyeing, etc. Besides that, there's a full arboretum of 16 1/2 acres of oak, maple, and rhododendrons. Open daily. Special hours for museum.

CENTER FOR ENVIRONMENTAL STUDIES: 621 Eagle Rock Ave., Roseland, Essex County. *Telephone:* 201-228-2210. Nature walks, slide lectures, classes for both children and adults. Center is also embarkation point for many daytrips — preregistration required. Open daily.

RIKER HILL PARK GEOLOGICAL MUSEUM: Livingston, Essex County. *Telephone:* 201-992-8806. Administered by Center for Environmental Studies. Reconverted army barracks now houses fossil museum with skeletal reproductions. Quarry with fossil digs open for tours in good weather (reservations needed for groups).

TRAILSIDE NATURE CENTER: Coles Ave. & New Providence Road, Mountainside, Union County. *Telephone:* 908-789-3670. Part of Watchung Reservation. New building, includes auditorium and a while museum display of stuffed animals, beehives, eggshells, arrowheads, etc. Weekend programs, nature walks. Planetarium also.

GREAT SWAMP OUTDOOR EDUCATION CENTER: 247 Southern Blvd., Chatham Twp., Morris County. *Telephone:* 201-635-6629. On one edge of the swamp and run by the county. Wooden building contains exhibits, library, classrooms. Nature trails, guided walks, wooden walkways into the swamp, special programs such as maple-sugaring. Closed July and August, when nature center moves to Schooley's Mountain Park, Route 24, Long Valley.

SOMERSET COUNTY PARK ENVIRONMENTAL EDUCATION CENTER: 190 Lord Stirling Park, Basking Ridge. *Telephone:* 908-766-2489. At the other edge of the Great Swamp. Modern solar building with classrooms, displays, separate solar-heated house. 8 1/2 miles of trails and wooden walkways. Bird-watching, guided hikes, cross country skiing.

PORICY PARK NATURE CENTER: Oak Hill Road, Middletown Twp., Monmouth County. *Telephone:* 908-842-5966. 250 acres of land with trails. Fossil bed in park, fossil walks. Museum has art and nature displays, art programs, school programs.

SANDY HOOK VISITORS CENTER: Gateway National Recreation Area, Highlands, Monmouth County, off Route 36. *Telephone:* 908-872-0092. Summer activities include canoe trips and dune walk. Center has slide show, exhibits. Year round weekend activities: holly forest walks and passes for lighthouse tours and Fort Hancock batteries. Classes by reservation.

HACKENSACK MEADOWLANDS DEVELOPMENT COM-MISSION ENVIRONMENTAL CENTER: 2 De Korte Park Plaza, Lyndhurst. *Telephone:* 201-460-8300. Emphasis on the urban salt marsh and history of the meadowlands. Exhibits on recycling. Trash Museum. *Hours:* Daily except Sun. & holidays.

MERRILL CREEK RESERVOIR ENVIRONMENTAL PRE-SERVE: 116G Montana Rd., Washington Twp., Warren County. *Telephone:* 908-454-1213. Primarily for hiking, wildlife observation and photography of 290 acre preserve. Visitor center, timber trail. *Hours:* Daily.

N.J. AUDUBON SOCIETY: — Besides their headquarters at Lorimar, the society operates several bird and wildlife sanctuaries and observatories and holds various programs of interest to birdwatchers and others. Among these are: **Scherman-Hoffman Sanctuaries**, Hardscrabble Road, Bernardsville (Tel. 908-766-5787); **The Cape May Bird Observatory**, 707 East Lake Drive, Cape May Point (Tel. 609-884-2736) - famous for its early May Cape May Weekend when millions of birds can be tracked; **Owl Haven**, Englishtown-Freehold Road, Tennent, (Tel. 908-780-7007); and **Rancocas Nature Center**, Rancocas Road, Mt. Holly, (Tel. 609-261-2495).

Note: Parents of young children should also check out the mini-zoos in such places as *The Newark Museum, The Morris Museum* and the *Bergen Museum.*

THE OUTDOOR LIFE

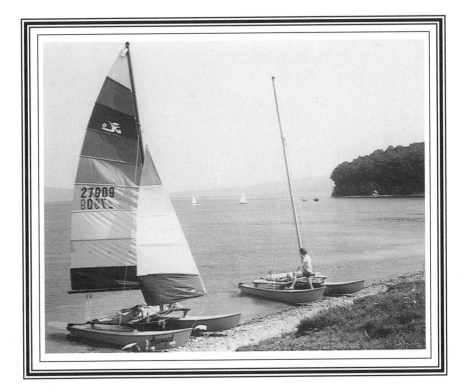

Photo: Courtesy N.J. Div. of Travel & Tourism

167

In This Chapter You Will Find:

Ski Areas
  New Jersey Ski Areas
  The Poconos Ski Area
  New York State Ski Areas
The Jersey Shore
  The Upper Shore
  Long Beach Island
  The Cape
Hiking, N.J.
Fishing, N.J.
Camping, N.J.
Pick-Your-Own Orchards, N.J.
Adventurous Outings, N.J.
State Parks and Forests, N.J.

SKI AREAS

New Jersey Ski Areas

GREAT GORGE — VERNON VALLEY: One ticket buys access to the whole complex. By far the largest ski area in New Jersey, this place can get awfully crowded on weekends with lines at both the lifts and the cafeteria. Ski instruction is available at all levels. Night-skiing and half-day tickets available. Altogether GG/VV has 13 double chairlifts, one triple chairlift, several tows, complete snowmaking equipment, 3 mountains, 52 trails, ski rentals, and nursery. Cafeteria and bar at both base lodges. Nighttime entertainment. Vertical drop of 1033 feet.

> **LOCATION:** Route 94 near McAfee in Sussex County.
> **TELEPHONE:** 201-827-2000 - for general information. 201-827-3900 — for ski report.

HIDDEN VALLEY: Once partially private, now a public ski area with day, twilight and night time skiing. 6 slopes, 12 trails, 620 foot vertical drop. Ski lessons plus separate racing program. Cafeteria, bar, lodge entertainment.

> **LOCATION:** Breakneck Road, Vernon Twp., Sussex County
> **TELEPHONE:** 201-764-4200, 201-764-6161

CRAIGMEUR: One chairlift, one T-bar, two rope tows. A popular family area which caters to intermediates and beginners. Four slopes, cross-country program, night lighting. It's conveniently located to the northern suburbs and can get quite crowded on weekends (actually it's the cafeteria that's crowded with mothers who sit and watch the clothing while Dad teaches the kids a few pointers). No difficult slopes here which is why it's so popular with the beginners.

> **LOCATION:** Route 80 to Green Pond Road (Route 513) Newfoundland, Morris County.
> **TELEPHONE:** 201-697-4501

BELLE MOUNTAIN (Mercer County): One chairlift, three rope tows, four ski trails including one intermediate 190 ft. vertical drop. Open evenings during the week and weekends.. Lighted for nighttime skiing. Lessons, snack bar, beginner packages.

> **LOCATION:** Valley Road (off Route 29), Hopewell
> **TELEPHONE:** 609-397-0043

CAMPGAW MOUNTAIN (Bergen County): For beginners and intermediates. 100% snowmaking equipment. Main slope and two learning slopes, two double chair lifts, one T-bar, vertical drop of 270 feet. Lighted for night skiing, cafeteria in lodge. Lessons.

LOCATION: Fyke Road, Mahwah
TELEPHONE: 201-327-7800

Note: Snowboarding available at all N.J. areas.

The Poconos Ski Areas

SHAWNEE MOUNTAIN: Close by. Shawnee offers eight double chairlifts, 17 slopes, snowmakers, ski school, accessory rental, cafeteria, bar and nursery. Trails include cross-country. Day, night and twilight skiing. Snowboarding.

LOCATION: Take Route 80 to exit 52, then north on 209 for six miles.
TELEPHONE: 717-421-7231

JACK FROST/BIG BOULDER: You buy a combination ticket for these two popular mountains. Each mountain has seven lifts, two J-bars and many trails that run the gamut from "Powderpuff" to "Thunderbolt." Rentals, ski school, restaurant, cafeteria, nursery. There are 11 slopes at Big Boulder, 19 at Jack Frost.

LOCATION: Lake Harmony and White Haven, Pennsylvania. Rte. 80 Exit 42 or 43.
TELEPHONE: 717-722-0104, 717-443-8425.

CAMELBACK: About a half-hour further on and part of the Big Pocono State Park. Camelback offers a variety of trails and attracts a pleasant crowd. 25 slopes, 11 lifts. This 2,100 ft. mountain is the largest in the area. Two base lodges.

LOCATION: Tannersville, Pa. Rte. 80 Exit 45.
TELEPHONE: 717-629-1661

New York State Ski Areas

HUNTER MOUNTAIN: For ski groups and more advanced skiers Hunter is very popular. A goodly drive away, but the mountain here offers a 1,600 foot vertical drop and a large variety of trails include plenty for beginners, intermediates and those who really want to hone their skills. Ten chairlifts, six tows, 45 trails, and all services available. Variety of eateries. Daytime only. Crowded.

    LOCATION: Take Garden State Parkway to New York Thruway, then exit 20 to Route 32 for 19 miles.
    TELEPHONE: 518-263-4223, 800-548-6648

SKI WINDHAM: 7 miles west of Hunter, perhaps a little less crowded. Two peaks, 33 trails, 7 lifts. Includes restaurant, cafeteria, ski school, nursery. Daytime skiing only.

    LOCATION: Windham, NY (Take NYS Thruway to Exit 21).
    TELEPHONE: 518-734-4300, 800-833-5056

STERLING FOREST SKI AREA: Really close at hand, in fact it is right over the border in Tuxedo. Once the site of a popular garden, this ski area now services families and is pleasant for beginners and intermediates. Four double chairlifts, six trails, 450 ft. vertical drop. Cafeteria, warming hut, lessons, rentals and snowmakers.

    LOCATION: Route 17 north to 17A north, just above Tuxedo, New York
    TELEPHONE: 914-351-2163

Note: Unless otherwise noted, snowmaking is available. Prices and number of trails (and trails available) change all the time. The number of chairlifts may be upgraded from one season to the next. It is always best to call first.

THE JERSEY SHORE

There are 127 miles of beach along the coast of New Jersey which offer swimming, boating and fishing. But for most people going to the shore means visiting one particular portion of that lengthy coastline. Here's a roundup of the various types of shore resorts that await the newcomer or oldtimer.

First of all, the beaches. Some are narrow, some are wide but few are free. Sandy Hook (government run) charges a parking fee, but can become crowded nevertheless. Atlantic City and the beaches of the Wildwoods are free. Island Beach State Park (State run) charges a per-car admission. Most other beaches require beach badges (which you buy from a man sitting there selling them), or admission through a private bathhouse. The price of badges varies depending on whether you buy per day, week or season. If you stay at a hotel which owns its own beachfront, you don't have to bother with all this. And then there are a few select beaches which are accessible to residents only.

Cottage and beach house rentals vary according to size, closeness to beach and the social status of the town. Guest houses remain the cheapest accommodation especially if you don't mind walking a few blocks to the beach. Most motels offer efficiency apartments for those who want to cook in, but still have motel convenience. Motel rates compare well to other beach areas along the Atlantic Coast. Major amusement areas are found at Point Pleasant, Seaside Heights, and Wildwood. (See chapter on Amusement Parks.)

The Upper Shore:
Sandy Hook to Island Beach State Park

The closest and most accessible to the crowded urban and suburban areas of northern New Jersey, the upper shore is naturally very popular for daytime and weekend trips as well as the two-week vacation. **Sandy Hook** beach is part of the Gateway National Park and is run by the Department of the Interior. The beach is free but there are parking fees during season. Besides the several beaches, Sandy Hook offers the oldest lighthouse in the U.S., a nature center, a visitor's center, tours of Fort Hancock and surf fishing.

Below Sandy Hook there begins a string of beachfront communities, each with a slightly different personality. Some, like **Belmar** and **Manasquan**, cater to a young, singles crowd who share cottages and guest houses.(Although Belmar has recently cracked down on "groupers".) Others, like **Deal**, are quiet and rich and interested only in full-time residents and full-summer rentals. You can find **Spring Lake** with its turreted late-Victorian homes and little old lady customers plus a good smattering of singles.

Asbury Park is a changing area with a wide beach, and many special events at its Convention Hall. One of the "old" resorts, with a rundown look, it is now best known for the **Stone Pony** where Bruce Springsteen began. There are only a few boardwalk amusements left. Separated from Asbury by a canal, **Ocean Grove**

is quiet, reserved and primly Victorian, with a well-known auditorium. The stick style houses here remain from the early camp meeting days.

Further on, are **Brielle** and **Point Pleasant,** towns with a large fishing fleet and large residential areas including an increasing number of condos. And a bit down the strip come more reasonable rentals. At **Seaside Heights** and **Seaside Park** there are over 1200 cottages, many of them minimal comfort types with just two rooms and a couple of screened windows. Hundreds of guest houses and almost 100 motels service the many vacationers who come to this popular area, with its large amusement center. Neighboring *Island Beach State Park* with its beach and nature area gets the daytime visitors. Parking at this popular public beach runs $7 on weekends, $6 on weekdays.

Long Beach Island

For many middle executive families the place to go is Long Beach Island only an hour and a half away from North Jersey's affluent suburbs. A long, narrow strip of beach that extends from Barnegat Light to Holgate, the island is actually a series of little towns connected to the mainland by a bridge. Here you will find closely quartered beach houses and a few motels leading up to the dunes. The friendly small-town atmosphere and spanking clean air remind one of Cape Cod. Since most people rent cottages or apartments for at least two weeks, there is an air of leisure and permanence about Long Beach Island.

Courses in art, photography, Yoga and such are offered at both the *Foundation of Arts and Sciences* and at *St. Francis Center.* A dinner theater assures visitors there's more to summer life than basking on the beach. An amusement area and boutique shopping center attracts both teenagers and families with kids to Bay Ave. between 7th and 9th Streets in Beach Haven.

Of course a trip to Long Beach Island would not be complete without a visit to "Old Barney" which is the main attraction at **Barnegat Lighthouse State Park.** The park allows picnicking, surf fishing and a view of the panorama from the red and white 122 year old lighthouse. It only takes 217 steps to climb.

The only access to Long Beach Island is the one road, Route 72 from the mainland to the center of the island. For the **Atlantic City** area (see separate chapter) you must return to Route 9 or the Garden State Parkway.

The Cape: Ocean City to Cape May

Like Atlantic City, this last strip of coastline is considered Philadelphia's shore as well as New Jersey's. However, people from all over come to these beaches, especially Canadians. **Ocean City**, the first down the line, bills itself as America's oldest family resort. It has never allowed liquor to be sold in its environs, the beach is wide and clean and the long boardwalk is filled with stores and arcades and several amusement centers. Right now, the town is experiencing a building boom.

Among the Wildwoods, **Wildwood Crest** may have the advantage of getting the biggest family crowd but the beaches all along this area are very wide and kept quite clean despite the huge crowds that come on weekends. The surf is definitely milder down here and shallow enough for a toddler to wade a little without fear of imminent drowning. Both Wildwood and the Crest are solid motels from start to finish with guest houses and rental houses a block behind. **Wildwood** has the nightclubs, the amusement park and the swinging crowd, while the Crest is more kiddie centered (although these things change from year to year). **Stone Harbor**, to the north, is rich and quiet with lovely homes and just a few very good motels.

Twenty minutes down the coast and at the very tip of New Jersey lies **Cape May City**. Here is a beautiful Victorian town with colorful gingerbread houses and green lawns set against a placid shore. Young couples and older folks seem to love the environment here. The beach in town has received new sand, but is still a poor relation to the neighboring wide swaths. Also, automobile congestion has become a problem in town.

As mentioned earlier in this book, one center of attraction here is the "Victorian Town," a series of renovated houses, quaint boutique shops, gaslight lamps and brick walkways. The shops lining Washington Mall offer an evening's entertainment in themselves with their art & crafts.

Beyond the town, **Cape May Point Beach** offers a wide beach, the recently refurbished lighthouse (you can now go in and climb all those steps), and those little pieces of quartz known as Cape May Diamonds. And at the very tip of the county, the line begins for the **Cape May-Lewes ferry**, a three hour boat ride that takes you to Delaware the slow but pleasant way.

HIKING

There are any number of County Parks which offer both easy and more difficult hiking trails. Popular among these are the trails in the Watchung Reservation in Union County, the South Mountain Reservation in Essex County, the Lenape Trail in Nutley, the Mahlon Dickerson Reservation in Morris County. Almost all State Parks include hiking trails and you will find the complete list of State Parks at the end of the chapter. There are, furthermore, two areas of extreme interest to outdoor enthusiasts in New Jersey — the **Pine Barrens** and the **Delaware Water Gap National Recreation Area**. Both of these include or neighbor state parks.

Information on hiking trails and other events at Delaware Water Gap is available at the Kittatinny Point Station right off of Route 80 as you travel toward the Pennsylvania border. Among the many activities sponsored by the Recreation Area are: the **Peters Valley Craftsmen** — a summer place where you may watch master potters, weavers, jewelry makers, at work; the **Walpack Art Center** (basically an art gallery); and **Slateford Farm**, an 1800's farmhouse over on the Pennsylvania side. **Millbrook Village**, a restored 19th Century town is mentioned separately in this book. The **Kittatinny Point Center** is also a staging area for canoeists (who bring their own) and includes picnic area, restrooms and lots of leaflets, including hiking trail guides. Whether you hike or take the car to an outlook point, a view of the Delaware Water Gap (which is a deep gorge cut by the river between two sets of mountains) is probably the most spectacular view in New Jersey. It should not be missed.

Stokes State Forest which is right nearby in the northern section of the State includes 17 named and marked trails plus a nine-mile stretch of the Appalachian Trail that transects the area. Here you will find Tillman Ravine. The 10,000-year-old ravine is preserved exactly as it was found with a host of natural wildflowers and trees. Five bridges have been installed to gain a better perspective for the hiker. The trails here are for the more experienced hiker.

High Point State Park, also in the northwestern portion of the state offers many hiking and nature trails, including a portion of the Appalachian trail. The highest point in the park is marked with the 220 foot High Point Monument which one can climb for a view of three states.

The **Pine Barrens** offer a completely different experience. The terrain is practically flat but the flora and fauna of the region are unusual. Trails and old sand roads wind through the pines and swamps. The Batona Trail is the longest, extending from Carpenter Spring in Lebanon State Forest to Batsto in Wharton Forest, for thirty miles. Another, shorter trail in the Pine Barrens is called the Absegami. Since trails in the Pine Barrens can be confusing and people have gotten lost, it is best to start your hike at Batsto where you can talk with the Rangers at the visitor's center and obtain hiking guides.

Those interested in hiking can obtain further information by writing to the *New Jersey Division of Travel and Tourism*, P.O. Box 400, Trenton, NJ 08625. Another good place to contact, especially if you are interested in joining group hikes is: **The Sierra Club**, 360 Nassau Street, Princeton, NJ. Telephone 609-924-3141. Although this club is primarily devoted to environmental protection, their hikes and canoe trips are graded according to difficulty and led by a responsible hiker. They are very knowledgeable in the area of New Jersey trails.

FISHING

Most people think of fishing in New Jersey as off-shore fishing. Indeed, there are fleets of boats from Atlantic Highlands to Cape May, just waiting to take customers out. Party boats go out seven days a week during the summer either for half or full day excursions. They come complete with tackle, bait, food and drink although you pay for the extras, of course. These boats can handle over a hundred people and are sturdy enough to go well out into the ocean in their quest for bluefish, weakfish, tuna, fluke, and striped bass.

Charter boats are hired by groups for the day and in the busy season must be reserved weeks in advance. **Brielle**, on the Manasquan Inlet is one of the largest centers of party and charter boats in the state. Check the Sports Section of your daily newspaper (the Friday edition, especially) for the names and rates of party and charter boats. You can also write or call The NJ Division of Fish, Game and Wildlife, CN 400, Trenton, NJ 08625 (609-292-2695) for a NJ Party & Charter Boat Directory.

Fresh-water fishermen have several favorite spots in New Jersey, two of them in State Parks. **Round Valley** is deemed to have the best sport fishing with 22 species of fish, including rainbow and lake trout and largemouth and smallmouth bass. The Round Valley Reservoir is part of the State Park about one mile south of Lebanon in Hunterdon County. It was created by two dams and is stocked by the State. In **Swartswood State Park** both Big and Little Swartswood Lakes are known for their fishing quality. This is a beautiful area high in the mountains of Sussex County.

The Pine Barrens is a magnet not only for hikers but for campers and fishermen as well. The **Bass River** in the State Forest of that name, the Batsto River and many lakes and inlets are dotted with fishing camps, both public and private.

While boating ramps are available at most of these state parks you must bring your own boat along. Anyone over 14 years of age must have a license for fresh water fishing. You may buy your Fishing License at any sporting goods store.

CAMPING

New Jersey has many state parks that offer beautiful, clean and well equipped campgrounds. All you have to do to enjoy them is to bring your own camping equipment, a minimum cash entrance fee, and tote your own garbage out (a new policy - they provide the bags). Best to call the campgrounds for details (a listing of state parks can be found at the end of this chapter.)

Bass River and **Swartswood State Parks** are excellent for family outings. Camp sites are adequately sized. Facilities include flush toilets and showers, and they are kept fairly clean. Swimming, boating and picnic areas are close to the sites. At Bass River, the shallow lake allows for canoeing and paddle boating. Swartzwood Lake is good for sailing as well. Canoes, rowboats and paddle boats can be rented.

The problem with these two attractive grounds (and many other state parks) is their popularity. For good weather weekend camping, reservations are recommended. At most state parks, half of the available sites can be reserved ahead so long as you stay a minimum of two days. So if there are 70 sites, 35 can be reserved. The rest are given out on a first come-first served basis. Sites are usually $10.00 a night plus $7.00 reservation charge. Group sites can always be reserved in advance. If you try for a site during mid-week, your chances are better of just driving up and finding one.

Waywayanda and **Worthington Parks** are definitely primitive. Waywayanda is especially suitable for group camping and day trips to the beach or for fishing. The group camp sites are served by outhouses. Flush toilets and bathhouses are located by the beach. No flush toilets are to be found at Worthington on the Delaware. Outhouses or bring your own potty have to suffice. Using the port-a-potty turned out to be the best amusement of the weekend for the six-year-old son of friends who tried this spot. Located a few hundred feet from the Delaware, this large open site will appeal to those who choose to fish, raft, or canoe on the river. There is no bathing beach.

For the truly hardy, scenic **Round Valley Reservoir** offers real wilderness camping. Campers must hike or boat to the sites. The key interest here is sailing, boating and fishing. (Round Valley's popular bathing beach with its excellent facilities is in a separate part of the reservoir.) **Spruce Run**, with facilities for boating, fishing and swimming, takes camping out of the woods and puts it in the sunshine, where, in the heat of summer, it doesn't belong. Sites are on a hill and there is no shade. Again, there is a beach for swimming with the usual facilities. During summers with low rainfalls, these sites may sometimes be closed.

At all parks, (remember, Worthington has no formal facilities), swimming, boating and fishing are open daily in season for noncampers. Check the parks to learn boat limits.

Aside from the camping facilities in the State parks, you can also find hundreds of sites in the many private campgrounds around the State. The Pine Barrens and the southern portion of New Jersey abound with these camps which usually offer more sophisticated facilities than the State-run sites (higher rates too, of course). A limited number of county parks offer camping also.

PICK YOUR OWN ORCHARDS

Who would have guessed that stooping over in the hot sun and picking strawberries, blueberries, etc. would become a "bonding" experience for young families. It's also attractive to people who want to save a little money and people who want to be sure their fruits and vegetables are fresh.

Usually you buy the empty basket and then fill it up, but arrangements vary. Also weather conditions can throw off standard picking times. Most orchards are open from June until Halloween when hayrides and contests often accompany the picking. Those places that specialize in one fruit (such as blueberries) of course are open only during that season.

The best source for a list of picking farms is the Rutgers Cooperative Extension which puts out a leaflet listing them by county and giving their farm specialties.

In Burlington County, there are seven farms specializing in blueberries in Pemberton alone. The extension suggests calling first to see what is pickable at the moment, getting directions (most farms are out-a-ways) and learning prices. Most farms also have already-picked stuff for those who get tired.

Some better known farms include **Terhune's** (330 Cold Soil Road, Princeton) which offers farm animals for petting and a busy cider mill also. **Matarazzo Farms** (Route 519, Belvidere) runs a strawberry festival and a winery next door. In Monmouth County you'll find **Casola Farms** with a variety of produce and the **Berry Farm** which specializes in raspberries. Both are on Route 34 in Colts Neck very close to **Delicious Orchards** which is a gorgeous indoors market with fruits, vegetables, baked goods and candies—definitely built for the gourmet who doesn't want the thrill of picking his own. Even in crowded Bergen County, there is the **Demarest Farm** at 244 Werimus Road, Hillsdale. And Mullica Hill in southern Jersey, known for its antique shops, has several pick-your-own places.

You can get the list from Rutgers Publication Distribution Service, Cook College, Rutgers University, Dudley Road, P.O. Box 231, New Brunswick, NJ 08903-0231. Also try your local county extension agent, and newspaper and magazine listings during picking season.

ADVENTUROUS OUTINGS

For those who like to add the element of adventure to their summer activities, there are a number of options available. You don't have to live in California to surf, skydive, parachute or raft down a river. Here are a few of the places where you can jump into action:

1. Skydiving/Parachuting: If you want to learn how to skydive and parachute (well, if you expect to land safely, you had better learn both) there is an outfit in New Jersey where they teach you both in one day. You get jump training on the ground, then they take you up and out. *Contact:* **Skydive East**, Sky Manor Airport, P.O. Box 84, Pittstown, NJ 08867. They are open weekends from Mar. 1- Dec. & weekdays, June 1-Sept. 1. Closed Tues. & Wed. *Telephone:* 908-996-6262.

2. Windsurfing: All you need for this one is wind, water and a surfboard with a sail attached. Popular areas are the lakes at such state parks as Round Valley and Spruce Run. The bay side of the Jersey shore also affords windsurfing territory for experienced practitioners. Sandy Hook is popular and you can find windsurfing rentals (along with rowboats & motorboats) on Long Beach Island and other shore resorts.

3. White Water Rafting: Rafting can run the gamut from lazy tubing down the Delaware to the more exciting white water stuff on the Lehigh River in Pennsylvania. New Jerseyans who want to try the Lehigh River can use either **Whitewater Challengers** which operates out of Whitehaven, PA (Tel. 717-443-9532) or **Pocono Whitewater** in Jim Thorpe, PA, (Tel. 717-325-4097). These outfits offer guided trips (the guides accompany the rafts on kayaks) and have graded outings ranging from easy to more challenging. Call for reservations and information on what to bring and what can be rented (wet suits, etc.).

Kittatiny Canoes in Dingman's Ferry, PA, (Tel. 717-828-2338) is not only one of the biggest of the canoe renters along the Delaware River, they also offer rafting and tubing trips. Further south you can find **Point Pleasant Canoes** which offers canoeing, leisure rafting, and river tubing. They operate out of three places: Point Pleasant in Bucks County, PA (Tel. 215-297-TUBE); Upper Black Eddy, PA (Tel. 215- 982-9282); and Martins Creek Base (215-252-TUBE). Picnic facilities are available at the bases, since the amount for food and drink allowed on trips is limited.

4. Hot Air Ballooning: For those of you who want to go back in time, hot air ballooning offers fancy flights (often with champagne included) over Hunterdon, Mercer and Somerset counties. Fancy prices, too. Flights are usually at sunrise and just before sunset. Some of the outfits currently operating are: The Flight Fantastic (908-479-6850), Festival Flights (800-446-8247) and Alexandria Balloon Flights (908- 479-4878).

5. Plane Gliding: You soar in a glider (which is pulled by an airplane) over the Delaware Water Gap, the Kittatinny Ridge and other scenic areas. Good picture taking possibilities. *Contact:* Eagle Ridge Soaring, 36 Lambert Road, Blairstown Airport, Blairstown, Warren County. *Telephone:* 908-362-8311.

6. Open Cockpit Bi-Plane Ride: A professional pilot takes you up in an antique (but completely restored) bi-plane for rides over Keyport, Sandy Hook, New York Harbor etc. There is also a World War II fighter plane on hand. Located at Old Bridge Airport, Englishtown. *Telephone:* 908-446-1300.

STATE PARKS AND FORESTS

Following is a listing of the State Parks and Forests of New Jersey. Most charge a parking fee: $7.00 for weekends, $5.00, weekdays for parks with swimming facilities, $4.00 weekends, $3.00 weekdays for others. A few are actually free. This charge is only operational from Memorial Day to Labor Day. Tuesdays are free. Some of these parks with historic sites or beaches, have been mentioned in greater detail elsewhere in this book.

State Parks

ALLAIRE STATE PARK, Monmouth County — 2,620 acres. Historic Howell Works and restored Allaire Village. Picnicking, hiking, nature study, horse trails, fishing, camping, old-time narrow gauge train rides. Lively calendar of events. *Telephone:* 908-938-2371.

ALLAMUCHY MOUNTAIN STATE PARK, Warren County — hunting, camping, fishing. *Telephone:* 908-852-3790.

BARNEGAT LIGHTHOUSE STATE PARK, Ocean County — 172-foot lighthouse with 217-step spiral staircase. Picnicking, fishing. *Telephone:* 609-494-2016.

CAPE MAY POINT STATE PARK, Cape May County — fishing, picnicking, nature center and tours of lighthouse. *Telephone:* 609-884-2159.

CHEESEQUAKE STATE PARK, Middlesex County — swimming, picnicking, fishing, camping, hiking. *Telephone:* 908-566-2161.

CORSON'S INLET STATE PARK, Cape May County — small boat launch, fishing, hiking. *Telephone:* 609-861-2402.

DELAWARE & RARITAN CANAL STATE PARK, Somerset County — Kingston or Bull's Island sections. Canoeing, fishing and hiking. *Telephone:* 908-873-3050.

FORT LEE HISTORIC STATE PARK, Bergen County — spectacular view; picnicking permitted, historic sites. *Telephone:* 201-461-3956.

FORT MOTT STATE PARK, Salem County — fishing, picnicking, playground. *Telephone:* 609-935-3218.

HACKLEBARNEY STATE PARK, Morris County — picnicking, hiking, fishing. *Telephone:* 908-879-5677.

HIGH POINT STATE PARK, Sussex County — 220 ft. monument, swimming, picnicking, hiking on Appalachian Trail, fishing, camping, nature tours. *Telephone:* 201-875-4800.

HOPATCONG STATE PARK, Morris County — on Lake Hopatcong, New Jersey's largest. Picnicking, swimming, fishing, boating. *Telephone:* 201-398-7010.

ISLAND BEACH STATE PARK, Ocean County — popular beach, ocean bathing, surf fishing, picnicking, wildlife sanctuary. *Telephone:* 908-793-0506. Year round parking fee.

LIBERTY STATE PARK, Hudson County — ferry to Ellis Island and Statue of Liberty, Liberty Science Center. Picnicking, special events. *Telephone:* 201-435-8509.

MONMOUTH BATTLEGROUND STATE PARK, Monmouth County — Visitor Center, picnicking, yearly re-enactment. *Telephone:* 908-462-9619.

PARVIN STATE PARK, Salem County — campsites, bathing, boating, hiking, picnicking, fishing, cabins. *Telephone:* 609-692-7039.

RINGWOOD STATE PARK, Passaic County — historic mansions, botanic gardens, swimming, fishing, canoeing. *Telephone:* 201-962-7031.

ROUND VALLEY STATE PARK, Hunterdon County — fishing, bathing, boating, wilderness camping. Second largest "lake" in New Jersey. *Telephone:* 908-236-6355.

SPRUCE RUN, Hunterdon County — fishing, small boating, bathing and picnicking. Reservoir area. *Telephone:* 908-638-8572.

STEPHENS STATE PARK, Warren County — *Telephone:* 908-852-3790.

SWARTSWOOD STATE PARK, Sussex County — excellent fishing, boating, camping, hiking, swimming. *Telephone:* 201-383-5230.

VOORHEES STATE PARK, Hunterdon County — picnicking, camping, nature study. *Telephone:* 908-638-6969. Free.

WASHINGTON CROSSING STATE PARK, Mercer County — museums, nature center, picnicking, outdoor theater during summer. *Telephone:* 609-737-0616.

WASHINGTON ROCK STATE PARK, Somerset County — picnic facilities, views of Watchung Mountains. Free.

WAWAYANDA STATE PARK, Sussex County — fishing, boating, swimming, picnics, camping.

State Forests

ABRAM S. HEWITT STATE FOREST, Passaic County — hiking and hunting. *Telephone:* 201-853-4462.

BASS RIVER STATE FOREST, Burlington/Ocean Counties — bathing, picnicking, hiking, nature study, hunting, fishing. Cabins and campsites. *Telephone:* 609-296-1114.

BELLEPLAIN STATE FOREST, Cape May/Cumberland Counties— bathing, picnicking, camping, hunting, fishing. *Telephone:* 609-861-2404.

JENNY JUMP STATE FOREST, Warren County — picnicking, camping, nature study, hunting. *Telephone:* 908-459-4366.

LEBANON STATE FOREST, Burlington County — bathing, picnicking, hiking, hunting, camping. *Telephone:* 609-726-1191.

NORVIN GREEN STATE FOREST, Passaic County — hiking, hunting.

PENN STATE FOREST, Burlington County — bathing, picnicking, hiking, hunting, fishing.

STOKES STATE FOREST, Sussex County — bathing, picnicking, hiking, camping, fishing, hunting.

WHARTON STATE FOREST, Burlington County — bathing, camping, picnicking, fishing, boating, hiking, hunting. Batsto Historical Area. Canoeing. *Telephone:* 609-561-0024, 609-561-3262.

WORTHINGTON STATE FOREST, Sussex County — hunting, fishing, hiking, picnicking, camping. *Telephone:* 201-841-9575.

Federal

SANDY HOOK NATIONAL PARK, Monmouth County. Several beaches, bathhouses, food concessions, picknicking, lighthouse, nature center, military tours. Seasonal parking fees. *Telephone:* 908-872-0115.

KITTATINNY POINT CENTER: Visitor's center for Delaware Water Gap National Recreation Area. Hiking, canoeing, historic sites, picknicking, nature trails, etc. on both sides of Delaware. *Telephone:* 908-496-4458; 717-588-2435.

THE GARDEN VARIETY

Photos by Laslo Vasko

185

In This Chapter You Will Find:

Longwood Gardens, PA
The Duke Gardens, N.J.
Brooklyn Botanic Gardens, N.Y.
New York Botanical Gardens, N.Y.
Central Park Trolley, N.Y.
Wave Hill, N.Y.
Hershey Rose Garden, PA.
Colonial Park, N.J.
Buck Gardens, N.J.
Branch Brook Park, N.J.
Skylands, N.J.
Frelinghuysen Arboretum, N.J.
Presby Iris Gardens, N.J.
Reeves Reed Arboretum, N.J.
Leaming's Run Gardens, N.J.
Well Sweep Herb Farm, N.J.

LONGWOOD GARDENS

Without a doubt the most extensive formal gardens in the area (and considered among the best in the United States), this impressive display by the Dupont family offers an amazing variety. The gardens are open all year round and there is always something of interest whatever the weather. Altogether 350 acres are open to the public, including some beautifully laid out conservatories, so bring good walking shoes.

You enter through the main Visitor's Center which looks like a standard institutional building from the front, but like an underground house from the back — it's cleverly concealed under a hillock of green. At the Center you purchase your tickets and watch a four-minute continuous film which introduces you to the highlights of the gardens and points out seasonal displays. There's a gift shop chock full of books and plants where you'll want to stop on your way out. But for now, be sure to get the brochure guide and map at the information desk — you'll need it to find your way around. Here are some of the highlights you will probably choose:

The *Conservatories* are huge glass-enclosed rooms that surround a patio. Inside there are hanging basket mobiles sprouting flowers; stone herons in a pond surrounded by azaleas and acacias; a ballroom featuring organ concerts spring and fall; and the hot and humid Palm House with its banana, breadfruit and traveler trees. There is one room for insect-eating plants another just for orchids. The main conservatory displays change four times a year. (The Christmas display alone, with its poinsettias and line of Christmas trees, attracts more than 100,000 people a year. However, this section is closed for renovations until 1996.) An indoor *Children's Garden* nearby allows a hands-on experience for kids.

Outside, directly in front of the conservatories (and below, because you watch from the terrace) is the main water fountain area. The fountain display, with its many spouting water jets is framed by trimmed boxwood. Certain nights during the summer, colored lights and music from the *Carillion* make a spectacular *"Son et Lumiere."* There are even fireworks added to the fountain displays on special Saturday nights — these must be reserved in advance. The carillion, by the way, is beyond the fountain area in its own little romantic nook. A high cascading waterfall, a rock garden and the stone carillion tower look like something out of a 19th century painting. Further on, on this west side of the gardens are the *Idea Garden, Heaths of Heather,* the *"Eye of God"* (a low, circular water sculpture), a topiary and a rose garden.

The right side of Longwood boasts the flower walk — a sort of main drag bordered by seasonal flowers, and the open air theater — a stage surrounded by sculptured trees and using a curtain of water fountains. You will also find the *Peirce-DuPont* House, open to visitors for an extra fee. This 1730 home has had only two owners — the original Mr. Peirce, who owned the basic park from which Longwood Garden was born, and the DuPonts, who saved the property from becoming a sawmill in 1906.

Further on there are wisteria and rose gardens, forest walks and meadows, a lake with gazebo and ducks, and last of all, a complete (though miniature) *Italian Water Garden* in the manner of the Villa D'Este. Luckily there are many benches and shaded spots at which to rest along the way.

The Terrace Restaurant, located near the conservatories, offers both regular dining and cafeteria-style buffet, and a nice view. No smoking is allowed at the gardens, and no food can be brought in, but there is no prohibition on strollers and children are welcome.

> **HOURS:** Daily. April - Oct., 9-6; Nov. - Mar. 9-5. Extended hours for special events.
> **ADMISSION:** Adults: $10.00, Children: $2.00, Under 6, free.
> **LOCATION:** Route 1, Kennett Square, Pa.
> **TELEPHONE:** 610-388-1000

THE DUKE GARDENS

Open from October to May, one of New Jersey's foremost attractions, the Duke Gardens, features a series of interconnecting hothouses with an amazing variety of plants. They are part of the Duke Estate in Somerville. Indeed, from the moment you board the little van in the parking lot that takes you through a winding road you are aware you are in Rich Man's country. The administration building where you get your tickets and wait for the tour is an English style gardener's cottage replete with rich woods and carpets. From here the guide takes you across to the hothouses where you enter a different world.

Each hothouse contains a shortened version of an international garden. The layout, the flowers and the walkways are all planned to reflect the atmosphere of that particular garden. The first one you enter is the *Italian Romantic garden*. Here you find statuary amid overgrown plants, standing orchids, and the type of Mediterranean setting that threw nineteenth century poets into ecstasy.

Each garden is controlled for climate and humidity. As you move from one to the other you find yourself shedding coats and sweaters according to the climate. Enter the *Edwardian Conservatory* and it's warm. Here, in a hothouse with tropical plants such as sego palms and elephant ears, the English gentleman would propose to his lady love (or at least he did in all those old movies on late night television). He would probably clip an orchid and hand it to her. For there are enough big, fat orchids in here to send an entire graduating class to the Senior Prom.

The long *English garden*, on the other hand, is temperate. A brick walkway takes you through sedate rows of hollyhocks, primroses and manicured boxwoods. A small herb garden is here also. The *French garden* is formal, with flowers set out in greenery shaped in a fleur-de-lis pattern. Lattice work covers all, and a far statue of a goddess reminds you that this is a small version of what you might find at Versailles.

The *Chinese garden*, with its overhanging willows, stone walkway and arched bridge over a goldfish pond is for serene meditation. The scent of the fragrant tea olive permeates the air. Among the other gardens you will find an Arizona desert with succulents and tall cacti; a Japanese rustic style meditation garden; a Persian with decorated tiles and fountains; and the lush foliage of a tropical rain forest with its banana trees and large ferns.

Twenty-five gardeners attend the plantings, so the Duke Gardens changes the flowers on display often, but the overall scheme remains intact. It is a favorite destination of garden clubs, but individuals enjoy the gardens as well. Advance reservations are required however. Cameras and high heels are not permitted (you'll understand why when you walk on those arched stone bridges).

HOURS: Oct. - May, 12-4 Daily, by reservation.
ADMISSION: Adults: $5.00, Children, Seniors: $2.50, Under 6 free.
LOCATION: Route 206, south of Somerville Circle.
TELEPHONE: 908-722-3700

BROOKLYN BOTANIC GARDENS

New Jerseyans often combine a trip to these gardens with one to the Brooklyn Museum (which is right next door) since parking in the museum lot can serve for both places.

The Brooklyn Gardens are known for the cherry blossom walk — a wide swath of lawn with Japanese double blossoms, white and pink, that come out in mid-April. Another other famous display is the *Japanese Gardens* which were originally designed and built in 1914, then reconstructed in 1960. Here a pagoda rises from the calm waters. The quiet meditation walks, the willow trees and the stone turtles create a duplication of a Kyoto scene set down incongruously in the midst of urban high-rises. The latest stellar attraction at the gardens are the brilliant new conservatories which house a variety of greenhouse plants.

The Brooklyn gardens follow the natural cycles: daffodils in March, then the lilacs, then the cherry blossoms, then the wisteria and rhododendrons in May. The rose garden is fenced off and opens only in June, so it's best you visit at the time of your favorite flower.

However, there are a number of attractions that are practically seasonless — the formal prospect that greets you as you enter from Eastern Parkway, the herbal gardens, the fragrance garden, the rock garden and of course all the desert cacti and tropical trees you will find in the conservatories.

There are 50 acres to the gardens and plenty of benches to sit on and brooks to walk by. A Terrace cafe offers interesting sandwiches and drinks (it is open only in good weather) and the gift shop has a wide assortment of flower related items. The administration is fairly strict about behavior here — no picnicking, no bicycles, no dogs, no sitting on the grass (except in the Cherry Esplanade) and no children under 16 unless accompanied by adults — and there are patrols to enforce these rules. Perhaps that is why the Brooklyn Botanic Gardens has remained a verdant oasis throughout the years. Free. (Fee for Conservatories).

HOURS: Apr.-Sept.: Tues.- Fri. 8-6; Weekends and Holidays: 10-6; Sept.-Apr.: Tues.- Fri. 10-4:30; Weekends and Holidays: 10-4:30.

LOCATION: Eastern Parkway and Washington Ave., Brooklyn, N.Y.

TELEPHONE: 718-622-4433.

NEW YORK BOTANICAL GARDENS

These gardens are a disappointment to some because much of these 250 acres are in such a natural state you might as well be in Central Park. Still, the gardens contain several areas of interest to garden clubs and plants lovers.

One is the imposing museum building which contains a library of 400,000 books and journals plus a herbarium of 4,000,000 plant specimens for staff and scientists. The museum also offers a first rate shop which sells plants, garden books, tools and related items.

The large conservatories, within easy walking distance of the parking lot, have been restored to their original 1901 crystal-palace look. Several galleries include the *palm dome, Old World* and *New World* deserts, an orangerie and one acre reserved for seasonal displays of lilacs, orchids, poinsettias, etc. These conservatories may be closed for renovations in 1995.

Outside, there are many pockets of flowering displays during the spring and summer. A rose garden with a succession of blooms from June to late autumn; a herb garden; a rhododendron slope; Daffodil Hill, Azalea Glen, and a flowering rock garden with many alpine plants are scattered about the extensive acreage.

The Bronx Gardens as they are often called, have much the look of a large, well-tended city park rather than a formal garden. Since areas of interest, such as flowering displays, the pine hill and the virgin hemlock forest, occur sporadically among the many acres, be sure to arm yourself with visitor's guide. And although the gardens are across the street from the Bronx Zoo, anyone who hopes to do both in one day is either an incurable optimist or has legs of steel.

HOURS: 10-6 Tues.-Sun. & Monday holidays. Conservatory: Call.

ADMISSION: Donation to grounds. $4.00 parking lot fee. Conservatory: Adults: $3.00; Children & Seniors: $1.00. Under 6 free.

LOCATION: George Washington Bridge & Cross County Expressway east to Exit 4B, to Bronx River Parkway North. Take Bronx Zoo exit.

TELEPHONE: 718-817-8705

CENTRAL PARK TROLLEY TOUR

A most pleasant way to see Central Park — from the "inside" is to take the trolley tour that runs three times a day (warm weather only) from a kiosk near the East 60th Street entrance to the park. This one-and-a-half hour guided tour includes some walking and covers areas both inside of the park and some important buildings on the fringe.

The greatest revelation of the trip is the fact that small formal gardens exist inside the park. They are opposite the Hospital on 104th Street and Fifth Avenue (once called Flower Fifth Ave. Hospital) and include a formal French garden complete with flowering bushes and fountains, an Italian garden with pergola and an English garden. The trolley group takes a walk through these. Other stops are the Bethesda Fountain and Strawberry Fields. The latter is a quiet area dedicated to John Lennon. The former Beatle was killed in front of the Dakota — a tall, Beaux Arts apartment building directly across from the west side of the park.

The guide is full of information and you discover all sorts of statues, flowers and greenery (the topiary of King Kong behind The Tavern on the Green, for instance). You also pass the carousel, the zoo, the sheep meadow, the rink, the ramble and all the nooks and crannies that Frederick Law Olmstead built into the park.

Charming as the tour is, the people who book group tours for garden clubs and such (The Gray Line runs the actual trolley tour although the information comes from the Central Park Conservancy) can be less than charming. If you book ahead, get everything in ironclad writing. If you're in New York, just hop aboard on a nice day.

> **HOURS:** Weekdays, 10:30, 1:30, 3:30
> **ADMISSION:** Adults: $14.00
> **LOCATION:** 5th Avenue and East 60th St. entrance to Central Park.
> **TELEPHONE:** 212-360-2727 (Info) 212-397-3809 (Reservations)

WAVE HILL

A public garden located in the upper reaches of the Bronx in a quiet section called Riverdale, Wave Hill still gives the sense of a private estate filled with beauty and serenity. There are lovely vistas of the Palisades and the Hudson from the many stone benches and balustrades on the "hill". There are greenhouses filled with tropical plants and desert cacti and there are outdoor gardens devoted to herbs and seasonal flowers. A small lake and many flowering trees dot the landscape.

Two houses stand on the estate. The one called Wave Hill, now sparsely furnished was once rented to such notables as Mark Twain, Theodore Roosevelt and Arturo Toscaninni. The building is currently used for Administration offices, a gift shop and a place for groups to enjoy a luncheon. French doors lead out to a stone terrace with yet another view.

While Wave Hill was built by William Morris in 1840 it later became home to several millionaires. The gardens and conservatories, under constant restoration by horticulturists, allow the plebian tourist a feel for the ambience of a private home landscaped for leisure and gracious living. Groups, families, mothers with children and adult hikers all come to enjoy these pleasant grounds.

HOURS: Tues.-Sun. 9:30-4:30. Summer: 9:30-5:30.
ADMISSION: Weekdays free. Weekends: Adults $4.00; Seniors, students $2.00. Under 6 free.
LOCATION: E. 249 St. & Independence Ave., Riverdale. Take G.W. Bridge to Henry Hudson Parkway to Exit 21.
TELEPHONE: 718-549-2055.

HERSHEY ROSE GARDENS AND ARBORETUM

Not far from the Hershey Hotel, the Rose Garden and Arboretum began as a small 3 1/2 acre plot devoted to roses and now covers over 23 acres with flowers, trees, lakes and shrubs. Individuals take a self-guided tour through terraces of roses and past a man-made lake filled with goldfish, ducks and swans and the statue of a *Boy with a Leaking Boot*. A holly collection, one hundred varieties of herbs, rhododendrons, and evergreens are part of the display all season long. Other major flowerings are: mid-April to mid-May — daffodils, tulips and early azaleas; May 15 — June 1 — azaleas, rhododendrons, peonies. Then, from June 1 to September 15, 27,000 rose plants bearing 1200 varieties of roses are in bloom. From September 15 to November 1 — chrysanthemums. Tapes available. Picnic area and sale shop.

HOURS: Mid-April - Oct.: 9-5.
ADMISSION: Adults: $4.25; Seniors: $3.75; Children 3-15: $2.00.
LOCATION: Hershey, Pa. on Route 322.
TELEPHONE: 717-534-3492

COLONIAL PARK ROSE GARDEN

The original garden, once part of the Mettler Estate, was redeveloped and expanded by a horticulturist so that it now covers an acre and displays a wide variety of roses. 275 species, 4,000 bushes form a formal display garden which exhibits the A.A.R.S. Award Winning Roses each year. Included here are the original York and Lancaster roses, tearoses, floribunda, and more. They are all labeled to show type and date of introduction into the horticultural world. A flagstone walk makes for easy ambling.

Behind the rose garden is the *Fragrance Garden for the Blind* which provides both braille plaques and a handrail for the handicapped. Both gardens are set inside of Colonial Park, one of those beautiful county parks that one comes upon so often in New Jersey. An arboretum and meandering stream border the gardens. Beyond that there are tennis courts, paddle boats and picnic tables for family get togethers. A lilac garden and wedding gazebo are popular picture-taking spots.

Garden clubs, school classes and other groups can arrange for guided tours for a fee. Otherwise the gardens are free. Major bloomings are the first week of June and the first week of September.

HOURS: Daily, 10-8 Mem. Day - Labor Day. Then 10-4:30 to Oct. 31.
LOCATION: East Millstone, Somerset County. Take Rte 206 to 514 (Amwell Rd) then left to Mettler's Rd.
TELEPHONE: 908-873-2459.

BUCK GARDENS

Only opened to the public for a few years, Buck Gardens is quickly becoming a major attraction in Somerset County where some of New Jersey's most interesting horticulture exists.

The former estate of Leonard J. Buck, a Far Hills millionaire, the tract is informal, grassy and treed, with many rock gardens (which were Mr. Buck's specialty) along the trails. The Buck

194

mansion still stands atop a winding, hilly path but is not open for viewing. There's plenty of walking here, with stops at various benches for the vistas. Terrain varies from low lying swamp to steep hillsides. The gardens are best seen in the spring when thousands of tiny flowers peek out from designed rock formations. There are many other plantings and unusual trees plus a pleasant lake that provides the ducks with a picturesque swimming area. Pick up a walking map at the visitors station. Free.

HOURS: Mon.- Sat.: 10-4; Sun.: 12-5.
LOCATION: 11 Layton Rd., (off Rte 512) Far Hills, Somerset County.
TELEPHONE: 908-234-2677

BRANCH BROOK PARK

More than 2,000 cherry trees in bloom in the middle of April beautify this Essex County Park which stretches from Newark to neighboring Belleville. The cherry blossom area covers 2 miles in length but only about a quarter mile in width. Originally donated by Caroline Bamberger Fuld, these pink and white, single and double flowering trees now outnumber those in Washington, D.C. Many special events are planned to coincide with the cherry blossom festival, in particular, a major foot race.

TELEPHONE: 201-482-7649/6294

SKYLANDS

A popular springtime attraction is the Skylands preserve flowering around the mansion in one section of **Ringwood State Park**. A half-mile alley of crabapple trees, 400 varieties of lilacs, azaleas and peonies and a small formal garden surround the castle-like 44-room home. In the back of the house there are interesting terraced gardens with greenery and statues. Because the mansion's owner was an avid horticulturist, there is a great variety of trees and bushes as well as flowering plants. A winter garden, an octagonal garden, a lily pond, and a number of vistas make this a beautiful place all year round. Since there are only six gardeners where there once were eighty, (back in the days of the millionaire owner) it is impossible to keep all the formal gardens up to par. Designated as New Jersey's state botanical gardens. Now if only the state would put some money into them. Tours of the house are available for groups only through the Skyland Association. Public tours four days in December. For location check Ringwood Manor entry.

HOURS: Daily
PARKING: $3 Weekends, in summer.
TELEPHONE: 201-962-7031; Association: 201-962-7527

FRELINGHUYSEN ARBORETUM

Tulips, azaleas, rhododendrons, a rose garden and a wealth of flowering trees are part of the display at this 127 acre tract that was once the home of the Frelinghuysens. Cherry trees, crabapple and magnolia blossoms along with a lilac garden and a dogwood copse bring color and contrast to the many evergreens in the collection. Run by Morris County Park System. At the Administration Building there is a botanical library and a meeting room where lectures, concerts and other activities take place. A gift shop specializes in garden items and books. Free.

HOURS: Daily: 9 AM - dusk.
LOCATION: 53 E. Hanover Ave. (Route 511) Morristown, Morris County
TELEPHONE: 201-326-7600

PRESBY IRIS GARDEN

From the last week in May to the second week in June, an outstanding display of irises can be found in this lovely suburban park in Upper Montclair. Hilly terrain and gracious homes are the setting for this local park where a Mr. Presby began his iris beds many years ago. Every color in the rainbow is reflected in irises. The 4,000 varieties are planted in beds that line a long walk. Free.

HOURS: Daily. Display runs approximately 3 weeks, beginning May 24.
LOCATION: Mountainside Park, 474 Upper Mountain Ave., Upper Montclair, Essex County
TELEPHONE: 201-783-5974

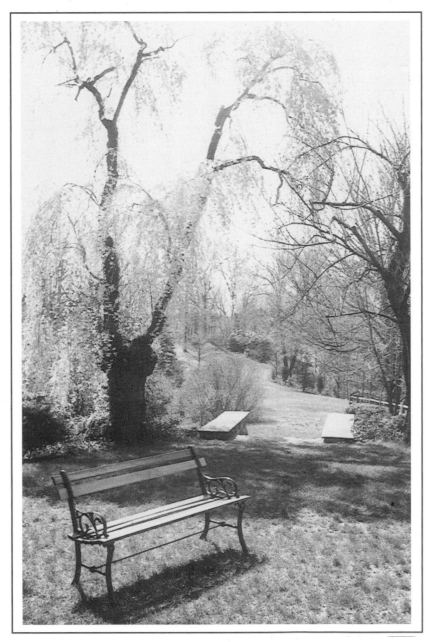

A tranquil spot in the Reeves-Reed Arboretum in Summit.

REEVES-REED ARBORETUM

A small 12 1/2 acre estate is the setting for this arboretum, hidden by tall trees on one of Summit's stately old streets. You follow a winding path down to the parking lot which has room for about fifty cars. The stone and shingle manor house on the rise above the lot was built in 1889 and is surrounded by trees, shrubs and flowering plants. But the major part of the gardens are out back, behind the house. It is rather like visiting the house of a rich old aunt and being allowed to wander through the backyard yourself.

You can follow the nature trails through oaks, maples, walnuts and beeches. The open area of this hilly site is devoted to both flower and herb gardens. A deep depression (called a kettle hole in geological terms) is the setting for a spectacular flowering of daffodils in April, followed by summer field flowers. Azaleas, rhododendrons and a small rose garden are also to be found along the walks.

The main house offers a variety of classes and free Sunday lectures. You can pick up literature there. Among the brochures is a garden guide to help identify the species in the arboretum. Free. They now have a gift shop also.

> **HOURS:** Grounds: Daily, daylight hours. Office: Mon., Tues., Thur., Fri.: 9-3.
> **LOCATION:** 165 Hobart Ave. Summit, Union County. Take Route 24 to Hobart Ave. Exit.
> **TELEPHONE:** 908-273-8787

LEAMING'S RUN GARDENS

Before the Garden State Parkway was completed, Route 9 was the only way to get to Cape May County, the southernmost section of New Jersey. When the parkway opened up, development slowed on the older Route 9. And that's just fine with Jack April, who created Leaming's Run Gardens as a bulwark of quiet woods and colorful plantings against the encroachments of motels and gasoline exhaust fumes.

This is one place that can transport you back to your childhood. Everyone has probably explored a forest at least once, felt the crackling of pine needles underfoot and heard the whipoorwill above. That's the sort of woods that covers thirty acres of sandy soil here, all interspersed with colorful gardens. You come across the gardens at a bend in the road. Many are assemblages of color. The yellow garden mixes gourds, gladiola, banana peppers and taller plants. Another garden is a medley of oranges. The English garden and reflecting pool typify a particular form. There are twenty-five gardens here, each planted to provide color and texture during the entire season from late spring to early fall.

One large area, (about an acre), is set aside for a Colonial farm. Here you will find the traditional log cabin (actually copied from the Swedish type used by early settlers in Salem County) and a fenced-in kitchen and herb garden. Beyond the farm there are other nooks and crannies — with snapdragons, pinks, a cinnamon walk and plenty of benches where you can sit and enjoy the view.

At the end of the one mile walk, you come to *"The Cooperage"*, a shop where you can buy a variety of dried flower arrangements and other gifts. There are a few rules for the gardens, by the way. No smoking, no pets, no drinks and no radios. During August, the Audubon Society conducts hummingbird tours here.

HOURS: Mid-May to mid-Oct.: 9:30-5.
ADMISSION: Adults: $4.50; Children 6-12: $1.00. Annual ticket available ($10.00).
LOCATION: Route 9, Swainton, Cape May County. Take Exit 13, GSP to Route 9, then go north one mile.
TELEPHONE: 609-465-5871

WELL SWEEP HERB FARM

A commercial herb-growing farm that is well known to buyers in the area, Well Sweep is a nicely laid out organic farm located way out in the hinterlands. Purchasers of herbs may browse the rectangular beds of rosemary and sage at any time, but special tours by the owner are reserved for groups. However, owner Cyrus Hyde does open up his farm twice a year to the general public. It is during these "Open Houses" that hundreds of people converge on Well Sweep Farm to sample homemade refreshments and watch craftsmen work. Rosemary chicken salad and herbed lemon bread are popular. But most popular of all are Mr. Hyde's lecture tours of his gardens.

Did you know that horsetail grass can be used for fine sanding? Or that tansy, planted next to the door, will keep ants away?

Want the recipe for rose geranium sugar? No wonder this tour is popular with garden clubs and other women's groups. Of course the principal activity here is growing and selling herbs so there is always a wide selection at reasonable prices.

Group tours are available to twelve people or more on a reserved basis and are given during the growing season (May-October). The Open Houses are usually on Saturday in June and September, and are free.

> **HOURS:** May-Oct.: Tues.-Sat., 9:30-5. Call before visiting. These hours are for selling herbs. Group tours must be booked.
> **LOCATION:** 317 Mt. Bethel Rd., Port Murray, Warren County.
> **TELEPHONE:** 908-852-5390

See Also: Formal gardens and landscaped lawns are often attached to the historic houses treated elsewhere in this book. For outstanding examples, see in particular, *Winterthur* (Restored and Reconstructed Villages, Homes, etc.) *Nemours, Lyndhurst,* and the *Vanderbilt Mansion* (Homes of the Rich and Famous) and *Buccleuch Mansion* (Where Washington Fought). The Hartshorn Arboretum (under "Nature Centers") should also be noted.

FLEA MARKETS AND OUTLETS

Photo by Linda Kimler

In This Chapter You Will Find:

OUTLETS

Reading, PA
Flemington, N.J. Outlets
Secaucus, N.J. Outlets
Woodbury Common, N.Y.
Franklin Mills Mall, PA
Other Outlets

FLEA MARKETS

Englishtown Auction Sales, N.J.
Chester, N.J.
Lambertville, N.J.
Rice's Flea Market, PA
Columbus Flea Market, N.J.
Other Flea Markets, N.J.
Antique Centers, N.J.
Indoor Markets, N.J.

READING, PENNSYLVANIA

Reading is the grandaddy of outlet towns. It was here that someone decided to take old factory buildings and turn them into stores that would sell direct to the customer. For years people would drive from all over to get these manufacturer's goods at 50% off.

Nowadays, with outlets all over the place, Reading has lost some of its draw. Still the busses and cars come and and some real bargains can be found. Things have changed over the years — most outlets now take charge cards (take your checkbook along, just in case) and there are several decent eating places around, and many of the shops are discount rather than outlet.

The original — **The Reading Outlet Center** is now a series of buildings, some of them the old factory, red brick variety, some new, white and modern. Building No. 1, the biggest is on Windsor St. between N. 9th and Moss. Building #2 is across the street, while Building #3 is cattycornered to #1. If you walk down N. 9th Street past Douglass and Oley you will pass Buildings Nos. 5 & 6 and later, Nos. 4 & 7 plus the Rawlings Building.

Each of these buildings is divided into rooms (some warehouse size, some small) with different outlets in each room. In Building #1, for instance, you'll find Bugle Boy, Polo, Coach, Joan & David, London Fog, Izod/Gant, Totes, etc. — and that's all just on one floor. There are two more floors of this. Buildings with later numbers are smaller and more modern.

Other popular stops in Reading are **David Crystal** (known for Izod LaCoste savings) at 13th and Rosemont Boulevard. **Heisters Lane Outlet**, the **Four Square Outlet**, and the **Burlington Coat Factory Warehouse** are all close together at Heister's Lane and Kutztown Road.

But most popular of all is the **VF Outlet** (at 801 Hill Ave.). This is a series of huge buildings which store racks and racks of Vanity Fair robes and nightgowns at half-price plus a whole lot of other goods. The complex is surrounded by gates and parking lots (with preferred parking going to the tour busses). Those companies owned by VF (Lee jeans, Jantzen sportswear, Healthtex) go for the straight 50% off (although styles may be limited.) Other renters in the complex may be discount houses with prices anywhere from 10% to 40% off.

Reading China and Glass takes up one whole building in the complex, while VF-Lee Jeans take up two connected buildings. The various buildings have colored flags and are designated as the Blue Building, the Red, the Purple, etc. That's so you don't get lost in the shopping canyons forever, and can find a landmark for your bus or car. It's worth checking out the nooks and crannies of these buildings, for shoes, silver, whatever. I particularly like the bargains at American Tourister in the basement of the Brown Building.

On heavy shopping days at the VF Outlet you may have to park blocks away and take a shuttle to the buildings.

HOURS: Most stores open Mon. - Sat., 9:30-5:30 or 9:30 and Sun. 12-5 (except Jan. & Feb.)
LOCATION: Rte. 78 to US 222 to 422W to Reading, Pa. VF Outlet is on Park & Hall Roads, Wyomissing.
TELEPHONE: 215-373-5495; VF: 800-772-8336.

FLEMINGTON OUTLETS

Flemington is a pretty Victorian town in the middle of Hunterdon County, an area that is still partially farmland. Over the years Flemington has grown from a town that offered a few discount shops to a name that has become synonomous for outlet shopping.

If you're driving down Route 202 from the north, the first outlet you see is **Dansk**, which is on the Flemington Circle itself. This building includes Dansk modern design items, Gorham Silver and other stores. If you proceed onto Route 12 and then to Main Street, you will find several shops including **Mikasa** (#95) and **Flemington Glass** (#156) and a number of nice lunchtime restaurants. Flemington Glass has sprouted annexes like crazy so you can find not only glass but pewterware and dinnerware also.

Next stop is **Liberty Village** (follow signs — it has a huge parking lot behind the railroad tracks). Liberty Village, started out in the 1970s as a restored colonial village, but converted into an outlet center years ago. The white clapboard buildings and brick walkways lend a pleasant air to the job of bargain hunting.

If the ambience is pleasant, the prices are higher these days. And although there are now 65 stores, the size of some seem to have shrunk. At the Van Heusen outlet, for instance, men's jackets were once available at good discounts. Now, the jackets have gone and it's down to shirts and ties. Which is not to say you can't find bargains anymore. Just that they won't be much different from department store sale prices. Hanes, Villeroy and Boch, and Corning offer a wide selection at discounts of 20% to 40%.

Next to Liberty Village is a small modern, enclosed mall called **Feed Mill Plaza**. Not only does it have drinking fountains, ladies rooms, air conditioning and a small sandwich shop — it has a few good stores as well. There are several clothing stores — including Cocoon, Barbizon and Izod/Gant. But it's the Oneida Factory Outlet upstairs that seems to have the best bargains — especially at holiday sales.

South of the Flemington Circle on Route 202/31 you pass yet another discount mall — this one called **Circle Outlet Center**. It contains another 16 stores, including chains like Bed, Bath and Beyond, Shoe-Town and Dress Barn.

Much of Flemington's uniqueness has gone by the wayside, as discount stores open up everywhere and outlets prices edge upward. But when it comes to pleasant surroundings and good, reasonably priced restaurants, Flemington, particularly around the Main Street and Liberty Village areas, certainly takes the prize. However, don't be surprised if some of your old favorites have closed or moved elsewhere.

LOCATION: Route 78 to 31 south, or Route 202. From Flemington Circle follow signs for "business district."
TELEPHONE: 908-806-8165; Liberty Village: 800-345-0010.

SECAUCUS OUTLETS

Set in one of the busiest areas of New Jersey, just the other side of the Meadowlands Sport Complex, the outlets here are dispersed over a huge area in between warehouses, office buildings, streets and flat open spaces. You will definitely need a map. Fortunately you can pick one up at the first outlet mall you hit **(Outlets at the Cove)** which is conveniently placed on Meadowlands Parkway. This small enclosed mall features air-conditioning, clean rest-rooms, and designer outlets such as Harve Bernard and Calvin Klein. At one of the stores here you can pick up a Secaucus booklet which not only includes a map but often offers discount coupons as well.

As you progress further to streets with names like Enterprise Avenue and Hartz Way, you will find the large outlet stores devoted to a single name which has made this complex so popular. Mikasa China and Glassware and Liz Claiborne have their own building, chock full of merchandise at 20% to 30% discount. Of course if you hit a sale you will get even further reductions, and many people put themselves on the mailing list to take advantage of sales. You will also find a number of discount chains (such as Linens 'N Things) in the complex. Syms Clothing (of TV commercial fame) takes up a full square block.

The **Harmon Cove Outlet Center** (20 Enterprise North) is a large enclosed mall with a variety of discount shops of varying value. But it also contains a food court ringed by food counters where you can rest your feet and partake of pizza, chicken, ice cream and other examples of fast food. And there's another small enclosed mall, the **Designer Outlet Gallery** at 55 Hartz Way, which includes designers with "names" like Anne Klein, Adolfo, Jonathan Martin, etc. If you check your map and drive back onto the Meadowlands Parkway above the Route 3 entrance, you'll find the **Swan Plaza**, a small strip mall that includes a delicatessen, Group USA Apparel, and best of all, a rather good Corningware outlet.

You'll also have to get in your car and drive all the way down Meadowlands Parkway to get to the **Castle Road Outlet Center**. This is a street full of individual stores, side by side, so walking is no problem once you've parked. You'll find a bunch of shoe stores down here, (including the ubiquitous Marty's), plus Flemington Fashions (plus and petite), and Passport Foods. There's a restaurant and kid's arcade on the street also.

Although the drive to Secaucus and the hunting for bargains can be exhausting, once you have found the store that fits your needs, or carries the name brand you usually buy, the trip is certainly worth it. And if you wait for the special warehouse sales (Mikasa has one, twice a year) you can stock up like crazy on all your presents.

HOURS: 7 days a week. Individual stores vary.
LOCATION: Secaucus. Take NJ Tpke to Exit 16W to Route 3 East to Meadowlands Parkway.
TELEPHONE: 201-348-4780

WOODBURY COMMON

For people who live in the northeastern section of New Jersey, this is a popular shopping stop. It's in New York State so you don't get the advantage of "no sales tax on clothes" that you do in New Jersey and Pennsylvania. However, the environs are pleasant (it's set up somewhat like Liberty Village, only larger) and all the shops are within walking distance - if you wear good shoes. Buildings are set up to look like New England houses built around a "common". None of them are too high or imposing.

There are 150 Outlet stores at Woodbury plus a number of eating places. Besides the usual line-up of outlets (Mikasa, Hanes, etc.) you can find the popular Jessica McClintock clothes and a Christian Dior outlet. One unusual place is The Ribbon Outlet which specializes in spools of the stuff. The Common also offers weekend special events such as a craft show in June. A farmers market with fresh produce and bakery items can be found near the Mark Cross outlet. Most stores open daily. May be reduced winter hours.

LOCATION: Route 32, Central Valley, NY, Exit 131, Route 17 at Harriman, (Exit 16 off NYS Thruway.
TELEPHONE: 914-928-4000.

FRANKLIN MILLS MALL

While many outlet centers evolved from nearby factories or the conversion of unused buildings, Franklin Mills is a huge, super-planned, hi-tech mall designed as a magnet for shoppers from Philadelphia and New Jersey. It combines the convenience of an indoor mall with the bargain prices of discount stores and outlets.

Inside the 1.8 million square foot complex, you will find hundreds of stores, food courts (this is a square of tables ringed by numerous fast food eateries), plus entertainment and resting courts. Each corner of the huge complex is anchored by a department store outlet — Sears, J.C. Penney's, etc. There was even an amusement complex for teenagers inside the mall, but it seems to have died — only a few arcade games still exist. Each section of the mall is color coded and everything is on one level. The planners seem to have thought of everything, except, (since they undoubtedly were men) enough ladies rooms!

Some of the best prices here are found at the department store outlets. Many of the bargains are clearly marked seconds, but if you're looking for bargain sheets for the guest room or curtains for the basement - this is the place. You can also find a Levi Strauss outlet in the mall plus chain discount shops such as Marshalls and Flemington Fashion among the many clothing stores.

Babysitting is available but serious shoppers who come from afar may find it easier to leave the kids at home and simply lose themselves among the inlets and outlets of this futuristic mall.

HOURS: Mon.-Sat.: 10-9:30. Sun.: 11-6.
LOCATION: Northeast Philadelphia. Take I-95 to Woodhaven Road Exit, turn right onto Franklin Mills Blvd.
TELEPHONE: 215-632-1500; 800-336-MALL.

OTHER OUTLETS

Close to the Jersey shore, the **Circle Factory Outlet Center** in Manasquan (just off Route 35) offers a smattering of outlets including Corning Ware, Mikasa, and Chaus. And in the northern part of the state, in Sussex County, you can find **Olde Lafayette Village** where Routes 15 and 94 meet just below the town of Lafayette. This "village" is half-and-half with colonial style attached buildings featuring bridal shops and fudge emporiums rubbing elbows with such outlet regulars as Corning Ware, Cape Isle Knitters and Van Heusen. Call 201-383-8323 for information.

Princeton Forrestal Village, at the juncture of Route 1 and College Road West is a newcomer to the outlet scene. This started out in the '80s as a yuppie mall with all sorts of boutiques and gourmets shops. Well, here it is the '90s, and there are over 35 outlets in there, including many regulars plus WestPoint Pepperell, Lady Leslie and some designer fashions. *Telephone:* 609-799-7400.

Besides these outlet "centers" there are individual outlets all over the state. For instance, **The China Outlet** at 443 Shore Road in Somers Point, Atlantic County, has a nice selection of china, crystal and kitchen gadgets at good discount. Check your local newspapers for these. Also check newspapers for once in-a-while warehouse sales at such places as Lenox China in Cranbury and department store warehouses.

FLEA MARKETS

The term supposedly originated in the Middle Ages when peddlers gathered at the marketplace to sell old clothing and assorted junk which came already infested with fleas. Nowadays the term covers a wide variety of sales, none of which have anything to do with insects. At Flea Markets you might find:

1. New merchandise from manufacturers overruns or seconds. Some "Flea Markets," such as the one outside of New Brunswick on Route One, are almost completely new merchandise. They are housed inside of defunct supermarkets or chain stores and the same dealers remain there all year round.

2. Antique and collectibles dealers. Both indoor and outdoor markets create a buying and selling arena for dealers of older merchandise. Traditionally, antiques must be 100 years old to be considered such and pieces dated before 1840 (the watershed date for the Industrial Revolution) are counted more valuable. Collectibles, on the other hand, include fairly recent items that have been discontinued or are considered desirable. Bubble gum trading cards, old postcards, Avon bottles, Depression glass enter this category. Prices vary drastically according to what's in and what's out.

3. Garage sale items. Since many outdoor flea markets rent their tables for the day and often for as little as 6 dollars, it is not unusual for local people to simply hold their garage sales at a popular market. Anything goes here!

4. Craft dealers. Generally craft people do better at Craft Fairs than at flea markets, since bargain hunters balk at the prices for new, hand-made items. However, at certain flea markets you might find someone selling seashell decorations or duck decoys, especially if the dealer has staked out this territory for himself.

5. Farmer's markets. Especially in Monmouth and Ocean Counties, summer markets include a food section where fresh corn, watermelons, beans and squash are on hand.

6. Antique centers. Sometimes they are near a flea market; other times they are in the center of town; but an Antique Center can be a barn, a mall, a house, a reconverted factory. Inside the structure, you find a series of rooms, stalls, niches or even huge quarters rented by individual dealers. Some centers are collectives. More often one dealer owns the building while the others rent.

THE ENGLISHTOWN AUCTION SALES

It is one of the world's largest flea markets—this vast dusty field set in the midst of Monmouth County's farm country. However, the term "flea market" is changing these days and anyone expecting acres of antiques on sale will be disappointed.

Right now, Englishtown Auction Sales consists of about 70 percent dealers in new discount merchandise and 30 percent dealers in collectibles. What you find is something like 300 garage sales going on side by side with 700 New York street hawkers all set up on tables covering a huge field. Add to that a farmer's market with tables of fresh corn, tomatoes, melons, apples and pumpkins. And then add several buildings filled with discount clothing booths, kielbasa stands, knish stands, booths selling hot dogs, hamburgers and oriental food and a complete bar and grill. Then add a cast of thousands worthy of a Cecil B. DeMille movie and you have some idea of the immensity of the place. In fact, Englishtown Auction Sales has everything but an auction — that term refers to the old days when cows were sold off too.

The Flea Market is open weekends only, but traditionally the day for "antique" bargains is Saturday, the earlier the better. The market actually opens early. However, chances of your finding the missing teapot to Catherine the Great's silver tea service is about the same as your chance of hitting the jackpot at Atlantic City. Even less. What you will find is a mass of memorabilia, knick-knacks, new shoes and old tires — practically anything in the world can be discovered here. A new bell for your bicycle, a collection of porcelain doorknobs, a reproduced stone plaque or garage sale "junque" all mixed in with bargain basement clothing and cosmetics.

Those who search for collectibles can certainly find something of interest. Depression glass, comic books, paper-weights and German World War I helmets and medals were some that I noticed the day I visited. More collectibles (along with food stands) can be found in the buildings called Red, Green, Blue and Brown.

Englishtown Auction Sales offers you a chance to buy that elusive whatnot you could never find anywhere else. Perhaps it will be a kitchen sink faucet or a car seat cover that's just right, a beat-up plant-stand or the missing Avon bottle to your set. A craft table pops up here and there also.

Outdoor tables in seasonable weather (well into fall). Lots of dust and dirt so dress appropriately. And they charge extra for parking.

HOURS: Sat.: 7 AM - 5 PM. Sun.: 9 AM - 5 PM all year.
LOCATION: Garden State Parkway to Exit 123. Route 9 South to Texas Road. Right on Texas Road to Route 527 for 3 miles to 90 Wilson Ave., Englishtown, Monmouth County.
TELEPHONE: 908-446-9644

CHESTER FLEA MARKET AND ANTIQUE STORES

Chester tried to be a quaint Revolutionary town for years, but what finally put it on the map was the Chester Flea Market. Run by the Lions Club in a field right outside the main hub of town, the Flea Market brought thousands of visitors every Sunday. Now that the land where the market used to stand has been sold, the Chester Flea Market has moved to Dover. I guess in a few years it will be called the Dover Flea Market.

Anyway, the vendors now sell their wares from stands on Main Street. One advantage of the change in venue is that you can now take the train on Sundays to Dover and walk from the station. The traffic in Chester on a Sunday used to be terrible.

Vendors here tend to book for the whole season, so there is some stability. Hot dogs and funnel cakes are available for snacking. Don't expect to find high quality antiques but there is a nice assortment of souvenir type collectibles, baseball cards and towels.

As for the town of Chester: a combination of specialty boutiques and antique shops has the streets bustling here in spring and summer. On East Main Street, stores with cutesy names like *Karen's Koop* and the *Country Mouse* offer a mix of antiques, quilts, coverlets, cookware, etc. An English tea shop and a few lunch places are nestled between antique stores with names like *Aunt Pittypat's Parlour*. The town center is on Route 510 near Route 206.

HOURS: (For Flea Market): Sundays only, May - Nov.
TELEPHONE: 800-555-6263

LAMBERTVILLE

Lambertville is another town that has benefited greatly from the presence of flea markets. Over the years it has become a genuine antique center. For years, Lambertville looked like a poor relation of its neighbor across the river, New Hope. But now the antique shops have brought a certain panache to this old canal town. New buildings along the river and reburbished row houses in town offer art stores, restaurants and second hand shops galore. Both Bridge Street, the main thoroughfare through town, and Union Street have a number of specialty antique stores worth looking at. And The *People's Store*, in this area, offers many interesting dealers under one huge roof.

As for flea markets, they are located outside of town, on Route 29 going south. This is where you will find both the *Lambertville Antique Market* and *Golden Nugget Antiques* side by side on warm weather weekends. The indoor sections of the market are extensive and some carry rather nice 19th Century items. The indoor part is open all year round, while the outdoor tables only last as long as the weather is good. One nice thing about the Lambertville market is there is hardly any new merchandise, so you do not have to contend with tables of jeans and sneakers. The outdoor tables have a variety of collectibles and garage sale type plates and jewelry.

If you cross the river, drive past New Hope and meet Route 202, then continue to **Lahaska**, you find a number of antique stores along the way. But the flea market at Lahaska has been replaced by a new outlet mart called **Penn's Purchase**.

> **LOCATION:** Lambertville: Rtes. 179 & 29, Hunterdon County. Lahaska: Route 202, Pa. 4 miles west of New Hope.

RICE'S FLEA MARKET

If it's Tuesday, it must be Rice's. That's the day this flea market comes to life on a flat field set on a back road near New Hope. Recently they've opened on summer Saturdays too.

Officially named Rice's Country Market and Auction, it has a reputation for quality. To the neophyte it doesn't look much different than any other flea market. In fact, many of the vendors who set up tables here on Tuesday can be found at other flea markets other days of the week.

The main virtue of Rice's seems to be its size. Although the dirt field where it is held is huge, getting past all the tables is not unmanageable. You can actually walk the whole market in a morning and get a chance to peruse all the bargains. Get there early — by 1 PM most vendors are packing up.

You can find specialty items here — one vendor sells only Guatamalan handmade goods; another specializes in ribbons and laces. There may be several booths of patterned sweaters. But the most common items tend to be college sweatshirts at reduced prices, tube socks, Chanel scarves at ten or twelve dollars, and some brand name toiletries.

Indoor stands sell coffee, bagels, doughnuts and Funnel Cakes (giant, intricately designed crullers with powdered sugar on top). There are also a few merchandise vendors inside the small buildings, but this is primarily an outdoor flea market. No real place for lunch — there are some hot dog vendors, plus locals with fresh bread and fresh produce.

As for toilets — there are none. Porta-potties are set out in the field.

HOURS: Every Tues., some holidays and Saturdays.
LOCATION: Route 202 to Aquetong, right to Green Hill Road, then another right.
TELEPHONE: 215-297-5993

COLUMBUS FLEA MARKET

This started out as a farmer's market and just grew and grew. Thursdays, Saturdays and Sundays are the days - from dawn until 2 p.m. with rows and rows of tables filled with pocketbooks, sweatshirts, sweaters, scarves, crazy items, knockoff perfumes, etc. It's also a traditional farmer's market with fresh produce brought in from the neighboring countryside. There is also the traditional big yard sale, with people selling used "garage sale" style items next to hawkers of new merchandise.

The indoor buildings include many permanent "niche" stores plus a number of eating spots (hamburgers, bagels, etc.) In one of the buildings you can also find several Pennsylvania Dutch delicatessen counters where you can buy Amish style cold cuts and breads and fresh grown produce. Don't be surprised to find furniture and other large items in the indoor sections, which are open Fridays also.

LOCATION: Route 206, just below Columbus, Burlington County.
TELEPHONE: 609-267-0400

OTHER FLEA MARKETS

NEW EGYPT MARKET: Again, a mix of old and new, with everything from foundry type to bicycle parts available. There are inside buildings which, though old, host plenty of dealers and in good weather over 50 outside tables are filled with garage sale items. Once in a while a real "find" is discovered among the junque. Antique day is Sunday when the market opens at 7 AM. Auctions at 1 PM Sunday. Open Sunday and Wednesday. New Egypt is located 6 miles west of Great Adventure in Ocean County (take Route 528). *Telephone:* 609-758-7440.

GREAT AMERICAN FLEA MARKET: Another popular market that attracts large crowds and bus tours. Now in a new building. Open all year on Friday, Saturday and Sunday. Located on Route 9, Howell, Monmouth County, between Freehold and Lakewood. *Telephone:* 908-367-1105.

BERLIN FARMERS MARKET AND SHOPPING CENTER: Traditional Jersey truck farm produce plus flea market mix. Indoor market houses over 85 stores, while the outdoor 70 spaces include new merchandise, flowers, shrubs, tools, garage sale stuff, etc. Services Camden County area. Located at 41 Clementon Road, Berlin, (on Route 30 between Atco and Voorhees). Runs Thurs.-Sun. 7 AM on. *Telephone:* 609-767-1284.

NESHANIC FLEA MARKET: Neshanic Station, Somerset County. This was considered very good, then dropped out of sight for a while. It is operating again on Sunday only, but call first. Antiques, collectibles. *Telephone:* 908-369-3660.

MEYERSVILLE GRANGE FLEA MARKET: A change of pace since this market is indoors and runs only in the cold weather. The building is tiny, but there are almost 30 tables inside. Glassware, china, urns, posters and one or two craft tables that feature duck decoys or handmade quilts. On Meyersville Road, Passaic Twp., Morris County. Sundays only, Oct. - May. *Telephone:* 201-832-7422.

Note: Flea market hours constantly change. Always telephone first.

ANTIQUE CENTERS

For those who do not relish the trudge through the dusty fields, there are plenty of antique stores and centers where you may browse in comfort — even air-conditioned comfort. There are over two thousand antique stores in New Jersey alone. Here is a short run-down on some of the better known centers.

The Antique Center at **Red Bank** hosts about 100 dealers in four large buildings within walking distance of one another. The shops are open daily from 11-5 and are located on Front Street and the 200s block. Take Garden State Parkway to Route 109, Monmouth County.

The Antique Mall in the Chestnut Ride Shopping Center, 30 Ridge Road, **Montvale**, in northern New Jersey has a collection of quality shops in comfortable surroundings. Take Exit 172 from Garden State Parkway.

A small enclave in north Jersey is *The Mill Market* in the quaint town of **Lafayette**, Sussex County. Forty dealers run a cooperative effort in a reconverted 1842 mill. The mill is on Route 15 in the center of town next to an old-fashioned General Store and is open Friday to Monday only. There are other interesting antique shops in Lafayette also. Both Sparta and Andover are other Sussex County towns with a good collection of antique stores.

Hunterdon and Somerset counties have a gaggle of loosely strung out country-store type antique marts. Some of these are individual dealers and some are centers that include over a dozen dealers. A few of the well-known names are: *Whitehouse Manor Antiques Center*, Route 22 West, **Whitehouse Station**, *Kitchen Caboodle* in **Mountainville**, Tewksbury Township, *Melody Cottage* in nearby **Oldwick**, *River Edge Farm, Smoke House* and *Yesterday's Barn Antiques* in **North Branch**, Somerset County and *Country Antiques* in **Pluckemin**. The town of **Summit** has several good antique stores such as *Kane Galleries* plus the *Summit Antique Center* open Friday to Sunday.

In southern Jersey the village of **Mullica Hill** has long attracted antique buyers to shops with quaint names like *The Eagles Nest, King's Row Antiques* and *Farm House Antiques* on Main Street. And visitors to the shore can always find antique shops open during the season, from *The Pink House Antiques* in **Cape May** to several shops on **Long Beach Island** that specialize in nautical antiques. One of the largest enclaves in the state is at the *Point Pleasant Antique Emporium* at Bay and Trenton Aves. at the shore resort. One hundred dealers, under one roof, offer furniture, quilts, dolls and collectibles, all in a beautiful air-conditioned building in the center of town. And close to Atlantic City in the Historic Towne of **Smithville**, the large antique filled building that once housed the Quail Hill Inn is now a genuine antique center with lots of good quality furniture and smaller pieces.

As I mentioned several pages before, towns like **Chester** and **Lambertville** have a full complement of antique and specialty stores besides their well-known flea markets. For neophytes, the best way to track down the antique marts is to pick up a copy of one of those free antique newspapers at the local flea market or antique dealer.

And don't forget all the antique fairs that go on from spring to fall in all the restored villages and indoor malls. The biggest one is at the **Atlantic City Convention Center** (it bills itself as the largest in North America.) One thousand dealers on 7 1/2 acres, all indoors. It takes place late in March.

INDOOR MARKETS

This is a growing group of markets that is fast taking over a big share of the bargain hunters brigade. Huge indoor marts, usually abandoned supermarkets, are divided into hundreds of stalls where entrepreneurs sell everything from bells to belts. Instead of *Two Guys* you get three hundred guys all touting discount merchandise. Market days are Friday, Saturday and Sunday.

The best known is probably the U.S. *#1 Flea Market and Antiques* situated on Route #1, New Brunswick (Telephone: 201-846-0900). This one still attempts to have an antique and collectible section. Another biggie is the *Route 18 Indoor Market*, 290 Route 18, East Brunswick (Telephone: 201-254-5080) which is almost completely new merchandise. *The Union Market*, Springfield Ave., Union, is an example of this new type of market where the fleas have all but disappeared from the flea market scene.

OTHER OUTINGS

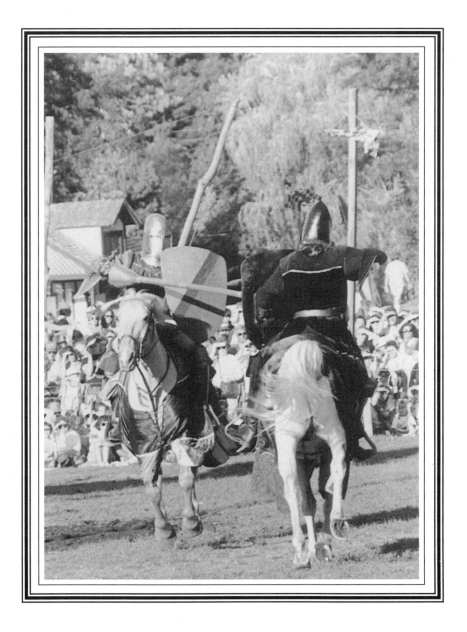

Photo: N.Y. Renaissance Festival

In This Chapter You Will Find:

Planetariums, N.J.
School Tours, N.J.
U.S.S. Ling Submarine, N.J.
Miniature Kingdom, N.J.
Sterling Hill Mine
Excursion Railroads
Excursion Boats
Twin Lights Lighthouse, N.J.
Bushkill Falls, PA
Renaissance Festival, N.Y.
Medieval Times, N.J.
Culinary Institute of America, N.Y.
Renault Winery, N.J.
Other Area Wineries
The Meadowlands, N.J.
Other Racetracks & Rodeos
Other N.J. Arenas and Auditoriums

PLANETARIUMS (NEW JERSEY)

Aside from the planetariums you find within major museums, (such as The American Museum of Natural History, the Newark Museum, etc.) there are a number of places star-seeking New Jerseyans can visit for sky programs. Children under six are sometimes not admitted to programs for good reason — once those doors shut in darkness, there is no escape. Luckily, many planetariums feature special "Stars for Tots" shows. Here's what is available.

OCEAN COUNTY COLLEGE: College Drive, Toms River. Robert J. Novins Planetarium. Outside the main hurly-burly of Toms River on a large campus, this planetarium not only schedules public shows all year round but has a special astronomy curriculum for school grades 1-6 during the public school year. (And this attracts students from outside counties as well.) Public shows are well attended. They do shut down every once in a while to prepare a new show, (although *not* when the college does) so call first. The planetarium holds 117 people and is quite modern. *Admission:* Adults $4.50; Children and students: $3.00. Under 6 not admitted except for special "tot" shows. *Telephone:* 908-255-0342.

TRAILSIDE PLANETARIUM: Coles Avenue and New Providence Road in Mountainside, Union County. Part of the Watchung Reservation's Trailside Nature and Science Center, this simple "down home" building is worth tracking down (it's just down the hill from the big Nature Center). Although it seats only 35 people, it is rarely overfilled and offers the same slide presentations, manufactured by a scientific company, that you see anywhere else, plus their own local star show. Sundays at 2 and 3:30 pm. Weekly after-school shows for groups — such as scouts — who reserve in advance. *Admission:* $2.00. *Telephone:* 908-789-3670.

RARITAN VALLEY COLLEGE: Lamington Road and Rte. 28, North Branch, Somerset County. The newest planetarium in New Jersey seats 100 people. Many school shows plus public showings on Saturdays at 1, 2 & 3 p.m. Special pre-school shows. Uses both the "canned" slide shows, and their own give -and -take lecture style sky show. Reservations required. *Admission:* $4.50. *Telephone:* 908-231-8805.

MORRIS COUNTY COLLEGE: Route 10 & Center Grove Road, Randolph. This automated 80-seat planetarium offers not only several programs to the local citizenry but also courses for those who really want to delve into the subject. Shows for school and scout groups are scheduled during the week and early Saturday. Public showings are every other Sat. evening while the college is in session. Reservations suggested. *Admission:* Adults: $5.00; Seniors, students: $4.00; Children: $3.00. *Telephone:* 201-328-5076.

SCHOOL TOURS

Almost any museum, zoo, historic house or park mentioned in this book is open to reserved guided tours for school groups, scout groups and members of adult schools. Here are a few more places, popular with school groups, that did not fit in the above-mentioned categories:

NEW JERSEY STATE HOUSE: Now that the long-term renovation is finished, the gold-domed State House is open for all tours. A standard trip for grade-school children, and one that is worth taking for adults also. Contact: School Reservation Service, N.J. State Museum, 205 W. State St., Trenton, N.J. 08625. *Telephone:* 609-292-6347.

ST. HUBERT'S GIRALDA: An animal shelter set up by Mrs. Geraldine Rockefeller Dodge which still has its quarters on the Dodge Estate. The education program for schools and scout groups includes movies, slides, handouts and a tour of the kennels. There are 16 different program that range from pre-school to eighth grade. Free. Location: Woodland Road, Madison, Morris County. *Telephone:* 201-377-2295.

THE U.S.S. LING SUBMARINE

The U.S.S. Ling is only 312 feet long and 27 feet wide, and when you consider that ninety-five men and twenty-four torpedoes were aboard during its short career as an active sub in 1945, you realize that this is no place for someone with claustrophobia. Nowadays, most of the torpedoes and many of the berths have been removed to allow for tour groups to move about. Indeed the inside seems surprisingly spacious compared with the outside.

Tickets are bought at the outside trailer museum which also houses lots of war pictures and paraphernalia — including the periscope of a Japanese sub. Tours leave about every 15 minutes and last about 45 minutes, depending on your guide.

You begin in the torpedo room where there are still two of these sleek weapons left. (No, they are not active). I learned that torpedoes do not go off by accident since they are activated only after they leave the tube. They also had to be aimed right, since a miss would give away the sub's position to an enemy ship.

I also learned that much of the time on the sub was devoted to eating and cooking. Besides three meals a day and night for all shifts, sailors could raid the refrigerator at any time. When the Ling first left port, space was so dear that fresh fruit and vegetables were stacked in one of the showerheads.

Since it was hot and cramped in the sub, showers were popular, as was Lifebuoy soap. And a huge laundry room throbbed night and day, cleaning the sailor's clothes. Smoking was allowed, surprisingly, until the air became so stale that the cigarette would not light.

Tours include the Control Room, Maneuvering Room, Main Engine Room, sleeping quarters and more; but the Conning Tower with its periscope is off limits. You are allowed to handle certain equipment, including the wheels and gauges, and the guide does sound the diving signal (memorable from a host of old war movies starring Cary Grant and John Garfield).

While modern submarines are larger and sleeker, this black, fleet-type vessel is a memorial to the World War II submariners who must have been a hardy lot. An interesting place, both for older children and ex-servicemen. Birthday parties, too.

> **HOURS:** Wed.-Sun.: 10-4
> **ADMISSION:** Adults $3.00, Children: $2.00
> **LOCATION:** Court & River Streets, Hackensack
> **TELEPHONE:** 201-342-3268

MINIATURE KINGDOM

When you approach this white concrete structure with its flags flying, you tend to expect an amusement park for children. Instead, what you find, once you enter the huge dimly lit room of the "kingdom", is a world of Lilliputian replicas of castles and harbors. For these are scale models of some of Europe's most famous landmarks.

Among the more spectacular exhibits is the shining white castle of Mad Ludwig of Bavaria, the major buildings and churches of the Kremlin, a German Festhaus, and a complete replica of an 11th Century fortress under seige. There are almost 10,000 miniature hand-painted hyacinths in one Dutch scene and thousands of cheeses in another. A model railroad chugs around the exhibits and serves to keep children interested while their parents explore the nooks and crannies of these miniature architectural wonders.

As you walk in, you can buy a brochure which describes the history and background of the exhibits. Lots of interesting reading here. Did you know that the towers of the Kremlin contained a secret escape route for the Czar? (Too bad he was someplace else when the Revolution broke out). Did you know that the scale at the Cheese Market in Alkmaar, Holland, was once used to determine whether or not a woman was in cahoots with the devil? If she weighed less than 150 pounds she was declared a witch and was burned at the stake. Gory, yes, but that piece of information alone is worth the price of admission for any number of dropouts from the Weight Watchers Club.

All in all, an interesting place for homesick Europeans, Americans who have lived in Europe, history buffs, architectural students and children, too, (although they are not allowed to touch). The kingdom is out of the way, but its cheaper and closer than the miniature kingdoms of Holland and Denmark.

HOURS: Daily, 10-5. Mem. Day - Labor Day: Closed winter. Weekends, fall, spring.
ADMISSION: Adults: $4.50; Seniors: $4.00; Children: $3.50; Under 5: $1.50.
LOCATION: Route 31, Washington, Warren County. Take Rte. 78 to Clinton Exit, then north on 31.
TELEPHONE: 908-689-6866

STERLING HILL MINE

The last operating zinc mine in New Jersey went out of business in 1986. You might wonder why anyone would want to keep and restore an old mine, but two brothers have put all their money and energy into it, and for good reason. Besides the primary zinc deposits there are 67 minerals in this mine, half of which are found nowhere else. The Hauck brothers, together with dedicated townsfolk, decided to keep the mine open for tours and some of the old buildings as a mining museum.

One thing you learn right away — wear a jacket. It is 56 degrees all the time, inside the mine, and it is often damp too. Wear good, heavy shoes. Because the area of Ogdensburg and nearby Franklin has the world's largest deposits of fluorescent stones, the most effective stop on the tour is the "Rainbow Room." This is a cutout of the wall which looks like ordinary rock when you first see it. The tour guide switches on an ultra-violet light, and the red-fluorescent calcite and green-fluorescent willemite begin to glow in the half-dark. It's like something from a science-fiction movie.

There's lots of walking on this 1 1/2 hour tour not only along the tracks of the mine itself but in the outer buildings as well. Inside the mine, the guide throws a pebble down a mine shaft. When you hear it hit, fathoms below, you realize how deep mines, like caves, can go. There are 3 tours daily in summer, two at other times.

Outside, you visit the building where the miner's once changed clothes. This is a huge exhibit hall now, with displays of everything from mining machinery to the metal baskets the miners used to dump their wet clothing in. At the end of the tour you return to mine-office building (where tickets are sold). Here you can buy a hot dog, use the restroom and peruse the gift shop, which includes, of course, a large number of rocks and minerals.

An interesting tour, both for scout troops or for grown-ups. It can easily be combined with a visit to the Franklin Mineral Museum, three miles away.

HOURS: Daily, 10-5. (May be closed Jan., Feb.)
ADMISSION: Adults: $6.50; Under 12: $4.50; Seniors: $5.50
LOCATION: 30 Plant St., Ogdensburg, Sussex County. Take Rte. 517 to Brooks Flat Road to Plant.
TELEPHONE: 201-209-7212

EXCURSION RAILROADS

New Jersey's best known excursion railroad is the **Black River and Western** that leaves from Mine Street and Turntable Junction in Flemington. In fact, the tracks are right next to the outlet shops of Liberty Village. Trains run in season, (usually mid-April until December) on weekends. It's a real old-fashioned steam engine that pulls the train (with real soot and ashes) and you travel through well-wooded Hunterdon County. The train makes stops at Ringoes and/or Lambertville, then back again. Call ahead for schedule. *Telephone:* 908-782-6622.

A popular attraction at *Allaire State Park* in Monmouth County is the **Pine Creek Railroad** which runs a ten-minute trip. The narrow gauge steam train ride is part of several attractions at this large park. The ride operates mostly during the summer season. Check the *Allaire Village* listing for further information.

Another train ride, this one well into Pennsylvania Dutch territory (and therefore, technically, beyond the periphery of this book) is the **Strasburg Railroad**. Located on Route 741, Strasburg, in Lancaster County, Pennsylvania, the ride is so well known that it attracts tourists from across the border. The 45-minute ride offers a steam train with pot belly stoves in the coaches and an observation car straight out of "Hello, Dolly!". It operates on weekends during March, April, November and December. Weekdays on May 1 through October 31. Call 717-687-7522 for time schedules.

The **New Hope** steam railroad is mentioned in the article on that town.

EXCURSION BOATS

Although there have always been sightseeing boats, they seemed, in the old days, to be secondary to the more popular fishing excursions. Nowadays, there is an increased popularity of the excursion type vessel, whether it is a motor launch or a re-created sidewheeler. These boats will offer entertainment, narrated tours, lunch, dinner or simple cruising depending on the time of year, and the place. Here are a few:

The *"Spirit of New Jersey,"* leaves from Weehawkin and sails into the Hudson River and New York Harbor. The trip may include brunch, lunch, cocktails and Broadway style entertainment. A similar excursion boat called *"The Spirit of Philadelphia"* leaves from Penn's Landing to circle around the Philadelphia harbor. Food is buffet style and the waiters turn into the entertainers after they clear the dishes. And The Circle Line (q.v.) offers New York Harbor tours.

At the Jersey shore you will find several versions of sightseeing and excursion boats. *"The River Queen,"* a simplified version of a Mississippi River paddle boat, cruises for lunch, afternoon sightseeing, etc. This boat, which sails from Bogan's Basin in

Brielle, and its sister ship the *"River Belle"* which leaves from Point Pleasant Beach are both popular with groups, especially senior citizens groups. The boats cruise the inland waters of the Manasquan River and Barnegat Bay so the water is calm and sightseeing is mostly of the docks and patios of shore homeowners plus an occasional bridge. Some cruises have narration, but there is no entertainment except for the special Dixieland band cruises that run on Wednesdays during the summer. *Telephone:* 908-528-6620.

The *"Sandy Hook Lady"* is the most recent addition to the excursion boat roster. It is an 85 foot custom built paddle-wheeler that leaves from Atlantic Highlands Harbor and cruises the calm Shrewsbury and Navesink rivers in northern Monmouth County. Sightseeting, sunset and moonlight cruises run about $12.00 per adult. Luncheon and dinner cruises. Two levels with dance floors and tables are cabaret style (4 or 8 people.) Reservations necessary. Season: May - Oct. *Telephone:* 908-291-4354.

Over at Atlantic City, Harrah's Marina Casino Hotel operates a paddleboat called *"Harrah's Belle"* during the summer. This one hour cruise of the Absecon waterway allows customers a change from the smoke-filled casinos.

Further down at Wildwood Crest, there is *Captain Sinn's Sightseeing Center* (609-522-3934) which runs sightseeing cruises as well as whalewatching trips and dinner cruises. And the *Cape May Fishing & Sightseeing Center* (609-898-0055) in Cape May operates whale and dolphin watching cruises plus a shorter wine and cheese harbor cruise. Of course the whale-watching trips go out into the ocean but whether or not they actually spot any whales depends on the time of year. There are a number of other short sightseeing cruises that leave from Otten's Harbor in Wildwood and the Cape May Yacht Basin in Cape May, most with narration (although the evening trips usually favor band entertainment).

All these excursion boats are available for group charter as well as weddings, bar mitzvahs, company picnics and whatever else you can think of.

TWIN LIGHTS LIGHTHOUSE

An unusual brownstone building that looks more like a castle than the lighthouse it once was, Twin Lights is perched on a mountainous bluff in Atlantic Highlands and affords a sweeping view of the ocean and coast. The "twin" lights, (one is square and one octagonal) are towers on either side of the main building. The first Fresnel lights were used here in 1841. The present fortress-like structure was built in 1862 and was the scene of many "firsts".

The museum inside includes exhibits on early life-saving equipment, a replica of the first rowing skiff to cross the Atlantic and displays concerning Marconi's first demonstration of the wireless in America.

Naturally part of the enjoyment of visiting a decommissioned lighthouse is making the climb up the stairs. The ascent up the spiral staircase involves only 167 steps and leads to an excellent view of Sandy Hook and the ocean. Downstairs, there is a small gift shop and outside you will find a picnic area and several historical markers. Free.

> **HOURS:** 10-5, Daily, summer. Closed Mon. & Tues. otherwise.
> **LOCATION:** Atlantic Highlands, Monmouth County,
> Take Route 36E make right turn just before Highlands Bridge, then another right. Follow signs.
> **TELEPHONE:** 908-872-1814

BUSHKILL FALLS

For families who wish to avoid the hurly-burly of amusement parks there are many scenic attractions which offer a day in the country with the simpler amusements of an earlier day. One of these is Bushkill Falls, set in a primeval forest in the foothills of the Poconos. The forest is cool in the summer and colorful in the fall, and while the main waterfall is nowhere near Niagara in width or grandeur, it does present both photographers and easy hikers with a pleasant outing. For Pocono tourists, the Falls have long been a standard attraction.

You first enter through a "nature" museum, then a pathway through a hushed forest. Although you get a good view of the cascading water from up top, it is more impressive to see it from below. That however, requires a climb down a "natural" log stairway. The Main Falls drop over the edge of a 100-foot cliff to a deep pool below. From that point the water now drops another 70 feet through a large gorge strewn with gigantic boulders. The falls are fairly narrow, but the drop is spectacular.

There are three routes to follow to the falls. The short route, with a green trail marker, takes only 15 minutes to walk. It is the "chicken" trail to a lookout where you can drink in the vistas, take a picture then sit down. The second or "popular" route takes 45 minutes and is for those who want their money's worth. This takes you down and around the bottom of the main falls, where from a bridge across the creek you get a full view from below of the majestic spill of white water.

The third route takes one and a half hours. Here you pass a series of three pretty, mist-laden falls on your trek. Following this path you also come upon a lookout where you can enjoy a panoramic view of the Delaware Valley. It is absolutely necessary for one to wear good walking shoes. Wedgies, Dr. Scholls, clogs and such are a disaster on these paths.

When visiting the Falls, check the map in the brochure you receive with your ticket. It clearly marks the trails to follow. Food service, concessions, and beer are available for those who need rest and relaxation after their exertions. Picnic tables also.

HOURS: April - Nov.: Daily, 9-5.
ADMISSION: Adults: $7.00; Seniors: $6.25; Children 6-12: $2.00; Under 6, free.
LOCATION: Bushkill, Pa. Take I-80 to Exit 52, then 209 N.Follow signs.
TELEPHONE: 717-588-6682

RENAISSANCE FESTIVAL, N.Y.

This festival has been running for many years now and has become quite popular. For eight weekends — from early August to mid-September — , the greenery at Sterling Forest in New York (close to the Jersey border) is taken over by knights in shining armor, ladies, peddlers dressed in motley, jugglers and mimes. A joust on horseback is the big attraction here, but it takes place during the last hour of the festival (5 to 6 P.M.) so allow time for that one. Otherwise a series of "shows" depicting outlaws, queens and jesters are part of the festival. However, the mud wrestling, juggling, Wagnerian puppets and other attractions are operated by free-lancers who expect the customers to come up with some coin of the realm so bring extra change along. Rides (some simple ones) and games (such as axe-throwing) are extra too. The main attractions - such as the Living

Chess Game, the Queen's Feast and the Joust, take place at particular locations at specific times - so it's really necessary to buy a program in order to enjoy everything.

There is plenty of food and drink here, but there is no prohibition to bringing your own. Veterans carry their own canteens or goatskins because there's plenty of hiking over the greensward. There are also gift "shops" which are set up in tents and offer such unusual items as brass rubbings and flower circlets for milady's hair. An Equity production of a different Shakespeare play is put on each year in the Festival's own Globe Theater — which has seating on a rustic hill and is about as comfortable as the original Globe.

> **HOURS:** Weekends, 11-6, Aug.-mid-Sept.
> **ADMISSION:** Adults: $15.00; Seniors: $13.00; Children 3-12: $6.00; Under 3 free
> **LOCATION:** Sterling Forest, Tuxedo, N.Y. Take Route 17N, look for signs.
> **TELEPHONE:** 914-351-5171 (Summer)

MEDIEVAL TIMES

Combine a horse show, a night club, a dinner theater and a Renaissance Festival, put it all in a circus-like arena inside of a huge stucco castle and plunk it down near one of New Jersey's busiest intersections (right near the Meadowlands) and you have the northern version of Medieval Times. Here you get not one, but six jousts, a steady narrative by a Master of Ceremonies and a chance to eat dinner without any utensils!

First you enter the cavernous castle, where you buy your tickets and are handed a paper hat with a special color. This color will determine which section you sit in and which knight you root for. These colored hats are a great gimmick, for it is in cheering on a particular champion that the audience becomes part of the show. But that comes later. You are first ushered into a greeting room where you pose for a picture with the local royalty. Then you go into a larger room where you have a chance to buy a drink and any number of medieval accoutrements including wooden swords and shields. Hungry yet? Well, you should have had a snack at home, since you are now herded into a reception room where the M.C. regales you with jokes. Finally you are ushered into the arena where chairs are set against long banquet tables. These are all set in tiers so that everybody in the huge oval arena does get a chance to see the show.

And now, the menu. As the serving wench tells you, there is soup (served in a porringer which you lift up and drink from), assorted raw vegetables, chicken, potato and ribs served in a steaming foil package, dessert, coffee or punch. You also get a huge napkin which is best tucked into your collar in standard Henry the Eighth style.

And now for the show! First a presentation by a magician and some fancy stepping by a trained horse and his rider. Then its on to the jousts. The various knights not only fight on horseback, but engage in choreographed swordplay after being unhorsed. This goes on for all six knights until the final victor is announced. All this while, the wenches are either serving supper or selling you pictures, banners, wines or whatever.

After the jousts, many couples stay on to dance at a small nightclub set up in the anteroom. Families often hang around until their knight shows up to autograph the picture, shield or whatever else their kids have bought. An interesting evening.

HOURS: Wed., Thurs.: 7:30 p.m.; Fri., Sat.: 8 p.m., Sun.: 4:30 p.m.
ADMISSION: Sun., Wed., Thurs.: Adults, $30.95; Children, $21.65; Fri., Sat.: Adults, $35.95; Children, $24.95 + tax.
LOCATION: 149 Polito Ave., Lyndhurst, Bergen County. From Route 3, take 17 S to Lyndhurst.
TELEPHONE: 800-828-2945; 201-933-2220

CULINARY INSTITUTE OF AMERICA

Any organization that wants to run a day trip and be assured of a well-filled bus, has only to mention the Culinary Institute of America and the seats fill up fast. The trick is to find a suitable date — for group bookings must often wait months for reservations. If you go on your own, you may find it easier to reserve a table at this school where budding chefs cook, clean and serve in the ever-expanding restaurants on the first floor.

What makes CIA so popular? Well prices are reasonable for a multi-course meal for one thing. And since many of the graduates go on to found chic, ultra-expensive restaurants there is the feeling of getting in on the ground floor of a good thing. But if the cooking is done by seniors, the waiters must be freshman, because the service can vary from efficient to inept. The food, however, is always good, if not necessarily in the sublime category.

Set high on a hill overlooking the Hudson Valley, the red brick Institute includes classrooms, student dorms, several restaurants and a well-stocked bookstore. **The Escoffier Room**, which specializes in the formal, multi-course European meal includes a large window which allows patrons to watch the chefs at meal preparation. (All we ever saw, however, was someone making butter curls). A typical formal meal might include a light hors d'oeuvre, a soup, a main course followed by salad, and then a handsome dessert table — a movable feast of tortes, tarts and eclairs — that winds its way around the room very slowly. The **American Bounty Room** offers faster service and includes such staples as roast beef and American pies.

Other eating areas include the informal **St. Andrew's Cafe,** and the Italian room, **"Caterina de Medici",** for formal fare. A tour of the CIA is available. You pass all the classrooms where students may be beheading fish or pushing pastry through a tube. There is a rolling graduation here, so classes go on continuously. If you are combining a trip to the Institute with a visit to the neighboring historic houses at Hyde Park be sure you allow plenty of time, as lunch is a leisurely affair here.

HOURS: Tues.- Sat., lunch & dinner, except cafe.
LOCATION: Hyde Park, NY (3 miles north of Poughkeepsie).
TELEPHONE: 914-471-6608

RENAULT WINERY

Let's face it, a winery tour is just about the most popular kind of industrial tour there is. The art of winemaking is so ancient, the slightly fermented air in the cellars so heady and the little old winemaker is usually so jolly that there is always a party air about these tours. And since wine-tasting is involved, no wonder everyone seems to have a good time.

Historic Renault Winery calls itself the best little tour-house in New Jersey and for good reason. It's fun! Yes, you learn about the early wine presses and dosage machines, but the tour leader may also play to the crowd, threatening to send the women in to stomp the grapes or the men in to clean the barrels. The tour includes a sip of wine and some history of the place. The winery is not run by the Renault family, by the way, but by the third family to buy this thriving business. It is situated way out in the Pine Barrens about 16 miles northwest of Atlantic City. Apparently this sandy soil lends itself well to grape production.

There are various stops in rooms full of antique winemaking equipment, Venetian glassware and small wine-tasting rooms. Then it's into the cellars where giant vats store the wine. These oak and redwood vats are fifty and sixty years old and would have to be replaced today by stainless steel as the old cooper's craft is lost. The guide explains how the wine is poured off and facts of vineyard life. If I learned one salient fact here it was to never-more buy cooking wine at the supermarket. It seems that food companies buy the wineries' rejects, then add salt to the already bad wine (that's a law), bottle it and sell it. As the tour leader mentioned — no cookbook every says to add cooking wine to your recipe.

Aside from it's tours, Renault Winery also serves lunches at a charming bistro outside the main building called "The Wine Garden." There is also a weekend gourmet restaurant, open to the public by reservation. In the fall, grape stomping festivals take over.

> **HOURS:** Daily. Tours are Mon. - Sat.: 10-4; Sun.: 11:30-5
> **ADMISSION:** $2.00 for tours. Under 18 free.
> **LOCATION:** Bremen Ave., Egg Harbor City, Atlantic County. Take Garden State Parkway exit 44 (if coming from north only!) and right onto Moss Mill Rd., then 6 miles to Bremen Ave. From Atlantic City: Route 30 to Bremen Ave.
> **TELEPHONE:** 609-965-2111

OTHER AREA WINERIES

Another Atlantic City sidetrip is the one to **Gross' Highland Winery**. Champagne tanks and equipment a specialty. Gift shop includes a wide selection of glassware. *Telephone:* 609-652-1187.

Wineries are a fast growing segment of New Jersey's agricultural scene and they seem to be popping up all over. New ones have sprung up in Warren, Hunterdon and Somerset counties. While many do not have traditional tours, they all welcome visitors on weekends and special occasions. Most of these wineries combine forces for a large spring and fall wine tasting festival, where food, entertainment, and an admission charge await. Hayrides and grape stomping also.

Even without festivals, tracking down wineries on fall weekends has become a popular activity. And tracking it is, because many of these places are on winding narrow roads where street signs don't exist. Luckily the Wine Council puts out a map, complete with directions. Call 609-292-8853 for this.

As for tours, the newer wineries (which often look like suburban ranch houses), are run scientifically with fiberglass and steel equipment. There isn't much to see and the information tends to be technical. The big thing is the wine-tasting. At a long bar, an attendant will pour wine into little cups and explain its type and texture. Often they start with light, dry wines and proceed to woody and fruit-flavored ones. Naturally, you are expected to buy a few bottles after all this work.

As for the barefoot grape stomping parties — these are usually reserved for groups and include food, wine and the right to enter an open barrel and squish grapes through your toes. Great anger therapy. Among the wineries in Warren County are the **Four Sisters** (908-475-3671), **Alba** (908-995-7800) and **Tamuzza** (908-459-5878). More southerly ones include **King's Road Vineyard** in Hunterdon County (908-479-6611) and **Cream Ridge**, near Great Adventure (609-259-9797).

THE MEADOWLANDS

You have only to drive through the battle-scarred South Bronx on your way to Yankee Stadium to realize what a stroke of genius it was to build the Meadowlands Sports-Arena Complex in the middle of a wide open area. It may have been a wasteland once, but now the sports-entertainment complex is breaking all box-office records. In fact, the biggest problem now is traffic tie-ups, especially when all three buildings are holding events. The complex consists of:

1. THE RACETRACK: Both harness and flat racing have their season at this modern, sparkling facility with its glassed-in, climate controlled Grandstand. There are several restaurants here for those who want to combine a night out with dining out. The fanciest of these is **Pegasus,** up on the top level of the track. It gives you a bird's eye view of the race, buffet stations, and high prices.

For those watching the race from the grandstand a large 15 x 36 foot video matrix screen allows you to watch the action on the far side of the field and also flashes the results almost immediately.

2. GIANTS STADIUM: So named because the football team of that name makes its home there. The stadium has a seating capacity of 76,000, color coded seats and a video matrix scoreboard that delights the kids. The stadium is used not only for sports events but for special concerts, antique shows, flea markets, petting zoos, a two-week carnival and other extravaganzas as well.

3. THE ARENA: (Officially the Byrne Arena). It boasts a striking modern design that arches eleven stories high. The arrangement of seats (approximately 20,000) allows good viewlines. However, a shortage of personnel often closes off the lower concourse so you may have quite a hike if you go for snacks. The Arena hosts basketball games, ice shows, Ringling Brothers Circus, rock shows and many other entertainments that New Jerseyans used to travel to Madison Square Garden to see.

FOR THE MEADOWLANDS COMPLEX

PARKING: Fee varies. Come early to avoid jamups.
LOCATION: East Rutherford, Bergen County.
DIRECTIONS: From N.J. Turnpike northbound - take Exit 16W for direct access. From Turnpike south - take Exit 18W. From Garden State Parkway northbound - Exit 153A to Route 3 East. From G.S.P. south-Exit 163 to Route 17S to Paterson Plank Road East.
TELEPHONE: 201-935-8500; Racetrack: 201-460-4092

OTHER RACETRACKS & RODEOS

MONMOUTH PARK: Oceanport, Monmouth County (Use GSP Exit 105). *Telephone:* 908-222-5100. Outdoor picnic area, indoor and outdoor seating, cafeteria and clubhouse at Jersey's oldest track, close to the seashore. Thoroughbred racing runs from May through September.

FREEHOLD RACEWAY: Park Avenue, Freehold, Monmouth County (Take Route 9 to junction of Route 33). *Telephone:* 908-462- 3800. A beautiful new track with flags flying, right in the heart of horse breeding country. Harness racing continues from January through December.

ATLANTIC CITY RACE COURSE: Junction of Route 40 and Route 322, Atlantic County (Atlantic City Expressway Exit 12). *Telephone:* 609-641-2190. Thoroughbred racing June 1 - September 30.

GARDEN STATE PARK: Rte 70 and Haddonfield Rd. Cherry Hill, Camden County. Telephone: 609-488-8400. Harness racing Wed.-Sat., Sept.-Dec.; Thoroughbred racing Tues.-Sun., Feb.-June.

COWTOWN RODEO: Yes, it does exist and it's a regular rodeo with bucking broncos and all that stuff. It runs every Saturday night from the end of May to the end of September, at 7:30 p.m. rain or shine. Audience sits on bleacher seats. *Admission:* Adults: $10.00; Children: $5.00; 12 and under free. *Location:* US Route 40 eight miles east of Delaware Memorial Bridge (Woodstown), Salem County. *Telephone:* 609-769-3200.

U.S. EQUESTRIAN TEAM HEADQUARTERS: Not that they're in residence that often, but there are several events open to the public at the team headquarters in Gladstone. One, *The Festival of Champions*, includes show jumping, dressage and things like four-in-hand competitions (for teams of horses). There is a charge for special events. The stables and show rings are located on Pottersville Road, Gladstone, Somerset County. *Telephone:* 908-234-1251.

OTHER NEW JERSEY ARENAS & AUDITORIUMS

GARDEN STATE ARTS CENTER: A beautiful white concrete ampitheatre designed by Edward Durell Stone is the setting for nightly concerts and loads of special events throughout the summer. The "shell" is covered and offers seating for 5,000 while an additional 4,000 people can be accommodated on the lawn. The lawn people, however, must bring their own blankets and chairs and risk the weather.

The shell is open on all sides so that there is easy access to seats and a delicious breeze from the nearby seashore wafts through the auditorium. Shows at the Garden State range from pop singers to symphony orchestras with a few ethnic festivals thrown in. Everyone from The Beach Boys to operatic divas have appeared here. The season runs from late June to early September.

LOCATION: Holmdel, Monmouth County. Take Exit 116 off Garden State Parkway, follow signs.
TELEPHONE: 908-442-9200

OCEAN GROVE AUDITORIUM: A cavernous 7,000 seat auditorium built in the late Victorian age is one of the attractions of this quiet camp-meeting town right next to Asbury Park on the shore. The Great Auditorium, with its majestic organ, has recently been refurbished and restored. It is now home to many familystyle entertainments plus a lecture series. Typical attractions are singers (including pop singers) choral groups and festivals. Again, this is for the summer season only.

LOCATION: 54 Pitman Avenue, Ocean Grove, Monmouth County.
TELEPHONE: 908-775-0035

WATERLOO VILLAGE SUMMER MUSIC FESTIVAL: As of now, the classical music concert inside the village has been discontinued. However, the big rock, pop and country concerts in the concert field one mile away are still going strong.

LOCATION: Waterloo Village, Stanhope, Sussex County.

INDEX

C

E

F

240

G

H

Z

REGIONAL INDEX

NEW JERSEY

ATLANTIC COUNTY
Atlantic City
  Casinos and boardwalk
  Atlantic City Race Course
  Historic Gardners Basin
Forsythe National Wildlife
  Refuge
Gross' Highland Winery
Lucy, Margate Elephant
Marine Mammal Center
Noyes Museum, Oceanville
Renault Winery
Smithville, Historic Town of
Pine Barrens
Somers Mansion
Storybook Land

BERGEN COUNTY
African Art Museum
Aviation Hall of Fame, Teterboro
Bergen Museum
Bergen County Wildlife Center
Campgaw Ski Area, Mahwah
Flat Rock Brook Nature Center
Fort Lee Historic State Park
Hackensack Env. Center
The Hermitage
Lorimar Nature Center
Meadowlands Sports Complex
Medieval Times
Montvale Antiques
NJ Children's Museum
Schoolhouse Museum, Paramus
U.S.S. Ling, Hackensack
Van Saun Park
Von Steuben House

BURLINGTON COUNTY
Bass River State Park
Batsto Village

Bordentown Tour
Burlington Tour
Columbus Flea Market
Lebanon State Forest
Mount Holly Tour
Penn State Forest
Pine Barrens
Rancocos State Park
Wharton State Forest

CAMDEN COUNTY
Barclay Farmstead
Berlin Farmer's Market
Camden
  Camden County Historical
  Society
  Campbell Museum
  State Aquarium
  Walt Whitman House
Clementon Lake Park
Garden State Discovery Museum
Garden State Park
Greenfield Hall, Haddonfield
Indian King Tavern, Haddonfield

CAPE MAY COUNTY
Belleplain State Forest
Cape May Bird Observatory
Cape May County Museum
Cape May County Park Zoo
Cape May-Lewes Ferry
Cape May Point State Park
Cape May (town)
Corson's Inlet State Park
Historic Cold Spring Village
Leaming's Run Garden
Ocean City
Ocean City Historical Museum
Stone Harbor
Stone Harbor Bird Sanctuary
Wetlands Institute
Wildwood
Wildwood Crest

250

CUMBERLAND COUNTY
Belleplain State Forest
Bridgeton Tour
Cohansic Zoo, Bridgeton
Pine Barrens
Wheaton Village, Millville

ESSEX COUNTY
Center for Environmental Studies
Grover Cleveland Birthplace
Edison Labs/Glenmont
Force House, Livingston
Hartshorn Arboretum
Montclair
   Israel Crane House
   Montclair Art Museum
   Presby Iris Garden
Newark
   Ballantine House
   Branch Brook Park
   New Jersey Historical Society
   Newark Museum
Riker Hill Geological Museum
Turtle Back Zoo

GLOUCESTER COUNTY
Gloucester County Tour
Hunter-Lawrence House,
   Woodbury
Mullica Hill Antiques
Red Bank Battlefield Park

HUDSON COUNTY
Afro-American Museum
Hoboken
Jersey City Museum
Liberty State Park
   Ellis Island
   Liberty Science Center
   Statue of Liberty
Secaucus Outlets

HUNTERDON COUNTY
Black River & Western Railroad
Clinton Historical Museum Village

Flemington Fair Flea Market
Flemington Outlets
Hunterdon Art Center, Clinton
Lambertville Antiques
Marshall House, Lambertville
Pick-Your-Own Farms
Round Valley State Park
Spruce Run State Park
Twp. of Lebanon Museum
Voorhees State Park

MERCER COUNTY
Belle Mountain Ski Area
Hopewell Museum
Kuser Farm Mansion
Howell Living History Farm
Princeton
   Bainbridge House
   Morven
   Princeton Art Museum
   Princeton Battlefield
   University Tour
Trenton
   New Jersey State House
   New Jersey State Museum
   Old Barracks
   William Trent House
Washington Crossing State Park

MIDDLESEX COUNTY
Cheesequake State Park
East Jersey Olde Towne
Edison Memorial Tower
Middlesex County Museum
New Brunswick
   Buccleuch Mansion
   Hungarian Center
   NJ Museum of Agriculture
   Rutgers Geology Museum
   Zimmerli Art Museum

MONMOUTH COUNTY
Allaire State Park
Allen House
Asbury Park

Belmar
Brielle
Deal
Englishtown Auction Sales
Freehold
  Covenhoven House
  Monmouth Battlefield State
  Park
  Monmouth County Historical
  Society
  Freehold Raceway
Garden State Arts Center
Great American Flea Market
Keansburg Amusements
Longstreet Farm, Holmdel
Monmouth Museum, Lincroft
Monmouth Park Racetrack
Ocean Grove
Owl Haven
Poricy Park Nature Center
Sandy Hook
Spring Lake
Spy House Museum
Stone Museum
Twin Lights Lighthouse

MORRIS COUNTY
Chester Flea Market
Cooper Mill
Craftsman Farms
Craigmeur Ski Area
Fosterfields
Frelinghuysen Arboretum
Great Swamp Outdoor Center
Hacklebarny State Park
Historic Speedwell
Hopatcong State Park
Meyersville Grange Flea Market
Morris County College
  Planetarium
Morris Museum
Morristown
  Acorn Hall
  Ford Mansion
  Jockey Hollow
  Macculloch Hall

Schuyler-Hamilton House
Museum of Early Trades and
  Crafts
St. Hubert's Giralda
Whippany RR Museum

OCEAN COUNTY
Barnegat Bay Decoy Museum
Barnegat Lighthouse State Park
Beach Haven
Island Beach State Park
Lebanon State Forest
Long Beach Island
New Egypt Flea Market
Ocean County College
  Planetarium
Ocean County Historical
  Museum
Point Pleasant
Popcorn Park
Seaside Heights
Seaside Park
Six Flags Great Adventure

PASSAIC COUNTY
Abram S. Hewitt State Forest
American Labor Museum
Dey Mansion, Wayne
Fairy Tale Forest
Norvin Green State Forest
Paterson
  Great Falls
  Lambert Castle
  Paterson Museum
  Paterson Tour
Ringwood Manor
Skylands
Van Riper-Hopper House, Wayne

SALEM COUNTY
Cowtown Rodeo
Fort Mott State Park
Hancock House
Parvin State Park
Salem Tour

SOMERSET COUNTY
Buck Gardens
Colonial Park Rose Gardens
Delaware and Raritan Canal State
Park
Golf House, Far Hills
Great Swamp
Neshanic Flea Market
Raritan Valley College Planetarium
Scherman-Hoffman Sanctuary
Somerset Environmental
Education Center
Somerville
Duke Gardens
Old Dutch Parsonage
Wallace House
U.S. Equestrian Team
Washington Rock State Park

SUSSEX COUNTY
Action Park
Delaware Water Gap
Franklin Mineral Museum
Gingerbread Castle
Great Gorge Ski Area
Hidden Valley Ski Area
High Point State Park
Millbrook Village
Old Monroe Schoolhouse
Olde Lafayette Village
Space Farms Zoo
Sterling Hill Mine
Stokes State Forest
Swartswood State Park
Vernon Valley Ski Area
Waterloo Village
Wawayanda State Park
Wild West City
Worthington State Forest

UNION COUNTY
Belcher Ogden Mansion
Bowcraft Amusement Park
Boxwood Hall, Elizabeth
Dr. Robinson Plantation

Drake House, Plainfield
Miller-Cory House
Reeves-Reed Arboretum
Scotch Plains Zoo
Trailside Nature Center
Trailside Planetarium

WARREN COUNTY
Alba Vineyards
Allamuchy State Park
Delaware Water Gap
Doll Castle Doll Museum
Four Sisters Winery
Jenny Jump State Forest
Land of Make Believe
Merrill Creek Reservoir
Miniature Kingdom
Pequest Trout Hatchery
Stephens State Park
Tamuzza Vineyards
Well Sweep Herb Farm

NEW YORK

HUDSON VALLEY AREA
Boscobel
Culinary Institute of America
Hunter Mountain Ski Area
Hyde Park
Kykuit
Lyndhurst
Philipsburg Manor
Renaissance Festival
Ski Windham
Sterling Forest Ski Area
Sunnyside
Van Cortlandt Manor
Vanderbilt Mansion
West Point
Woodbury Common

NEW YORK CITY

MANHATTAN
American Museum of Natural
  History
Central Park Trolley
Chinatown
Circle Line Tour
Cloisters, The
Empire State Building
Forbes Galleries
Frick Collection
Lincoln Center Tour
Metropolitan Museum of Art
Museum of Modern Art
NBC TV Tours
N.Y. Stock Exchange
South Street Seaport
U.N. Headquarters
World Trade Center

BROOKLYN
Brooklyn Botanic Gardens
N.Y. Aquarium

BRONX
Bronx Zoo
N.Y. Botanical Gardens
Wave Hill

STATEN ISLAND
Staten Island Zoo

PENNSYLVANIA

BRANDYWINE VALLEY AREA
Brandywine Battlefield State Park
Brandywine River Museum
Longwood Gardens

BUCKS COUNTY
Andalusia
Green Hill Farm
Lahaska
Mercer Mile, Doylestown
New Hope
Pennsbury Manor

Rice's Flea Market
Sesame Place
Washington Crossing Park

PHILADELPHIA AREA
Fairmount Park Houses
Franklin Institute
Franklin Mills Mall
Independence Mall
Museum of American Art
Philadelphia Museum of Art
Philadelphia Zoo
Please Touch Museum
United States Mint

POCONOS AREA
Big Boulder Ski Area
Bushkill Falls
Camelback Ski Area
Delaware Water Gap
Jack Frost Ski Area
Shawnee Mountain Ski Area
Shawnee Place

OTHER PENNSYLVANIA AREAS
Dorney Park -
  Wildwater Kingdom
Hershey Rose Gardens
Hersheypark
Reading Outlets
Strasburg Railroad
Valley Forge

DELAWARE
Cape May-Lewes Ferry
Hagley Museum
Nemours
Winterthur

254

Can't find a copy of NEW JERSEY DAY TRIPS in your local bookstore? Want to send a copy to a friend in another state? Just photocopy the coupon below and send, with check or money order, to:

THE WOODMONT PRESS
P.O. BOX 108
GREEN VILLAGE, N.J. 07935

Please send me _____ number of copies of NEW JERSEY DAY TRIPS @ $12.95 a copy. Postage and handling are $2.00 extra.

I am enclosing .... $ _____
Postage $2.00

TOTAL .... $ _____

Send book to:

NAME _____

ADDRESS _____

CITY/STATE/ZIP _____

*For 2 or more copies add .50 to postage for each additional copy.